D1505741

THE GREEN WOMAN

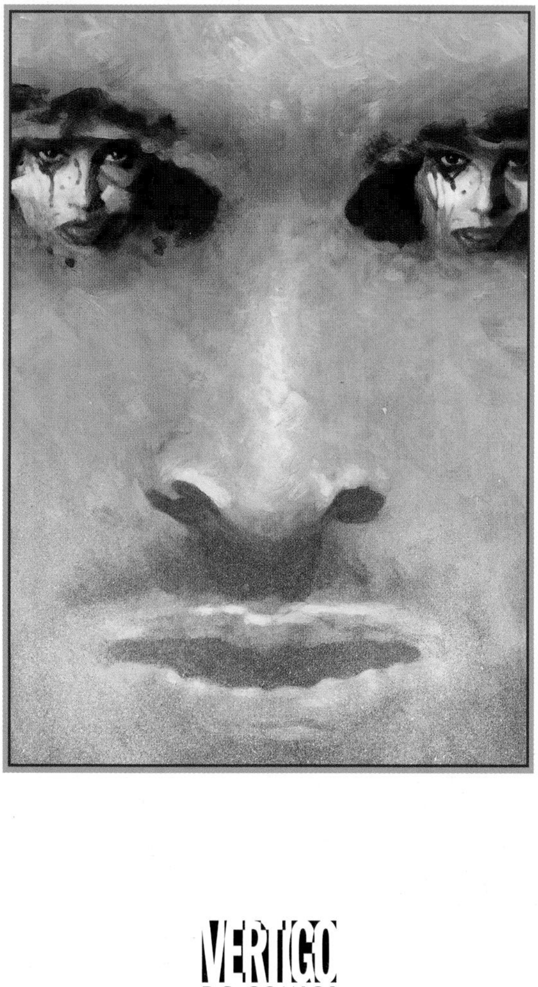

VERTIGO
DC COMICS

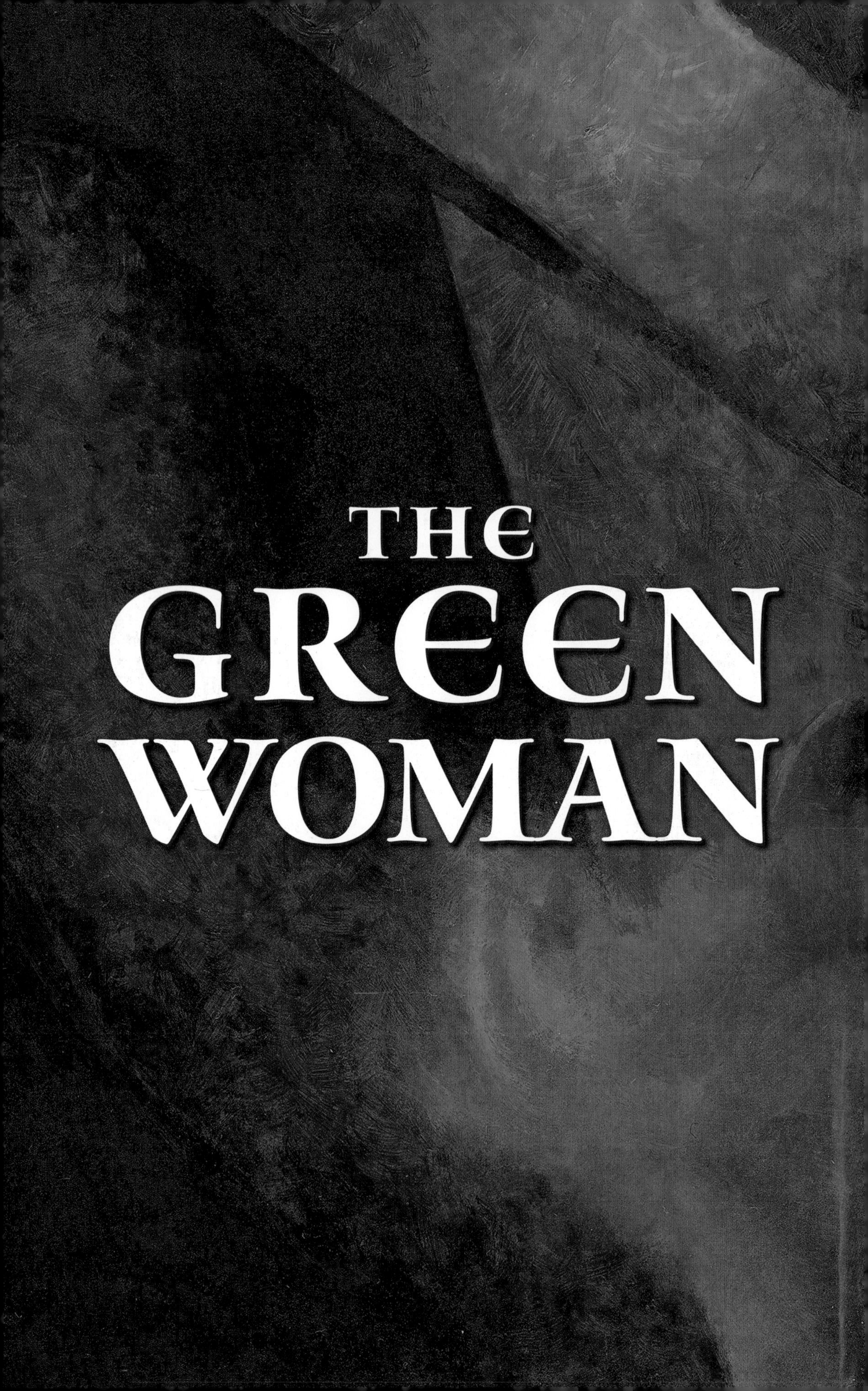

THE GREEN WOMAN

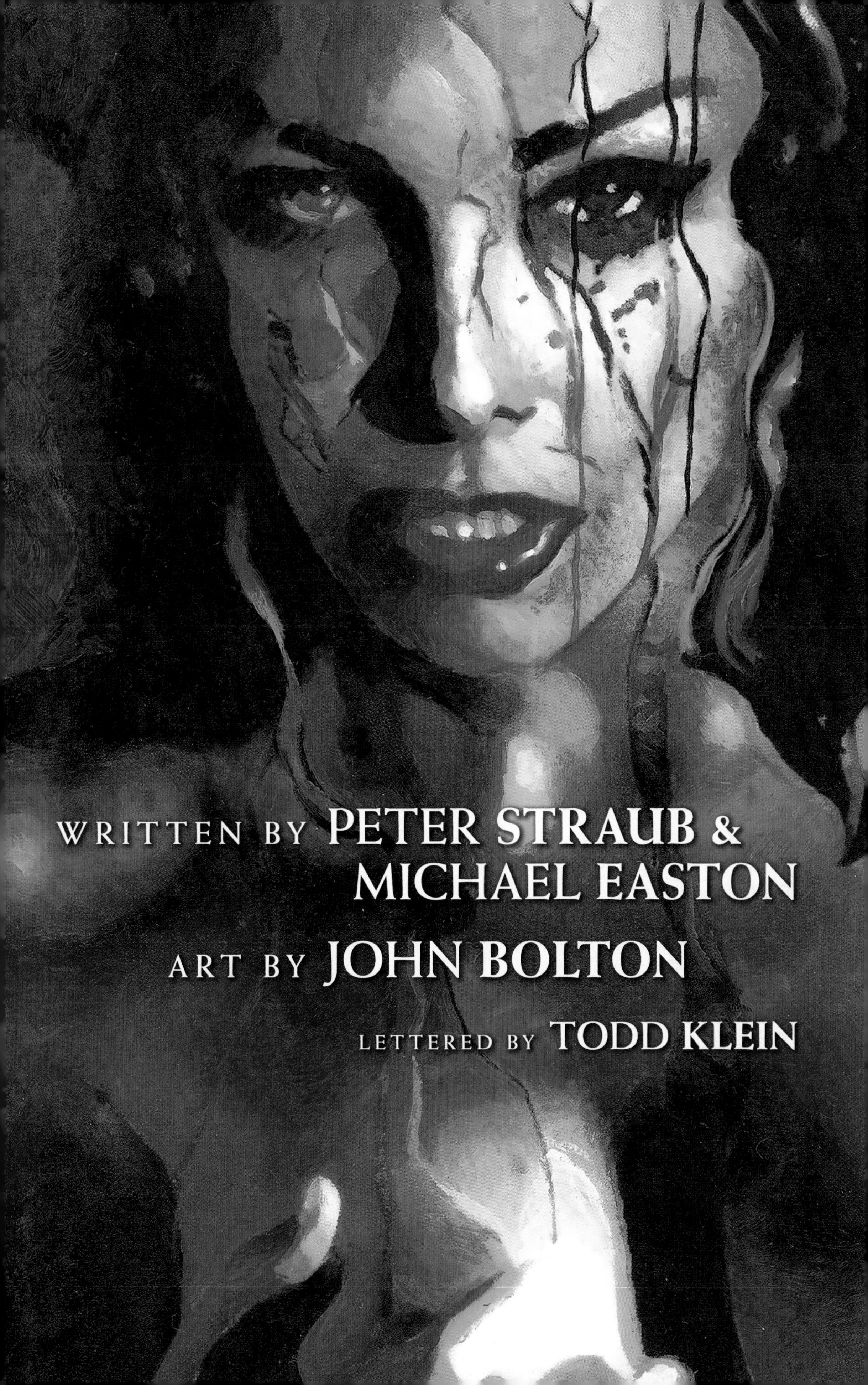

WRITTEN BY PETER STRAUB & MICHAEL EASTON

ART BY JOHN BOLTON

LETTERED BY TODD KLEIN

Dedications

Peter Straub & Michael Easton
For Robert S. Woods.

John Bolton
To my friend the actor
Peter Capaldi for being
the perfect villain.

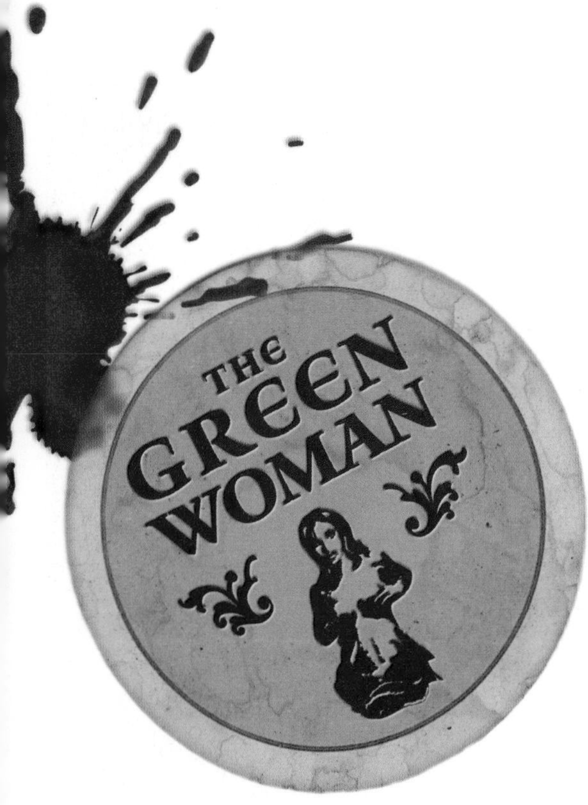
THE GREEN WOMAN

Karen Berger SVP-Executive Editor
Jonathan Vankin Editor
Sarah Litt and Mark Doyle Assistant Editors
Robbin Brosterman Design Director-Books
Curtis King Jr. Senior Art Director
DC COMICS
Diane Nelson President
Dan DiDio and Jim Lee Co-Publishers
Geoff Johns Chief Creative Officer
Patrick Caldon EVP-Finance and Administration
John Rood EVP-Sales, Marketing and Business Development
Amy Genkins SVP-Business and Legal Affairs
Steve Rotterdam SVP-Sales and Marketing
John Cunningham VP-Marketing
Terri Cunningham VP-Managing Editor
Alison Gill VP-Manufacturing
David Hyde VP-Publicity
Sue Pohja VP-Book Trade Sales
Alysse Soll VP-Advertising and Custom Publishing
Bob Wayne VP-Sales
Mark Chiarello Art Director

THE GREEN WOMAN
Published by DC Comics, 1700 Broadway, New York, NY 10019.

Printed in the USA. First Printing.
DC Comics, a Warner Bros. Entertainment Company.
HC ISBN: 978-1-4012-1100-4.
SC ISBN: 978-1-4012-1101-1.

SUSTAINABLE FORESTRY INITIATIVE
Certified Chain of Custody
Promoting Sustainable Forest Management
www.sfiprogram.org
Fiber used in this product line meets the sourcing requirements of the SFI program.
www.sfiprogram.org NFS-SPICOC-C0001801

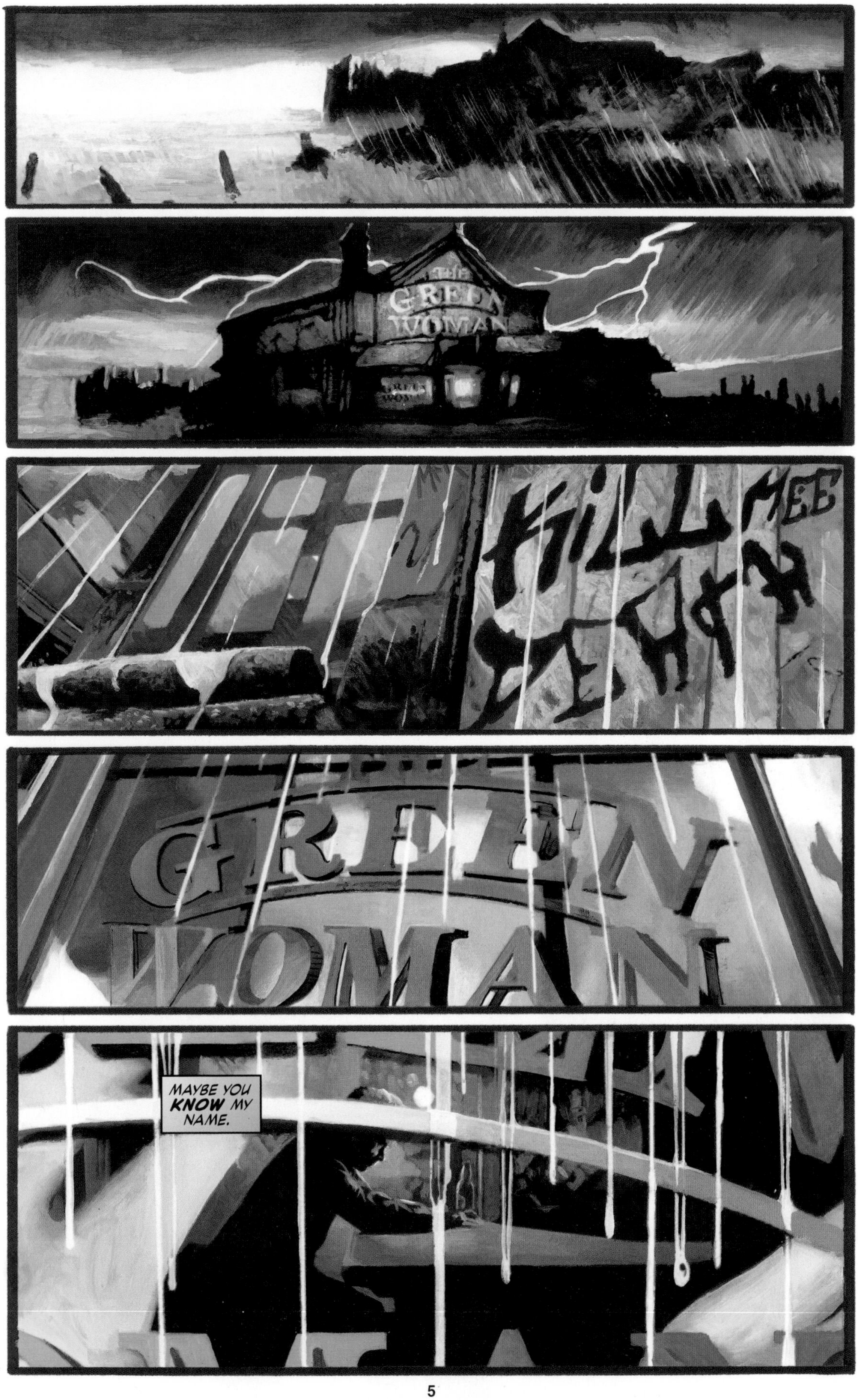
THE GREEN WOMAN
MAYBE YOU KNOW MY NAME.

YEAH, YOU MAY HAVE HEARD OF ME. GUY WROTE A **BOOK** ABOUT ME ONCE.

HE WANTED A NICE, PRETTY ENDING TO HIS STORY. HE THOUGHT IT WOULD PUT A LITTLE **BOW** ON TOP IF I GOT KILLED.

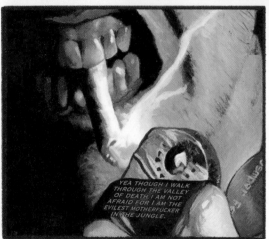

YEA THOUGH I WALK THROUGH THE VALLEY OF DEATH I AM NOT AFRAID FOR I AM THE EVILEST MOTHERFUCKER IN THE JUNGLE.

WRITERS. ISN'T A WRITER BORN WHO DOESN'T TURN INTO A LYING **PIECE OF SHIT** THE SECOND HE PICKS UP A PEN.

BEING GOOD WITH WORDS DOESN'T EXACTLY MAKE YOU A FUCKING VISIONARY, EITHER.

ALLOW ME TO INTRODUCE MYSELF. I'M **FIELDING BANDOLIER.** OF COURSE, OVER THE YEARS I HAD TO USE SOME **DIFFERENT** NAMES.

ACTUALLY, A *LOT* OF DIFFERENT NAMES.

WHEN I WAS A GREEN BERET, THEY CALLED ME FRANKLIN BACHELOR. WHEN I WAS A COP, THEY CALLED ME FRANK BELKNAP.

YOU GET CONFUSED, JUST CALL ME *FB*. A MAN LIKES TO HAVE A TRADEMARK.

Millhaven lager

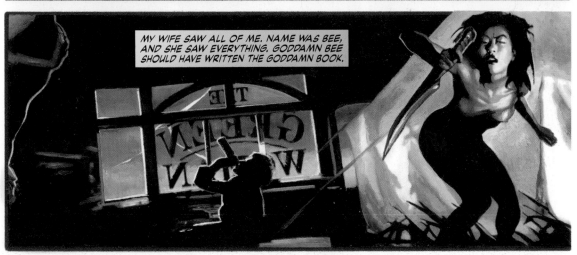

MY WIFE SAW ALL OF ME. NAME WAS BEE, AND SHE SAW EVERYTHING. GODDAMN BEE SHOULD HAVE WRITTEN THE GODDAMN BOOK.

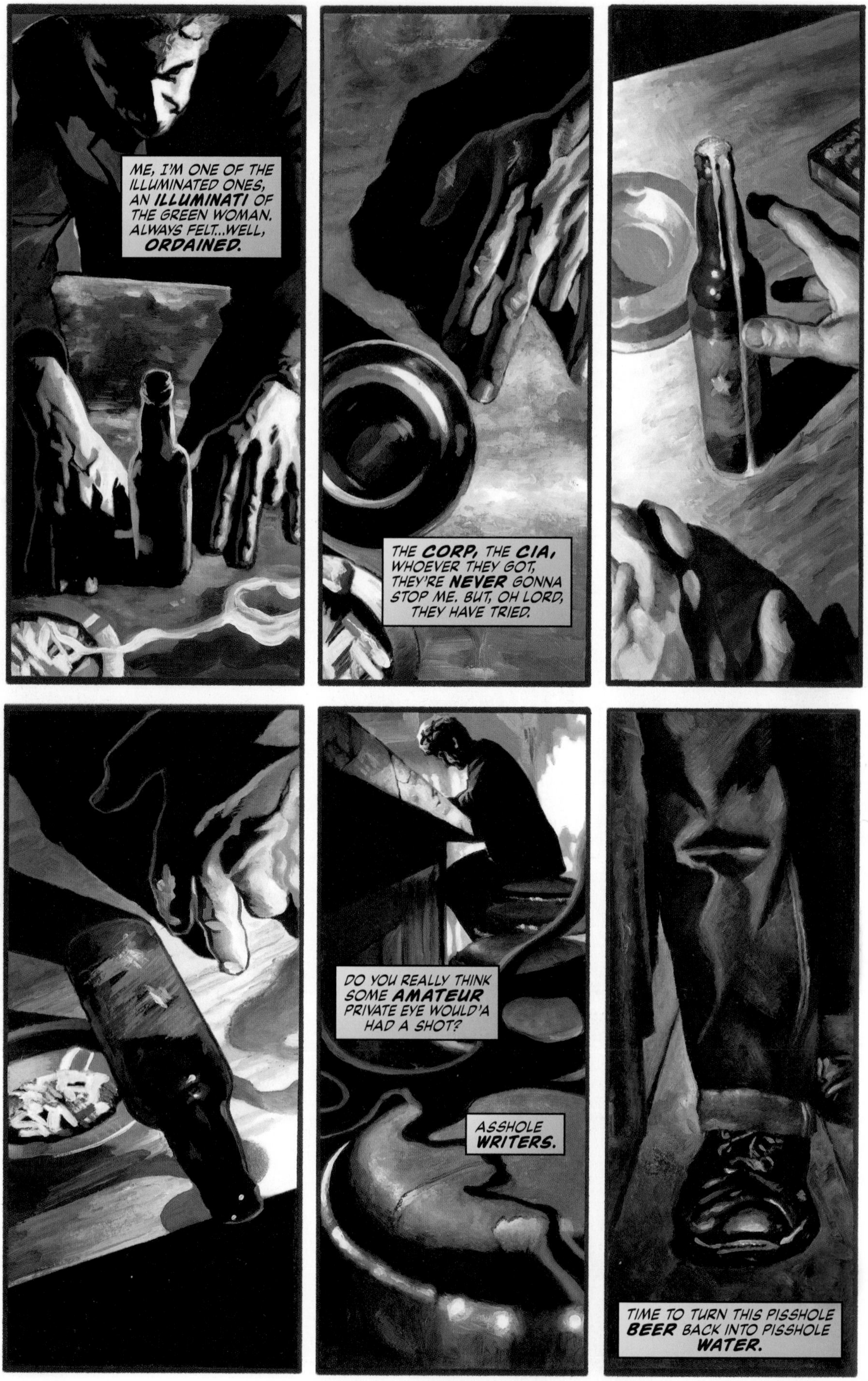
ME, I'M ONE OF THE ILLUMINATED ONES, AN ILLUMINATI OF THE GREEN WOMAN. ALWAYS FELT...WELL, ORDAINED.
THE CORP, THE CIA, WHOEVER THEY GOT, THEY'RE NEVER GONNA STOP ME. BUT, OH LORD, THEY HAVE TRIED.
DO YOU REALLY THINK SOME AMATEUR PRIVATE EYE WOULD'A HAD A SHOT?
ASSHOLE WRITERS.
TIME TO TURN THIS PISSHOLE BEER BACK INTO PISSHOLE WATER.

Call me
GODDAMMIT.

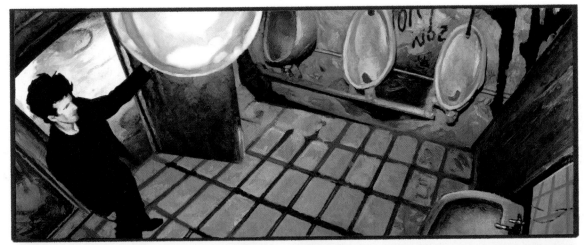

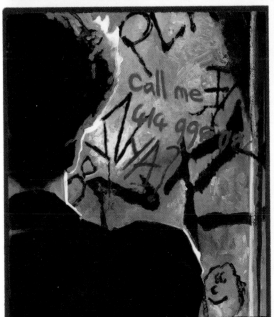

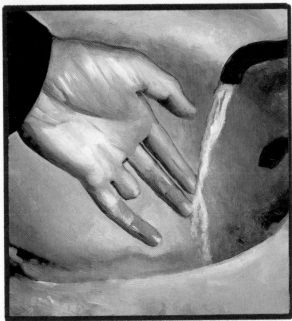

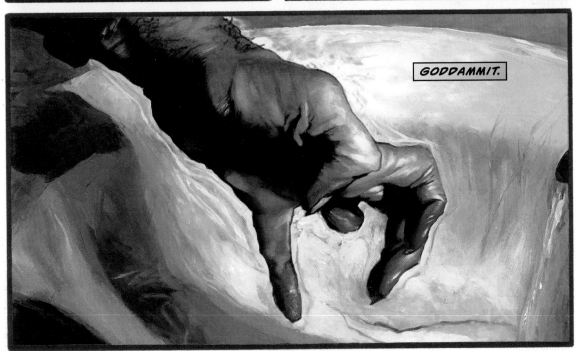

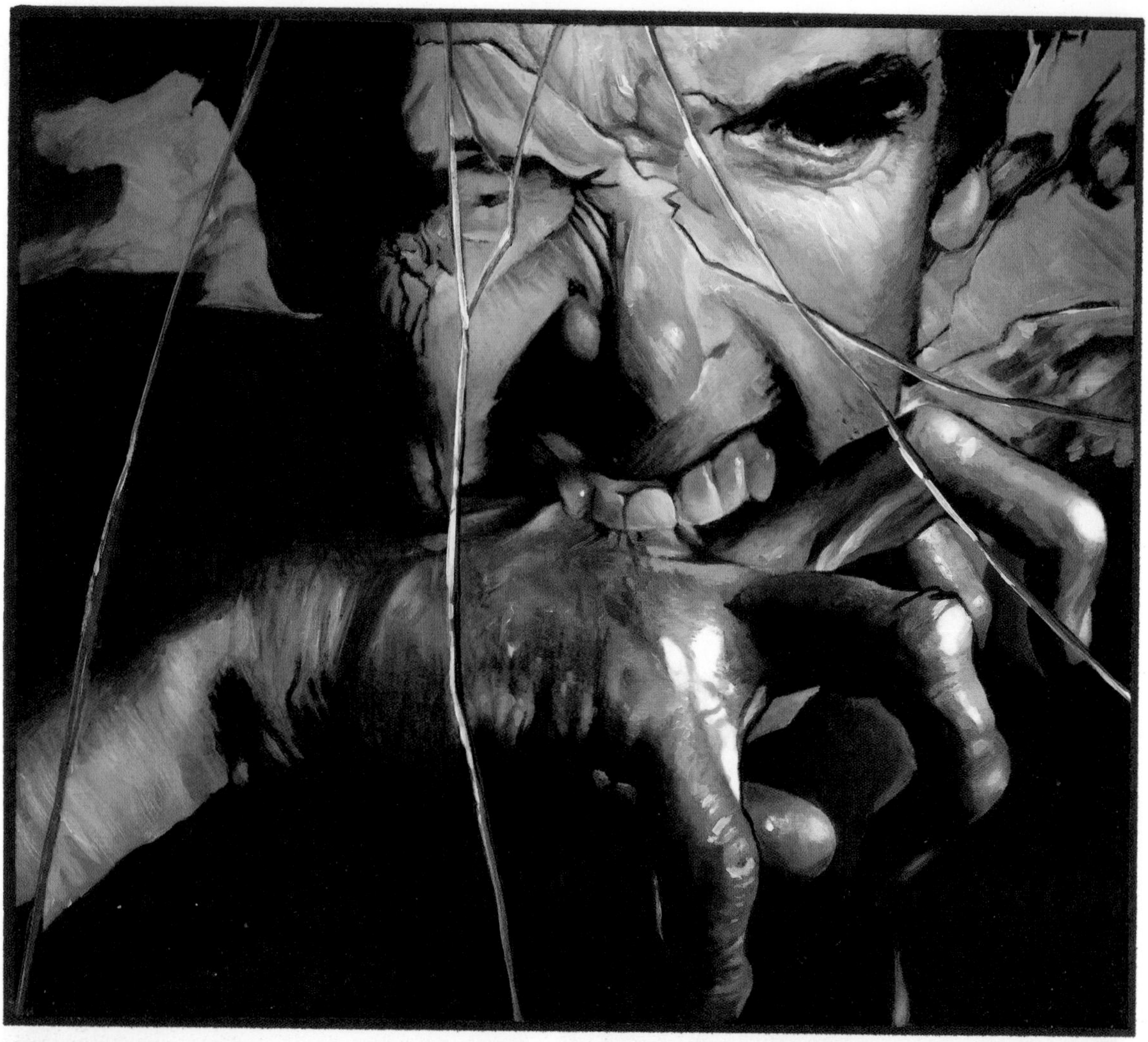

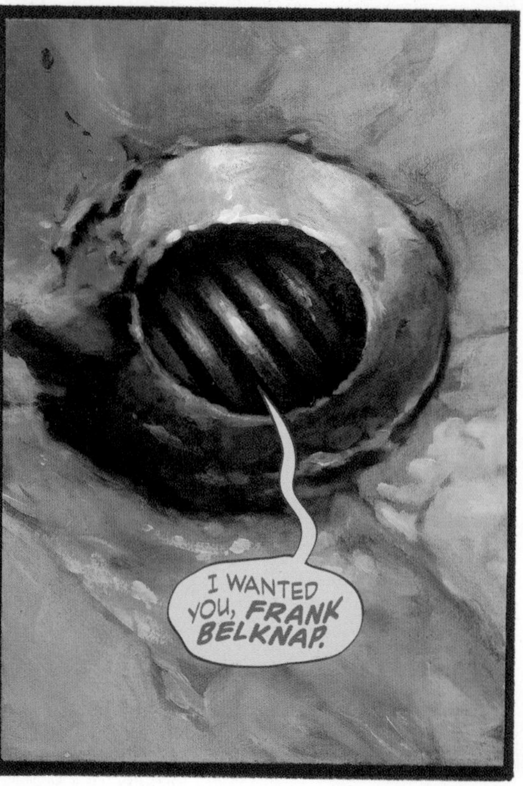
I WANTED YOU, FRANK BELKNAP.

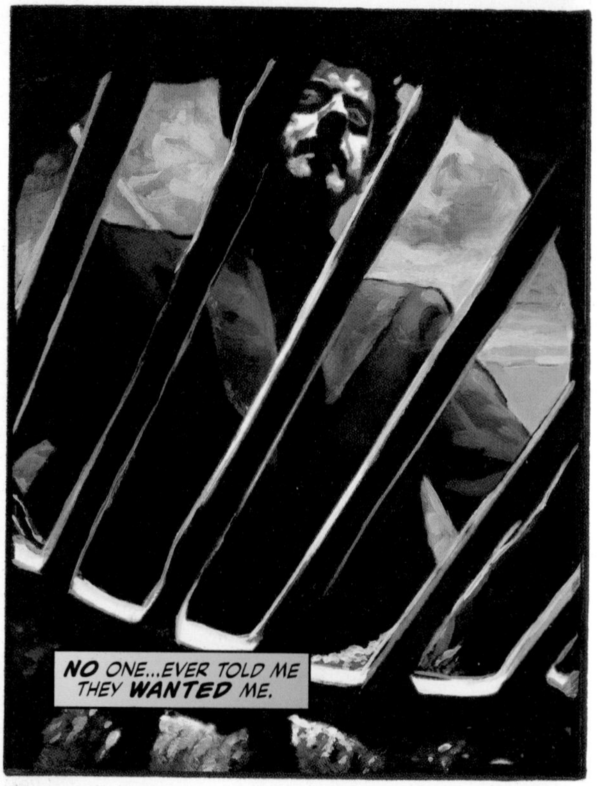
NO ONE...EVER TOLD ME THEY WANTED ME.

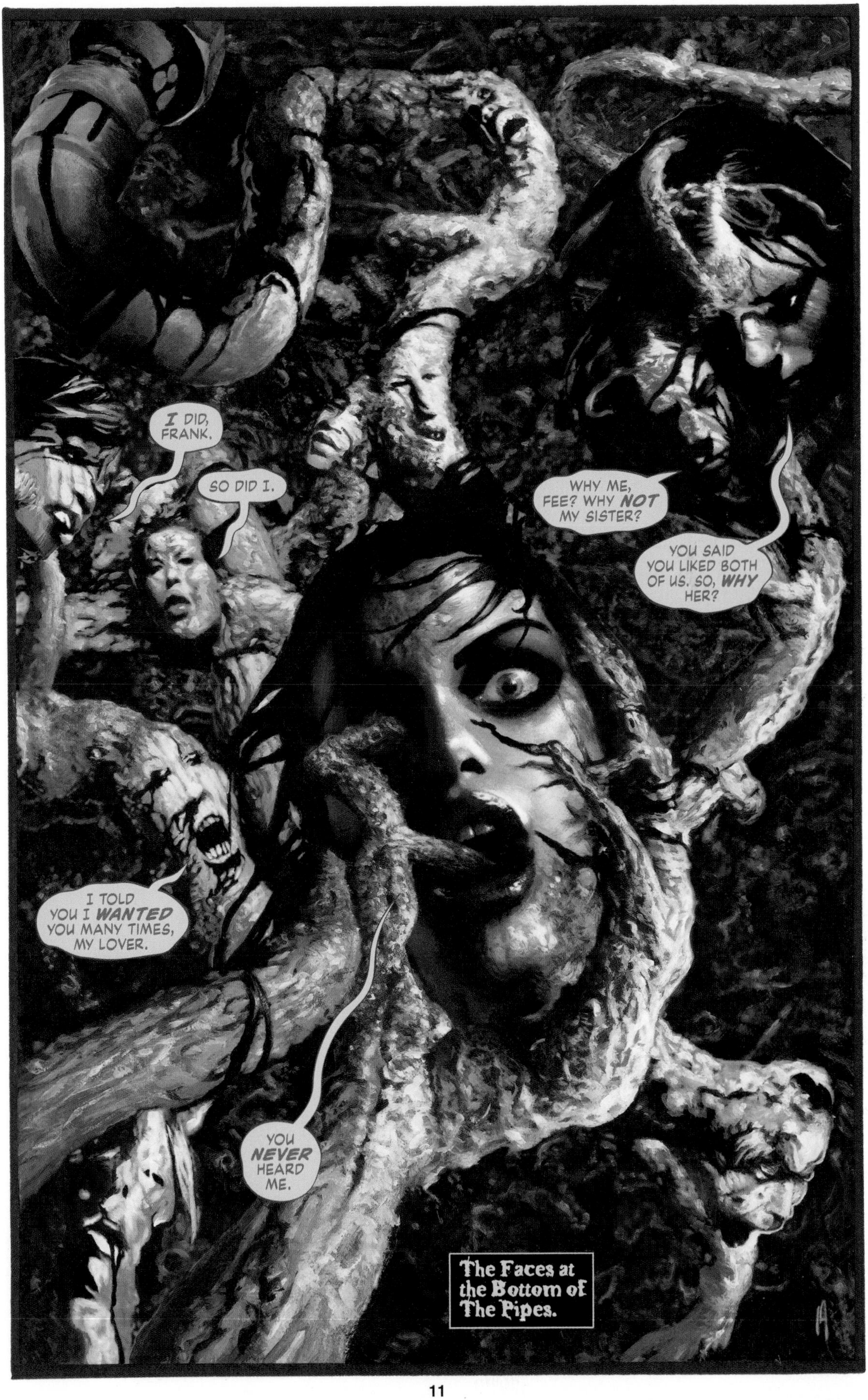
I DID, FRANK.
SO DID I.
WHY ME, FEE? WHY NOT MY SISTER?
YOU SAID YOU LIKED BOTH OF US. SO, WHY HER?
I TOLD YOU I WANTED YOU MANY TIMES, MY LOVER.
YOU NEVER HEARD ME.
The Faces at the Bottom of The Pipes.

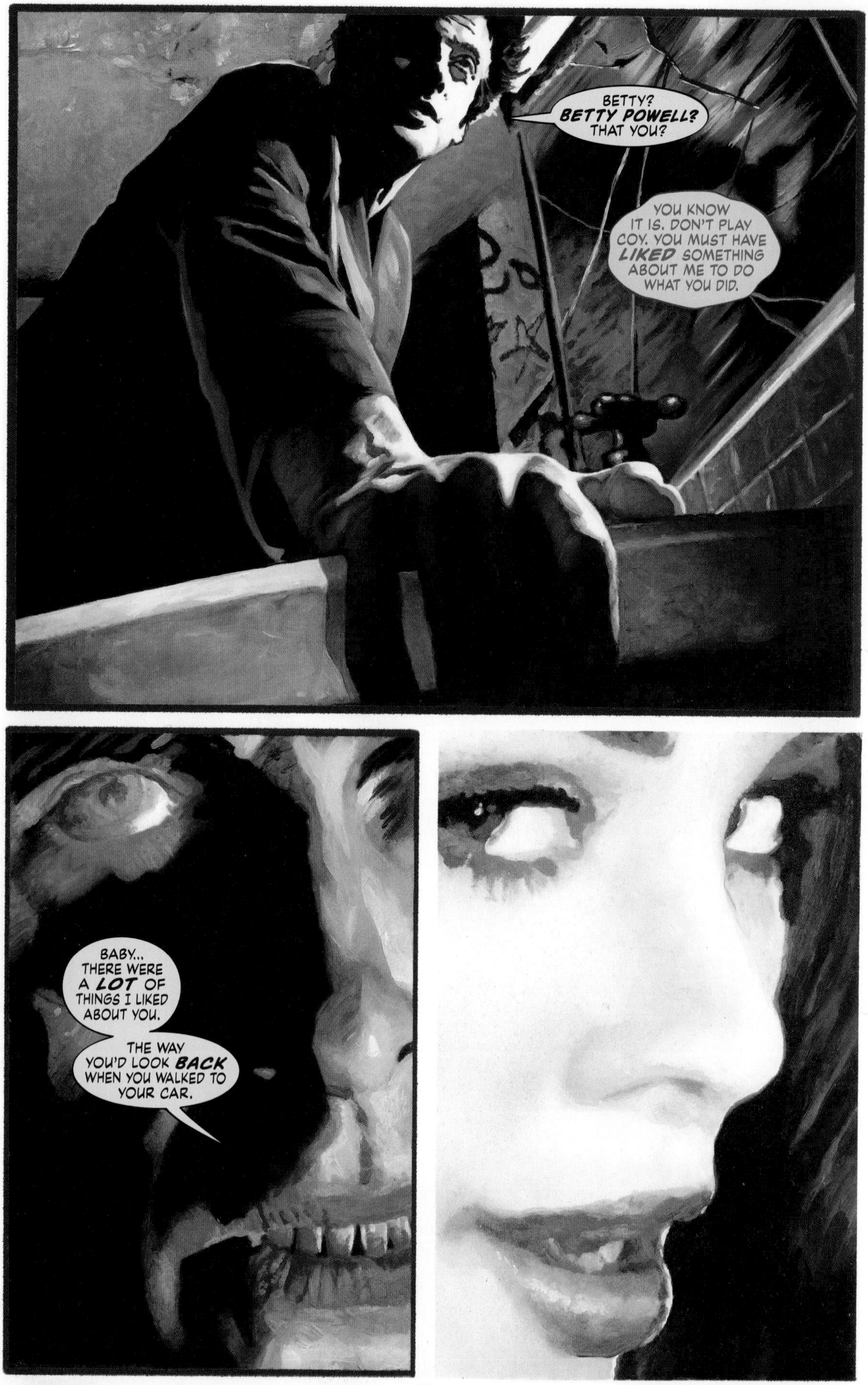
BETTY? BETTY POWELL? THAT YOU?
YOU KNOW IT IS. DON'T PLAY COY. YOU MUST HAVE LIKED SOMETHING ABOUT ME TO DO WHAT YOU DID.
BABY... THERE WERE A LOT OF THINGS I LIKED ABOUT YOU.
THE WAY YOU'D LOOK BACK WHEN YOU WALKED TO YOUR CAR.

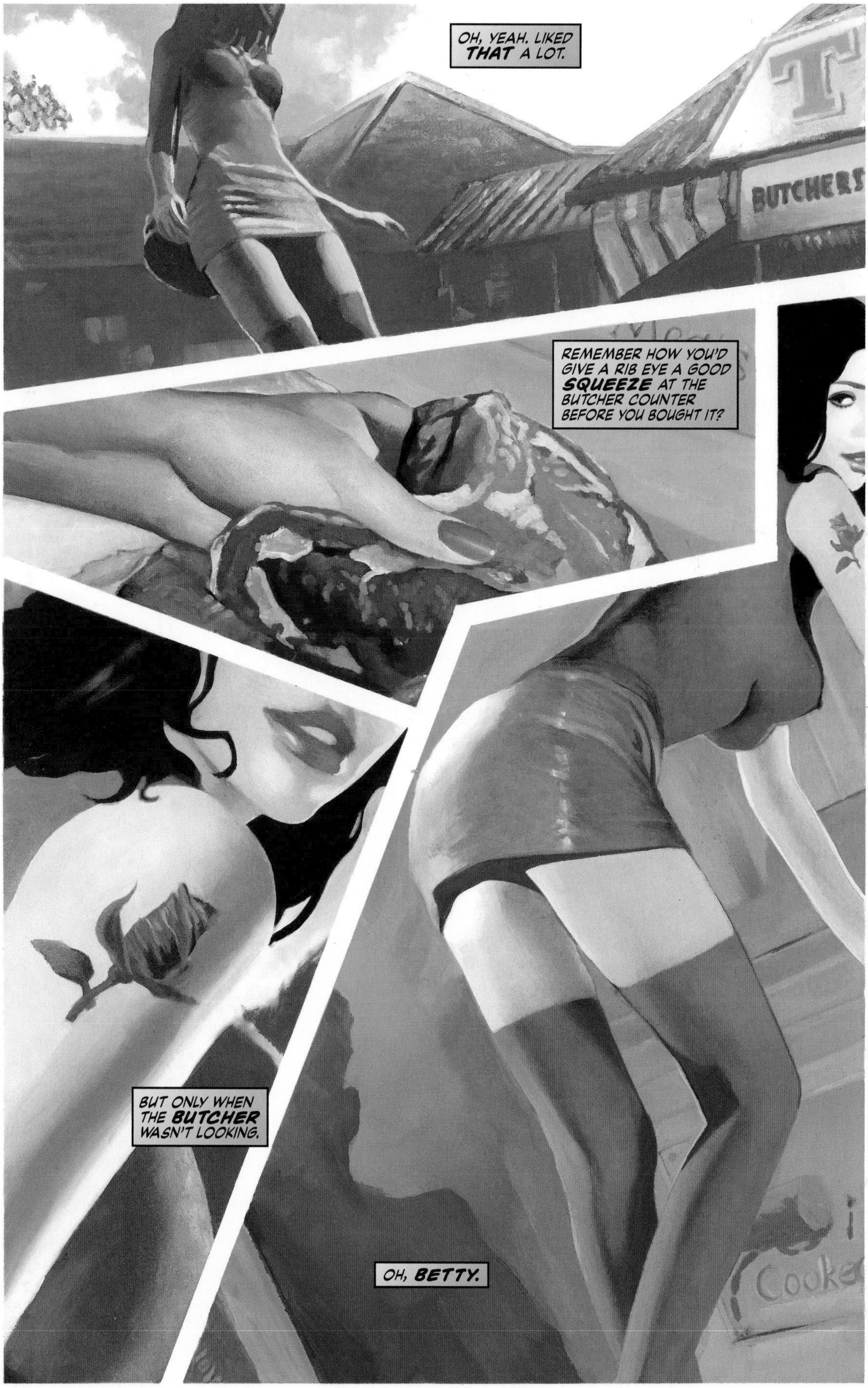
OH, YEAH. LIKED THAT A LOT.
BUTCHERS
REMEMBER HOW YOU'D GIVE A RIB EYE A GOOD SQUEEZE AT THE BUTCHER COUNTER BEFORE YOU BOUGHT IT?
BUT ONLY WHEN THE BUTCHER WASN'T LOOKING.
OH, BETTY.

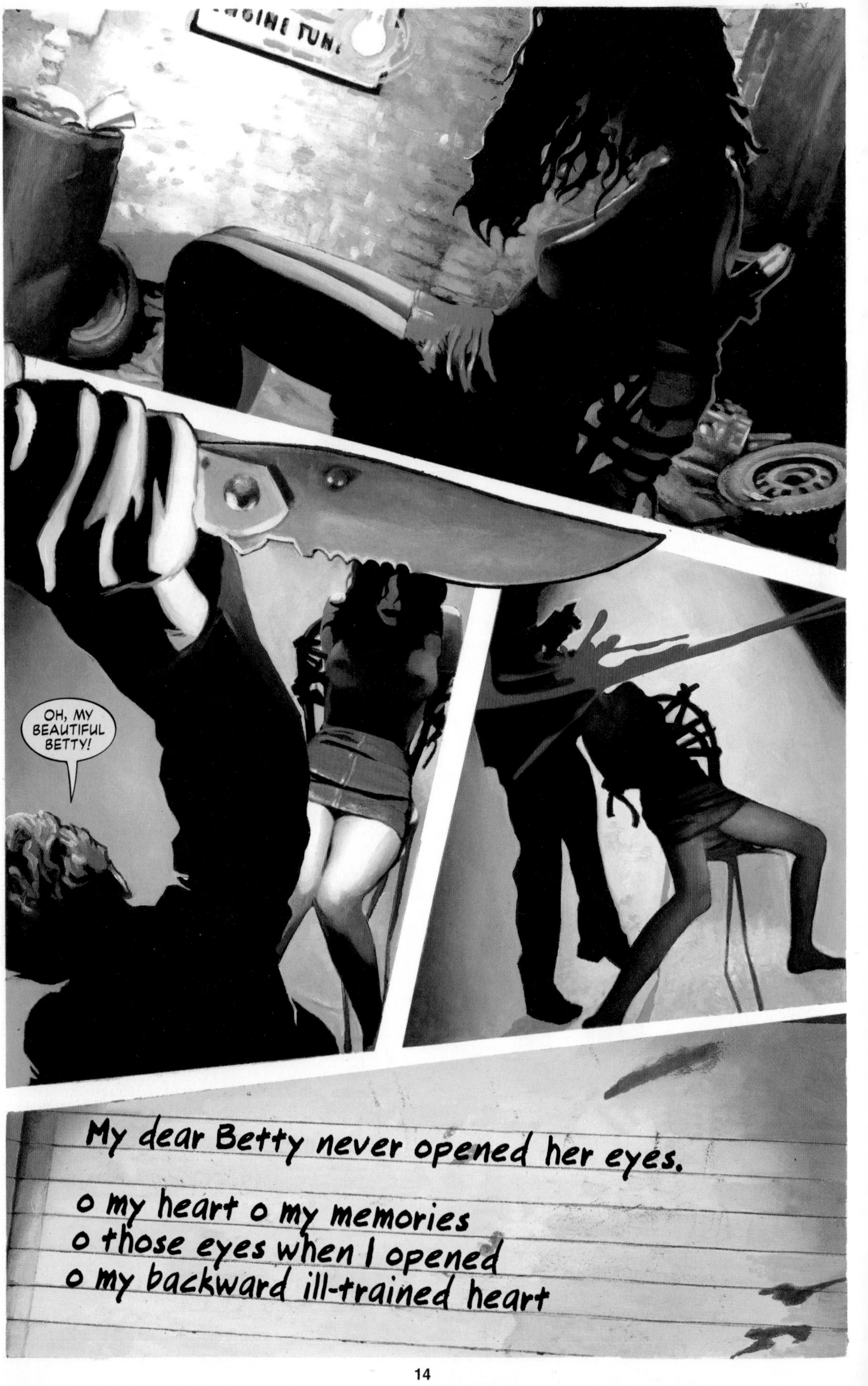
OH, MY BEAUTIFUL BETTY!
My dear Betty never opened her eyes.
o my heart o my memories
o those eyes when I opened
o my backward ill-trained heart

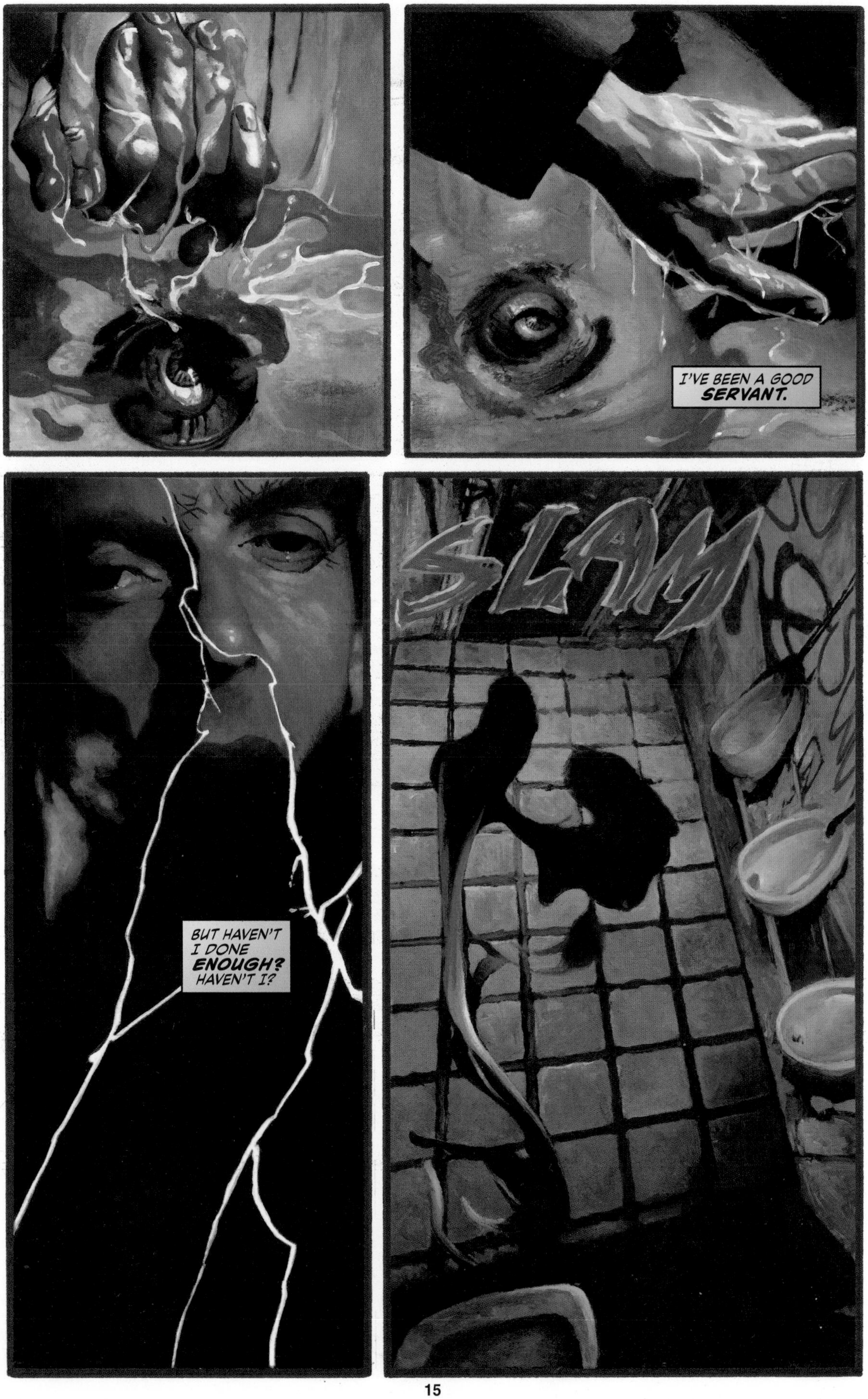
I'VE BEEN A GOOD **SERVANT.**
BUT HAVEN'T I DONE **ENOUGH?** HAVEN'T I?
SLAM

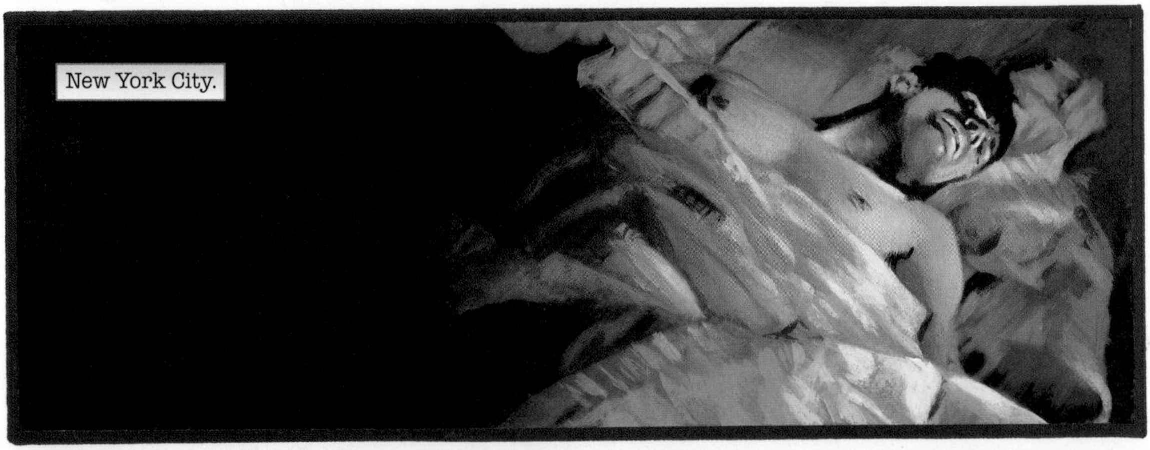
New York City.

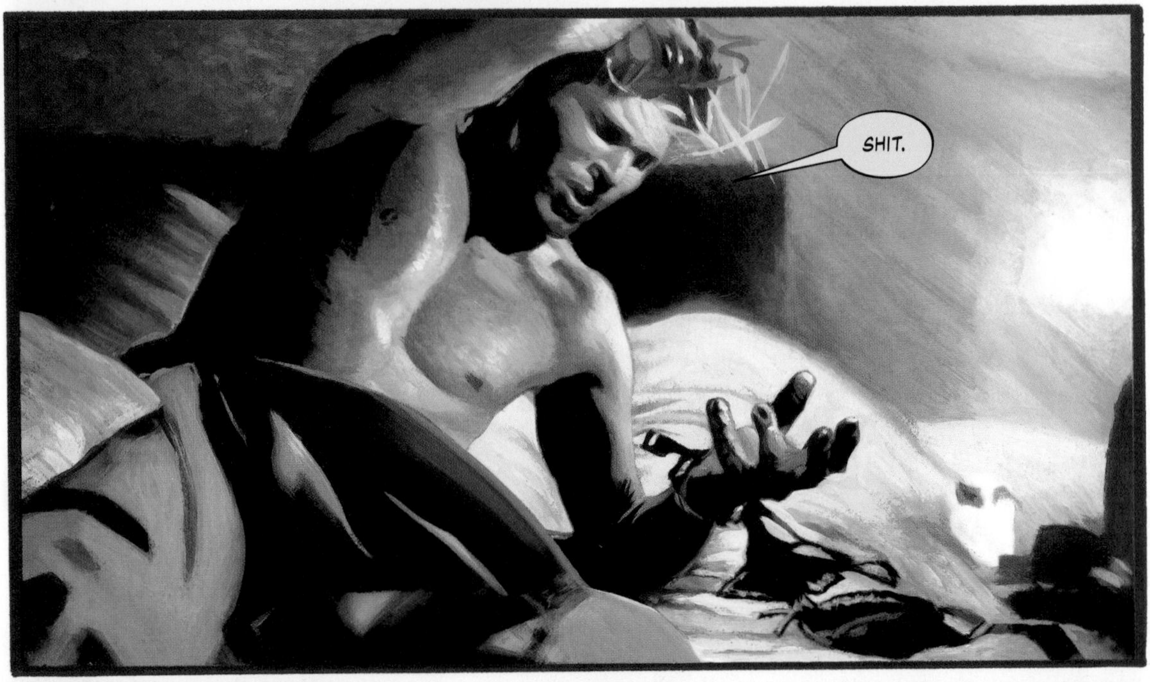
SHIT.

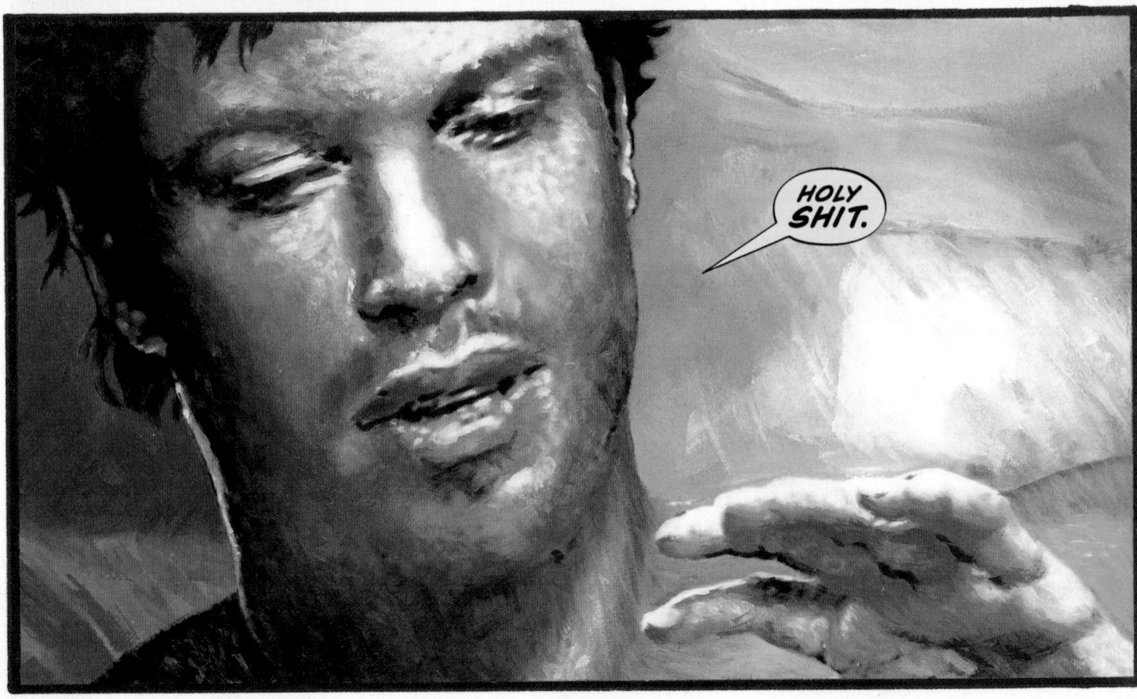
HOLY SHIT.

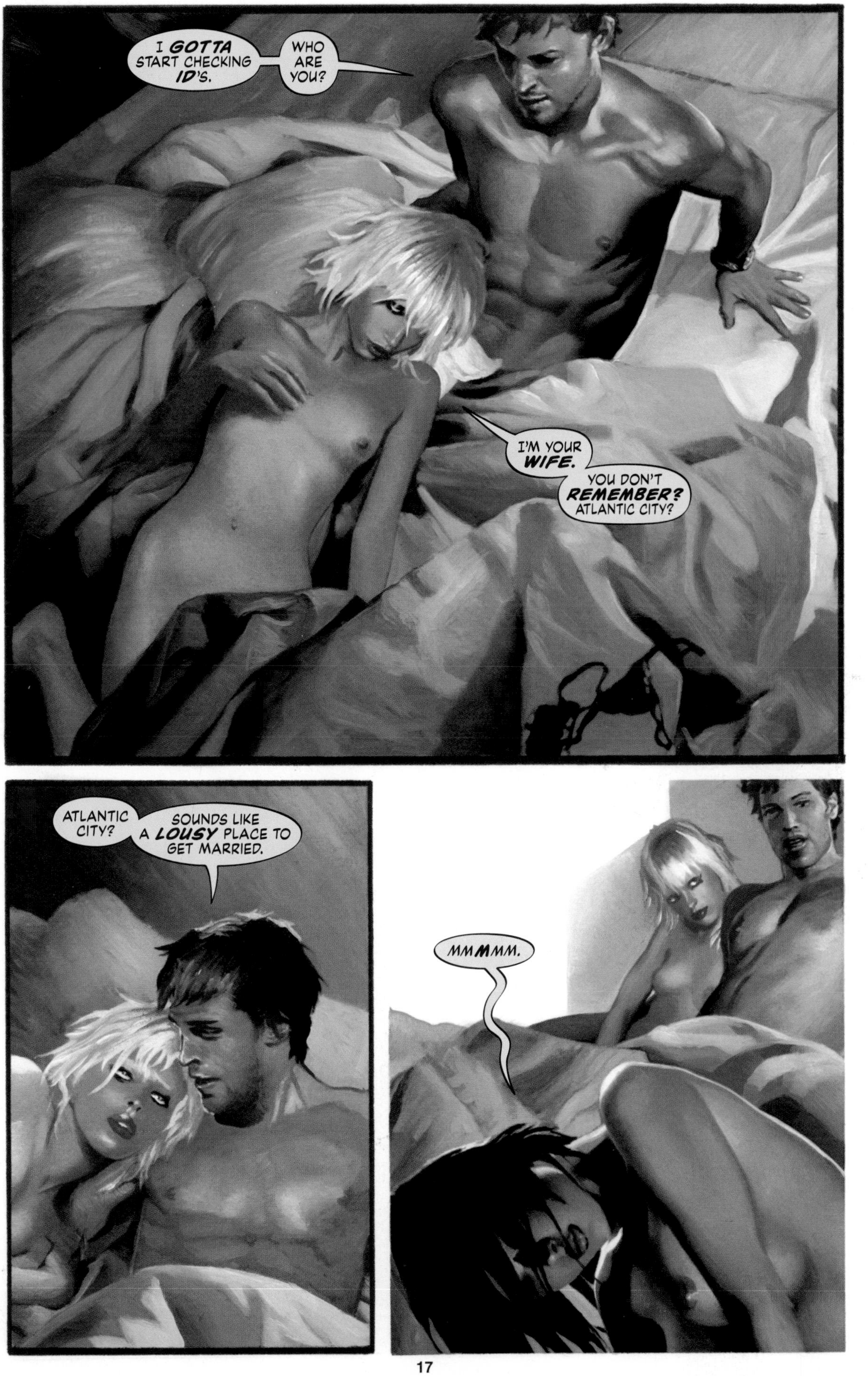
I GOTTA START CHECKING ID'S.
WHO ARE YOU?
I'M YOUR WIFE.
YOU DON'T REMEMBER? ATLANTIC CITY?
ATLANTIC CITY?
SOUNDS LIKE A LOUSY PLACE TO GET MARRIED.
MMMMM.

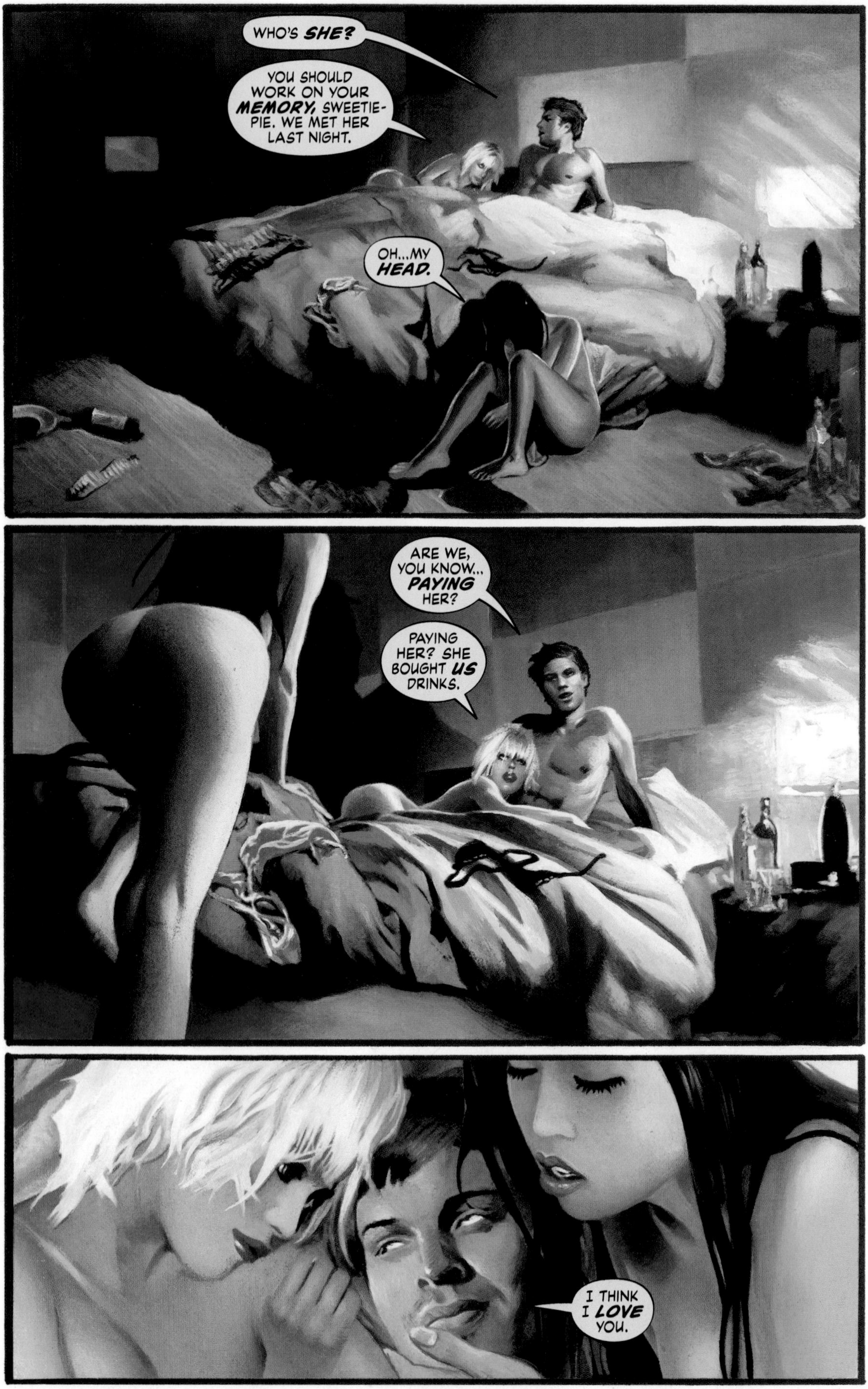
WHO'S SHE?
YOU SHOULD WORK ON YOUR MEMORY, SWEETIE-PIE. WE MET HER LAST NIGHT.
OH...MY HEAD.
ARE WE, YOU KNOW... PAYING HER?
PAYING HER? SHE BOUGHT US DRINKS.
I THINK I LOVE YOU.

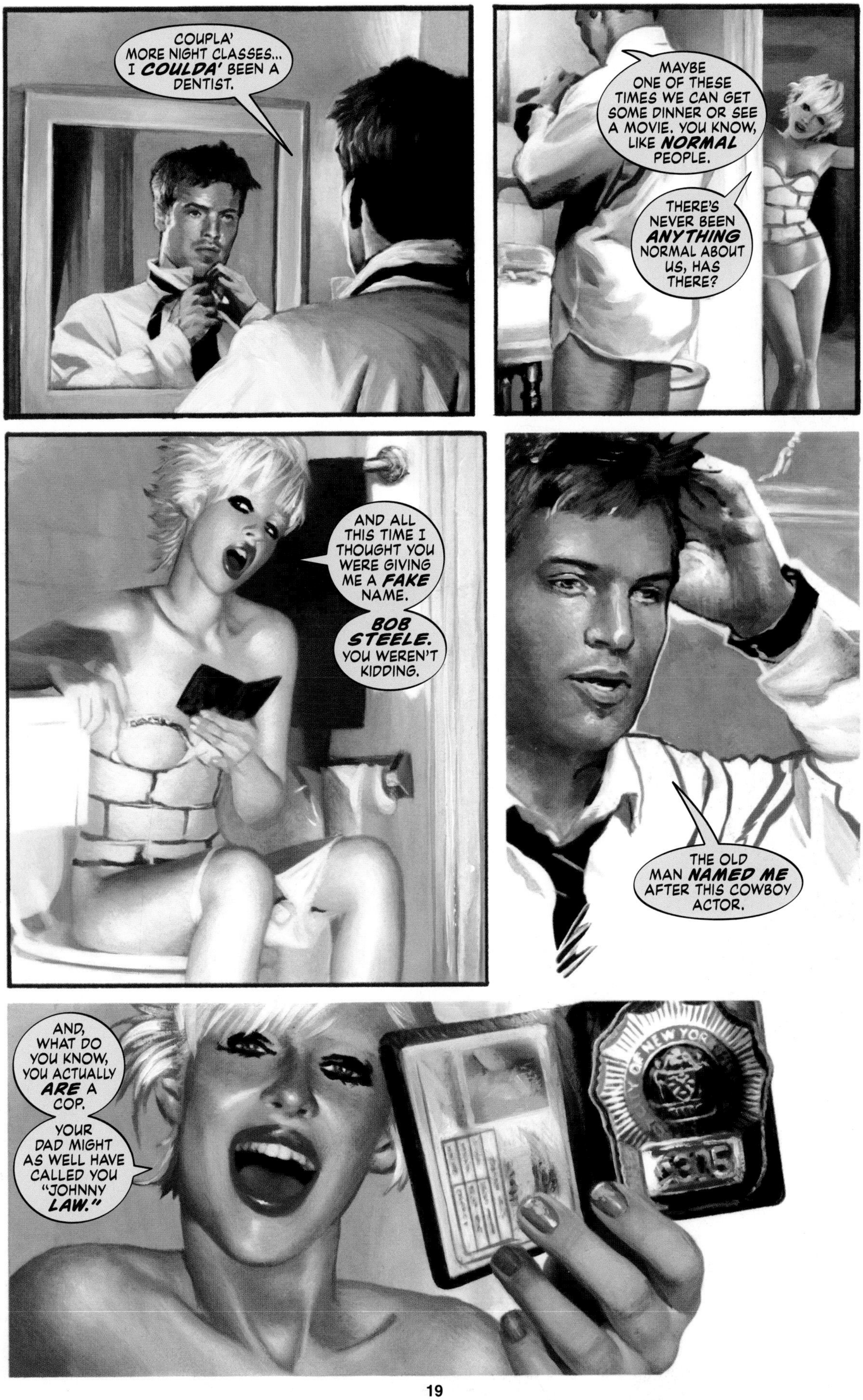
COUPLA' MORE NIGHT CLASSES... I **COULDA'** BEEN A DENTIST.
MAYBE ONE OF THESE TIMES WE CAN GET SOME DINNER OR SEE A MOVIE. YOU KNOW, LIKE **NORMAL** PEOPLE.
THERE'S NEVER BEEN **ANYTHING** NORMAL ABOUT US, HAS THERE?
AND ALL THIS TIME I THOUGHT YOU WERE GIVING ME A **FAKE** NAME.
BOB STEELE. YOU WEREN'T KIDDING.
THE OLD MAN **NAMED ME** AFTER THIS COWBOY ACTOR.
AND, WHAT DO YOU KNOW, YOU ACTUALLY **ARE** A COP.
YOUR DAD MIGHT AS WELL HAVE CALLED YOU "JOHNNY **LAW.**"

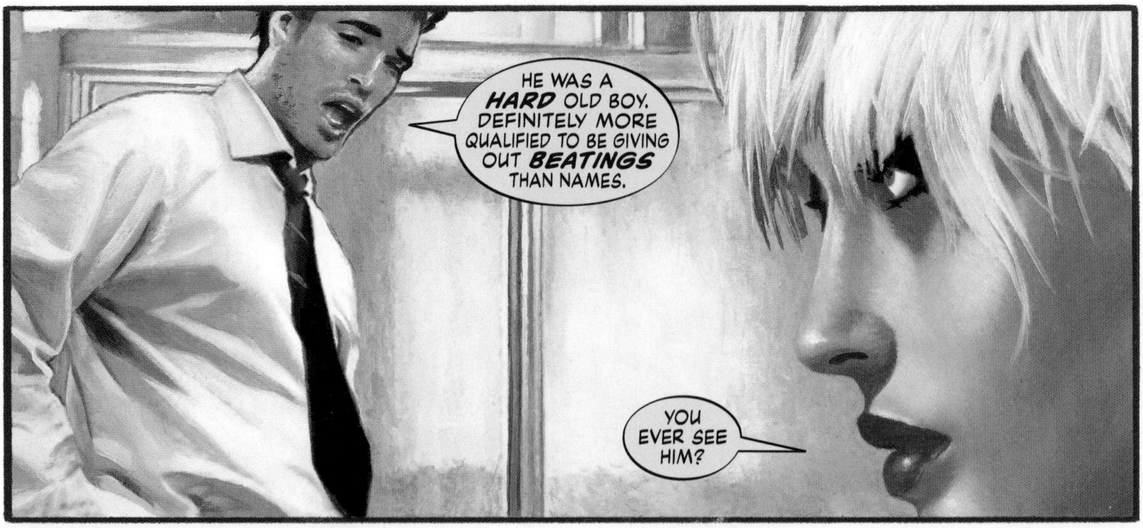
HE WAS A HARD OLD BOY. DEFINITELY MORE QUALIFIED TO BE GIVING OUT BEATINGS THAN NAMES.
YOU EVER SEE HIM?

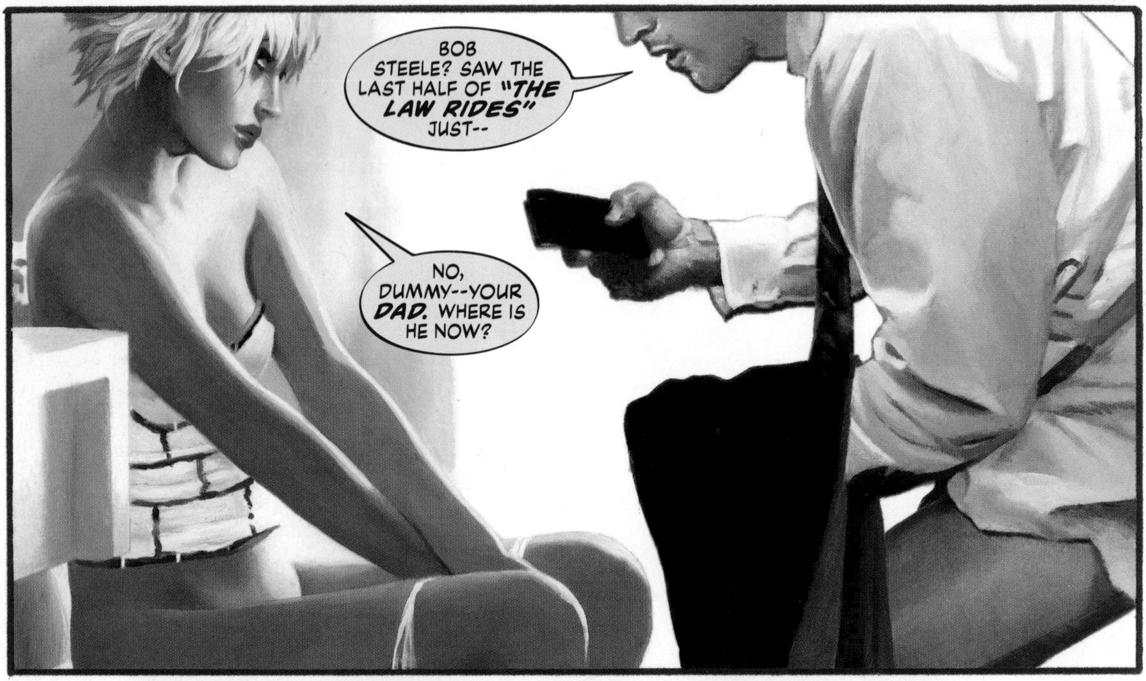
BOB STEELE? SAW THE LAST HALF OF "THE LAW RIDES" JUST--
NO, DUMMY--YOUR DAD. WHERE IS HE NOW?

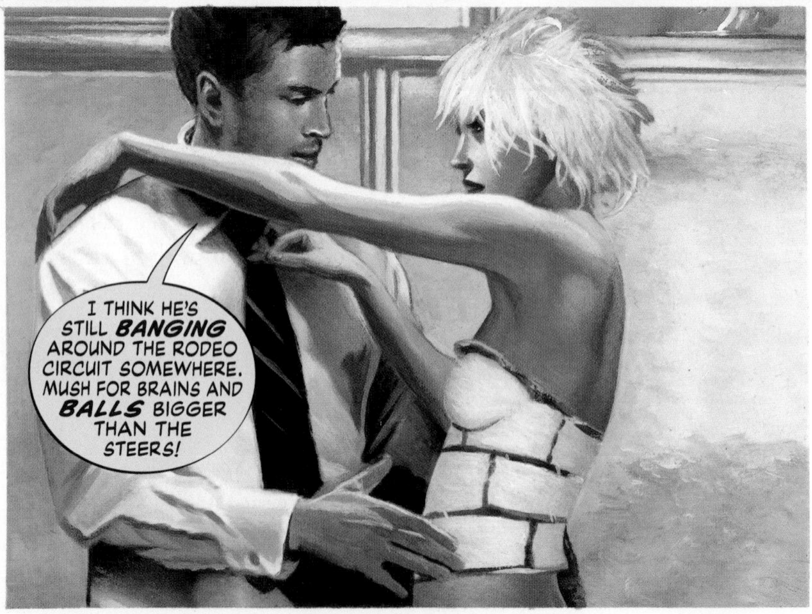
I THINK HE'S STILL BANGING AROUND THE RODEO CIRCUIT SOMEWHERE. MUSH FOR BRAINS AND BALLS BIGGER THAN THE STEERS!

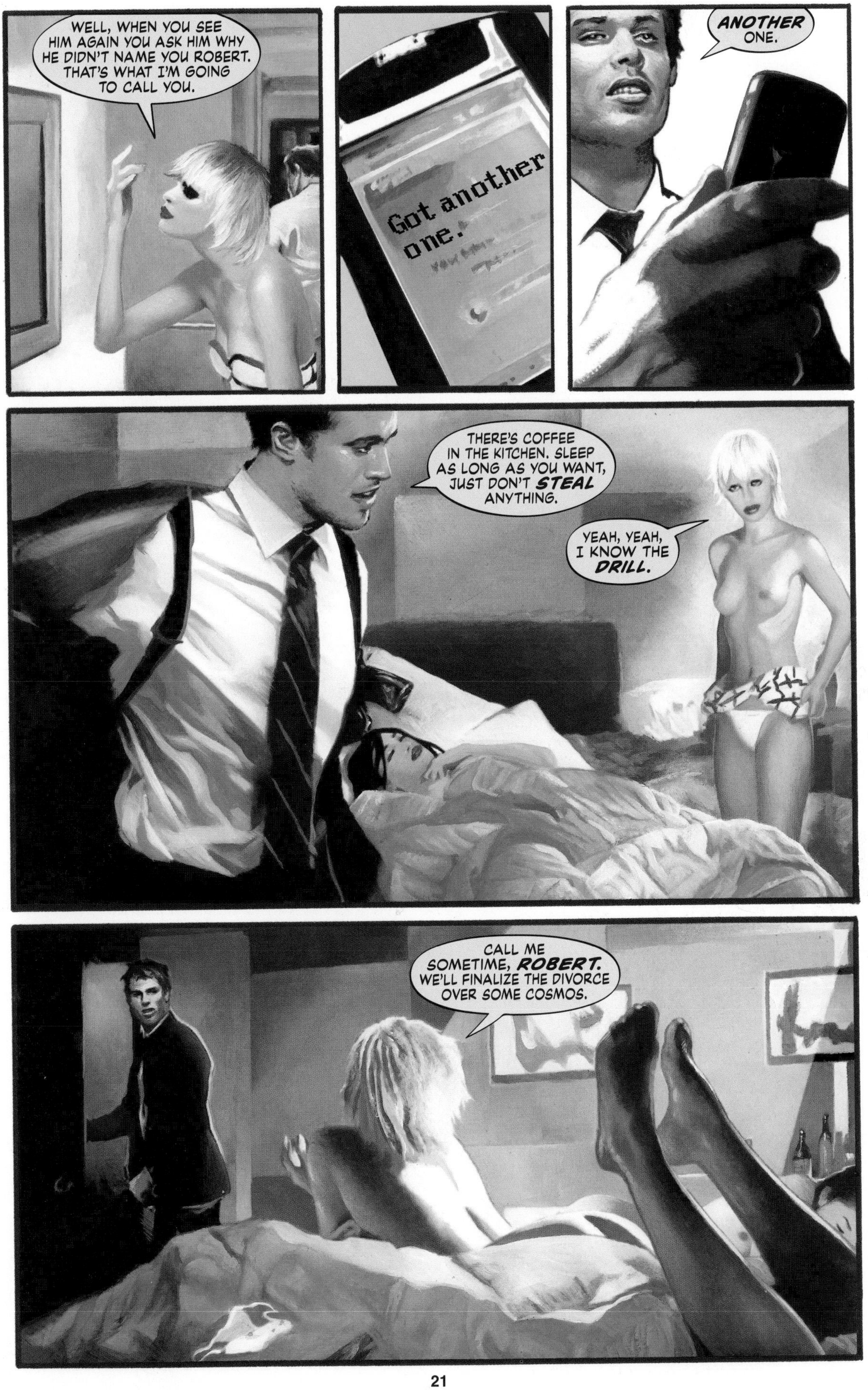
WELL, WHEN YOU SEE HIM AGAIN YOU ASK HIM WHY HE DIDN'T NAME YOU ROBERT. THAT'S WHAT I'M GOING TO CALL YOU.
Got another one.
ANOTHER ONE.
THERE'S COFFEE IN THE KITCHEN. SLEEP AS LONG AS YOU WANT, JUST DON'T STEAL ANYTHING.
YEAH, YEAH, I KNOW THE DRILL.
CALL ME SOMETIME, ROBERT. WE'LL FINALIZE THE DIVORCE OVER SOME COSMOS.

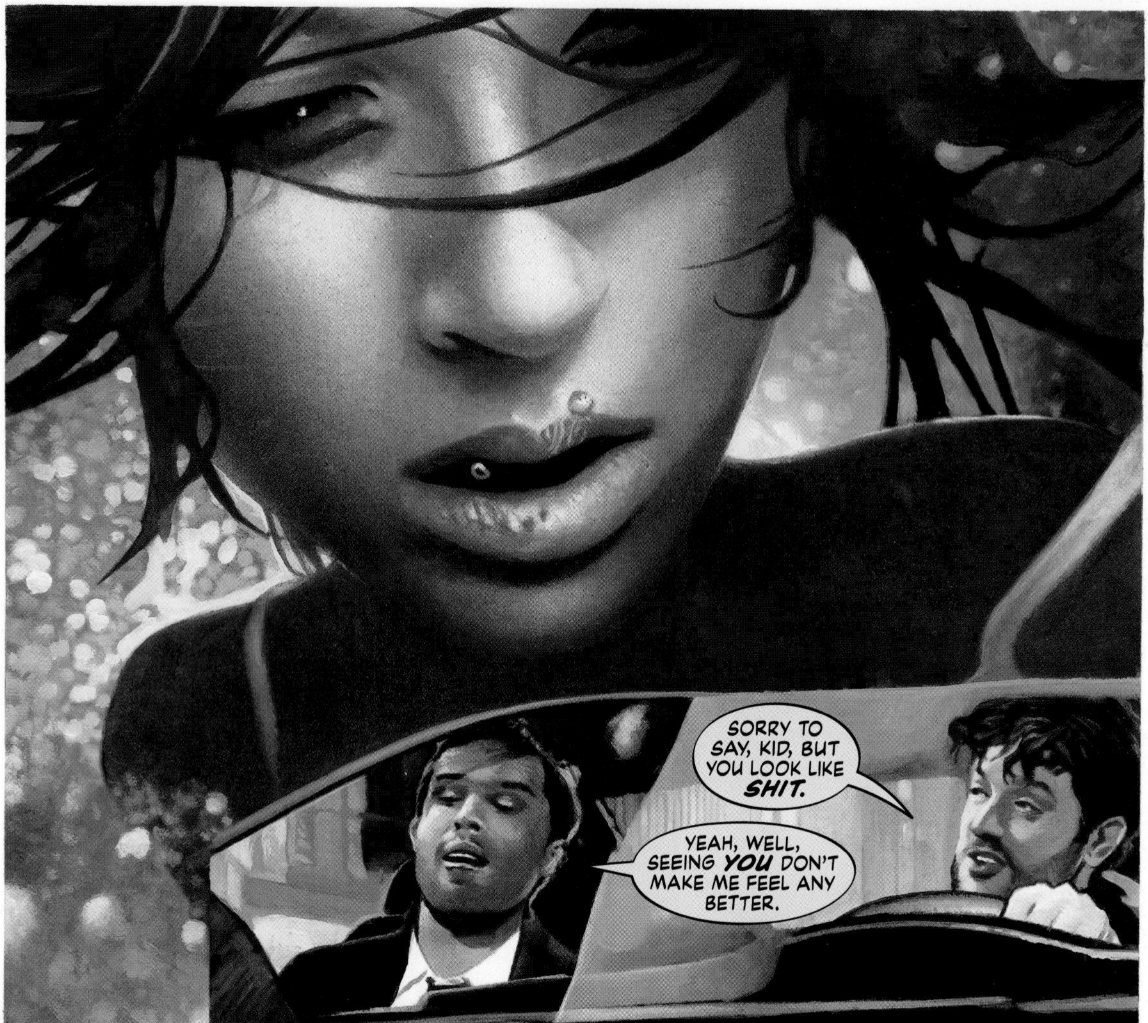
SORRY TO SAY, KID, BUT YOU LOOK LIKE *SHIT.*
YEAH, WELL, SEEING *YOU* DON'T MAKE ME FEEL ANY BETTER.

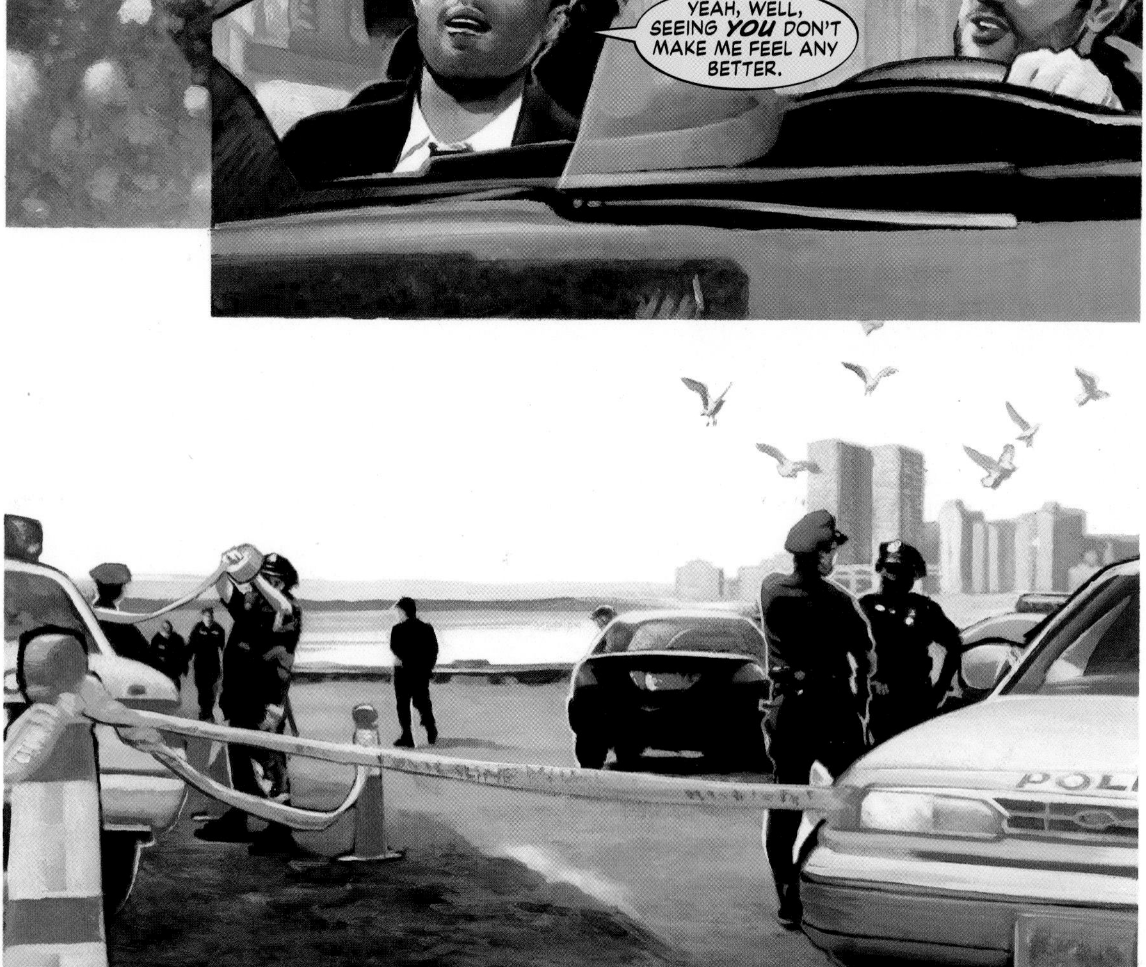

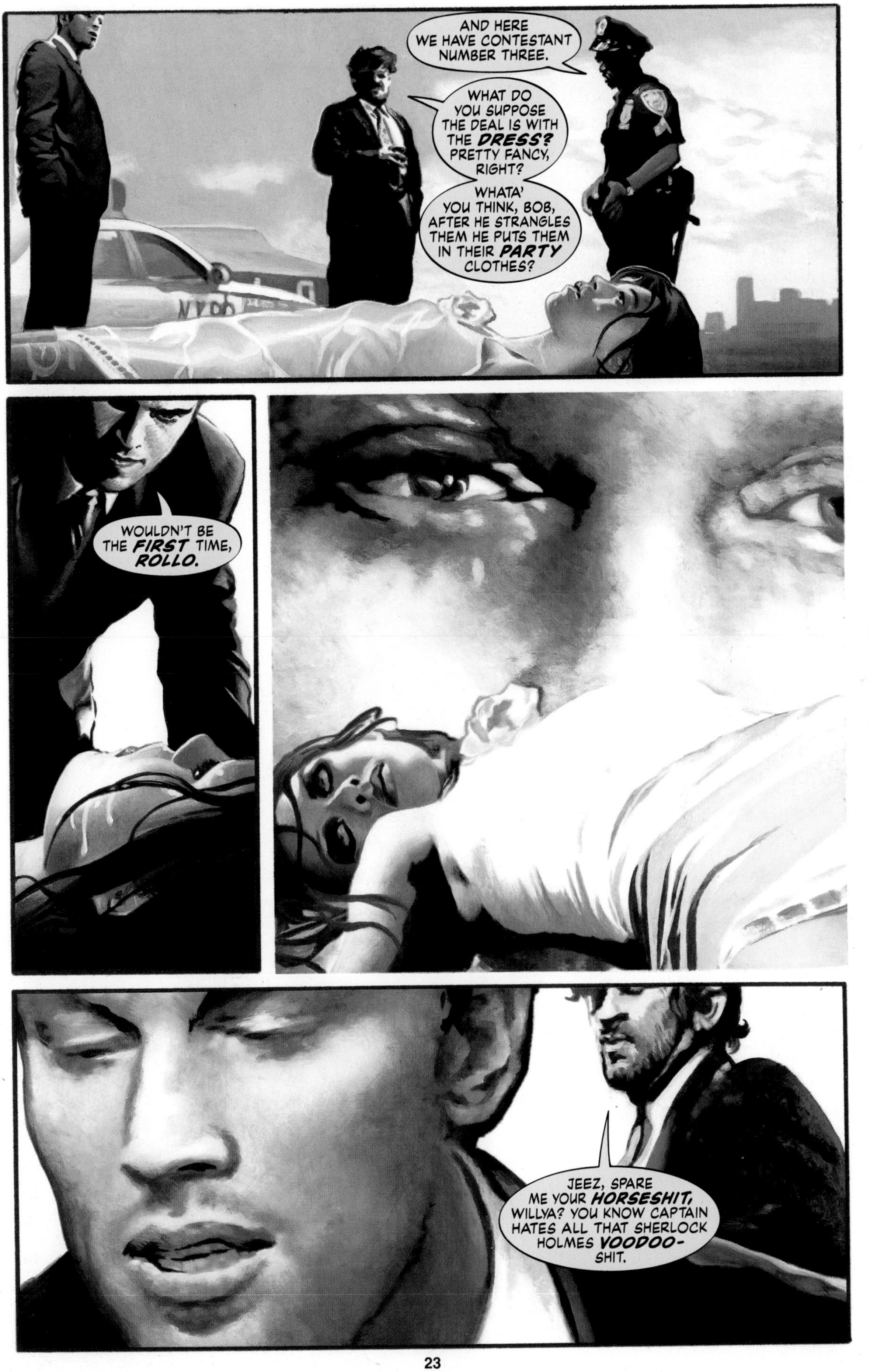
AND HERE WE HAVE CONTESTANT NUMBER THREE.
WHAT DO YOU SUPPOSE THE DEAL IS WITH THE DRESS? PRETTY FANCY, RIGHT?
WHATA' YOU THINK, BOB, AFTER HE STRANGLES THEM HE PUTS THEM IN THEIR PARTY CLOTHES?
NYPD
WOULDN'T BE THE FIRST TIME, ROLLO.
JEEZ, SPARE ME YOUR HORSESHIT, WILLYA? YOU KNOW CAPTAIN HATES ALL THAT SHERLOCK HOLMES VOODOO-SHIT.

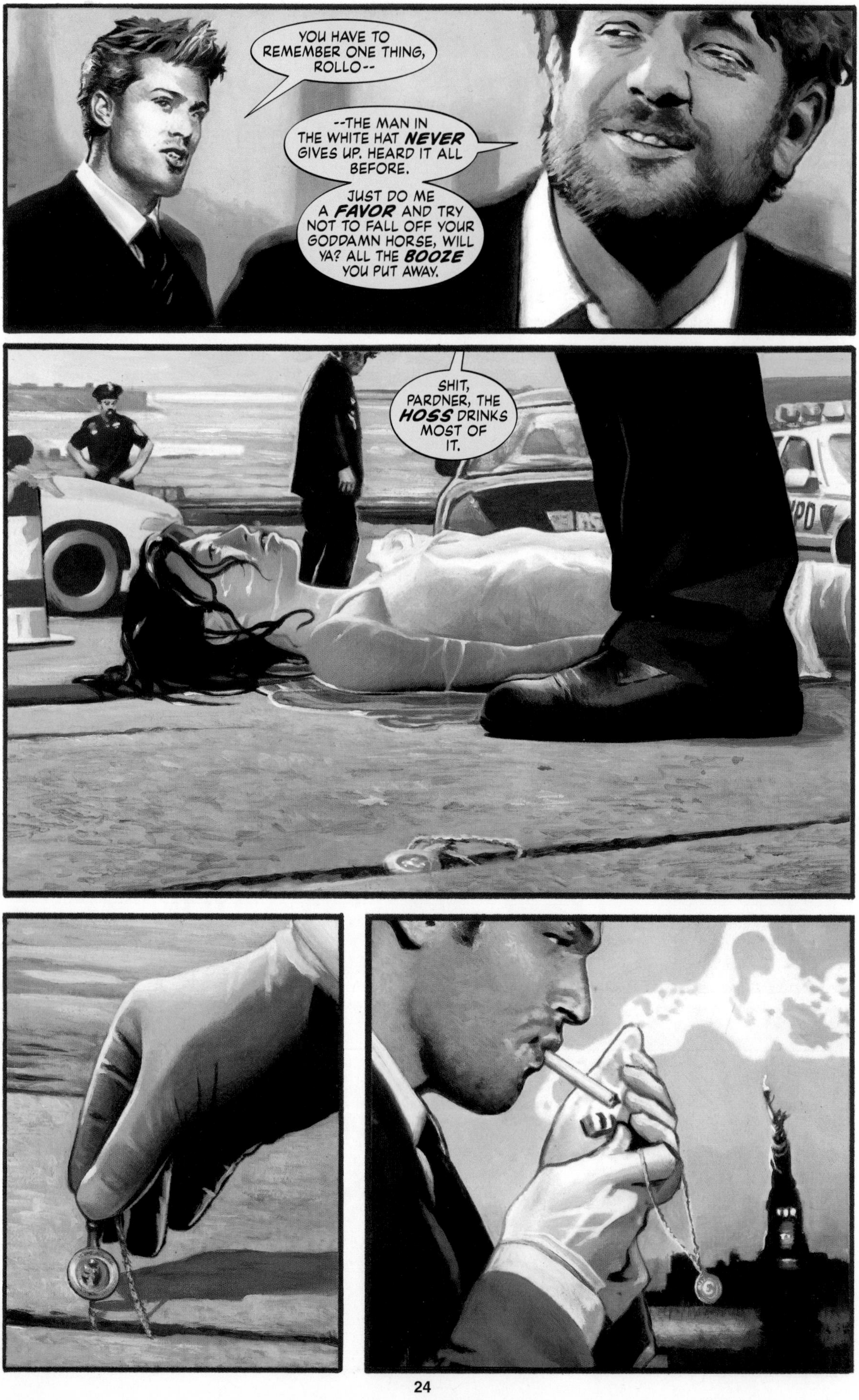
YOU HAVE TO REMEMBER ONE THING, ROLLO--
--THE MAN IN THE WHITE HAT NEVER GIVES UP. HEARD IT ALL BEFORE.
JUST DO ME A FAVOR AND TRY NOT TO FALL OFF YOUR GODDAMN HORSE, WILL YA? ALL THE BOOZE YOU PUT AWAY.
SHIT, PARDNER, THE HOSS DRINKS MOST OF IT.
NYPD

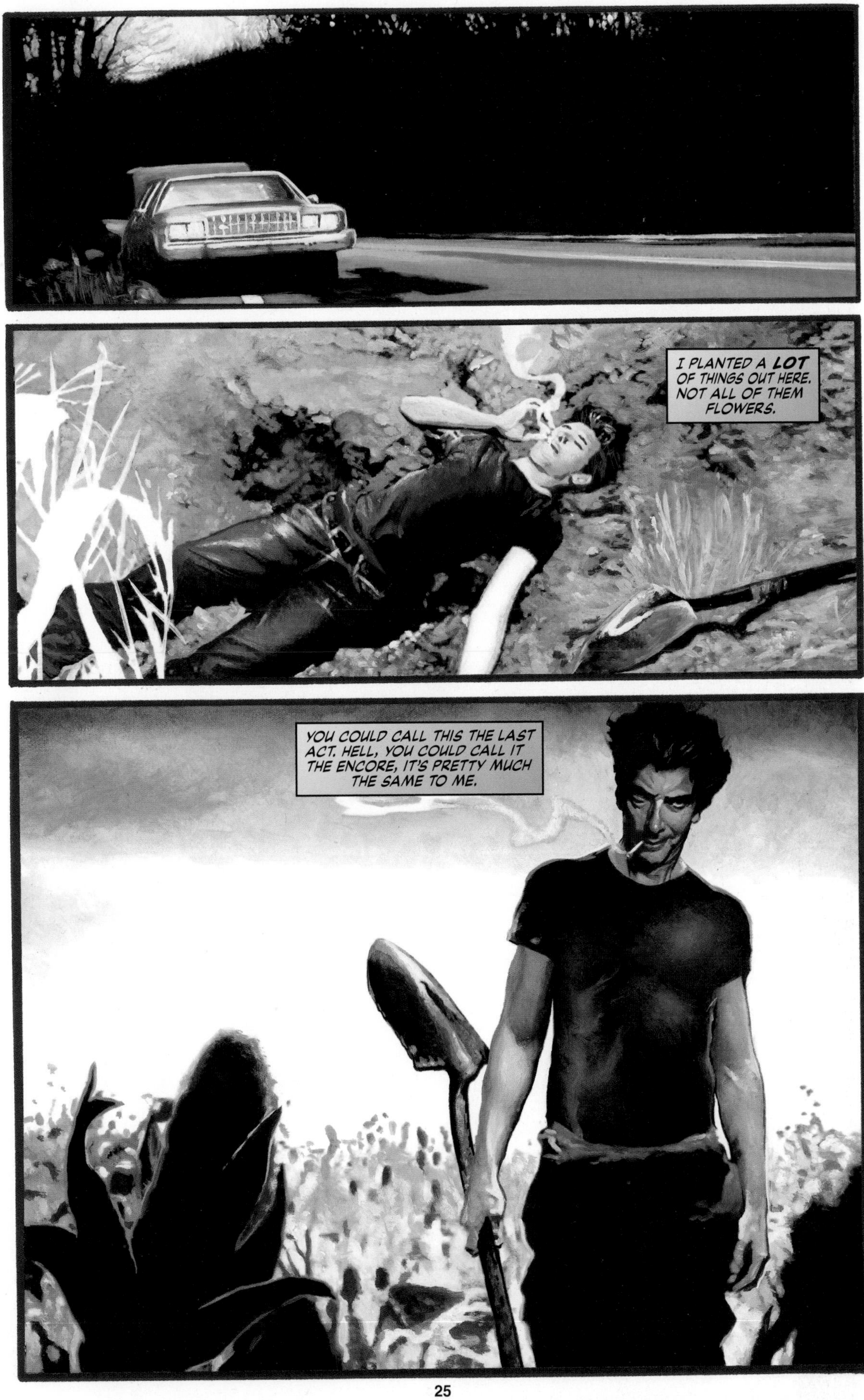
I PLANTED A **LOT** OF THINGS OUT HERE. NOT ALL OF THEM FLOWERS.
YOU COULD CALL THIS THE LAST ACT. HELL, YOU COULD CALL IT THE ENCORE, IT'S PRETTY MUCH THE SAME TO ME.

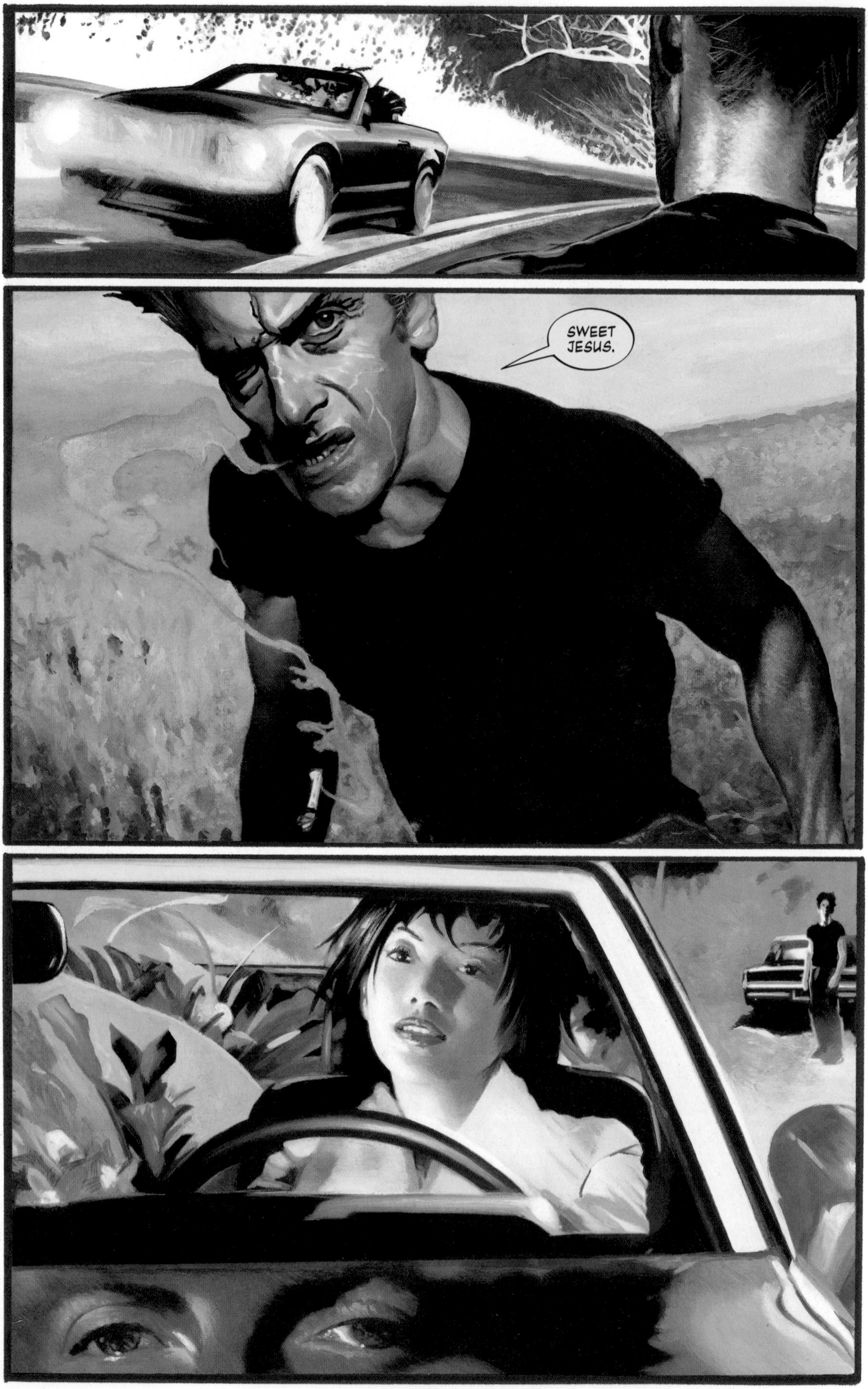
SWEET JESUS.

After Dark.

LADY, IF THERE'S ONE BITCH IN ALL THIS WORLD I *DON'T* WANT TO PISS OFF, IT'S YOU.

IN THE MIDDLE OF THE *NIGHT*, I HEAR THE SHIT YOU *WHISPER*.

PUSSY.

GODDAMN *PUSSY* IS WHAT YOU'VE BECOME.

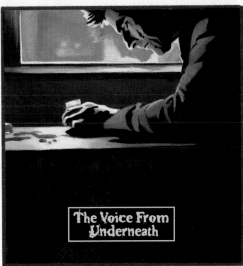

The Voice From Underneath

LOOK AT YOURSELF, FEE. DICKLESS WONDER.

THE *OLD* YOU WOULD'VE BEEN ON THIS ALREADY.

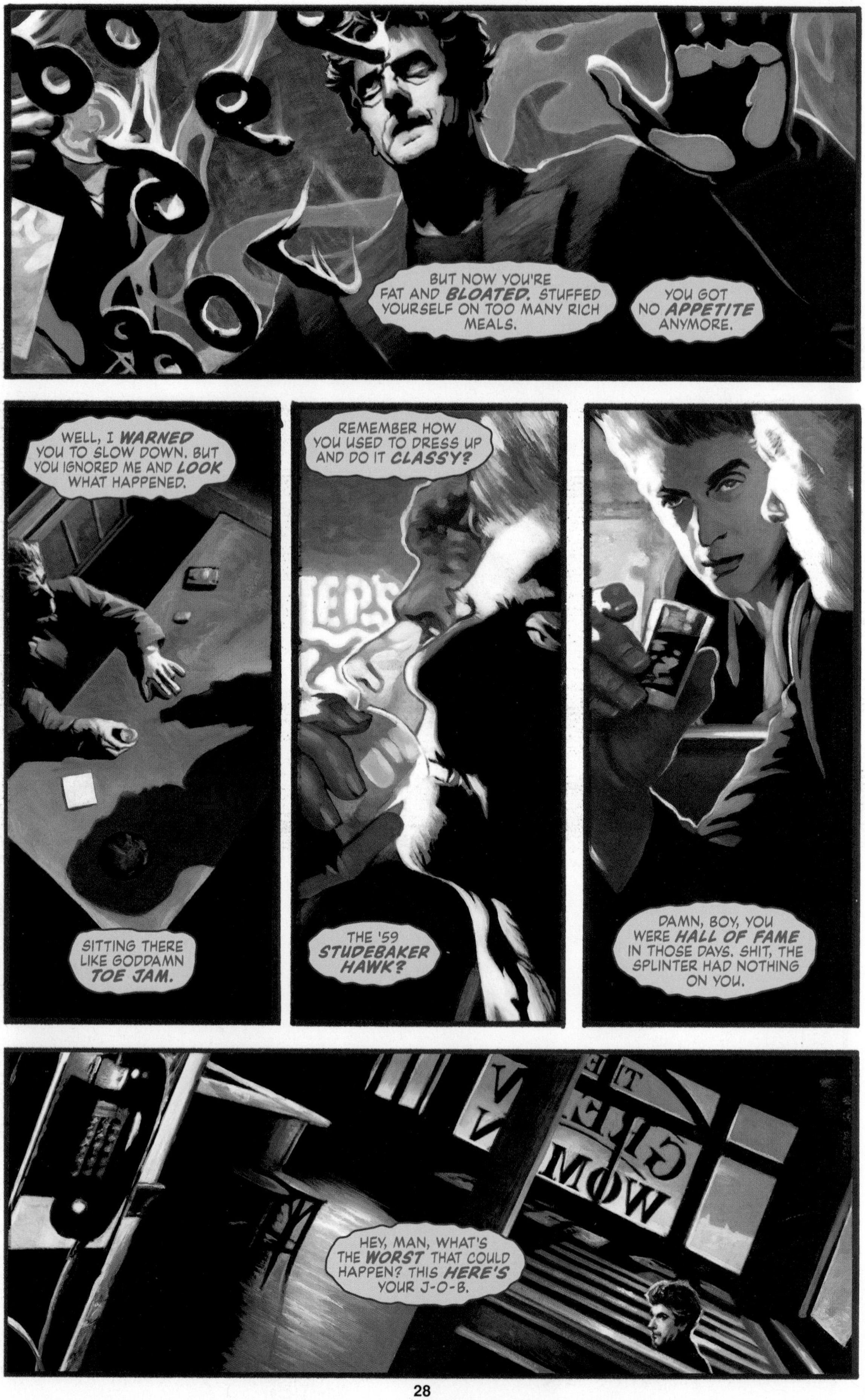
BUT NOW YOU'RE FAT AND BLOATED. STUFFED YOURSELF ON TOO MANY RICH MEALS.
YOU GOT NO APPETITE ANYMORE.
WELL, I WARNED YOU TO SLOW DOWN. BUT YOU IGNORED ME AND LOOK WHAT HAPPENED.
SITTING THERE LIKE GODDAMN TOE JAM.
REMEMBER HOW YOU USED TO DRESS UP AND DO IT CLASSY?
THE '59 STUDEBAKER HAWK?
DAMN, BOY, YOU WERE HALL OF FAME IN THOSE DAYS. SHIT, THE SPLINTER HAD NOTHING ON YOU.
HEY, MAN, WHAT'S THE WORST THAT COULD HAPPEN? THIS HERE'S YOUR J-O-B.

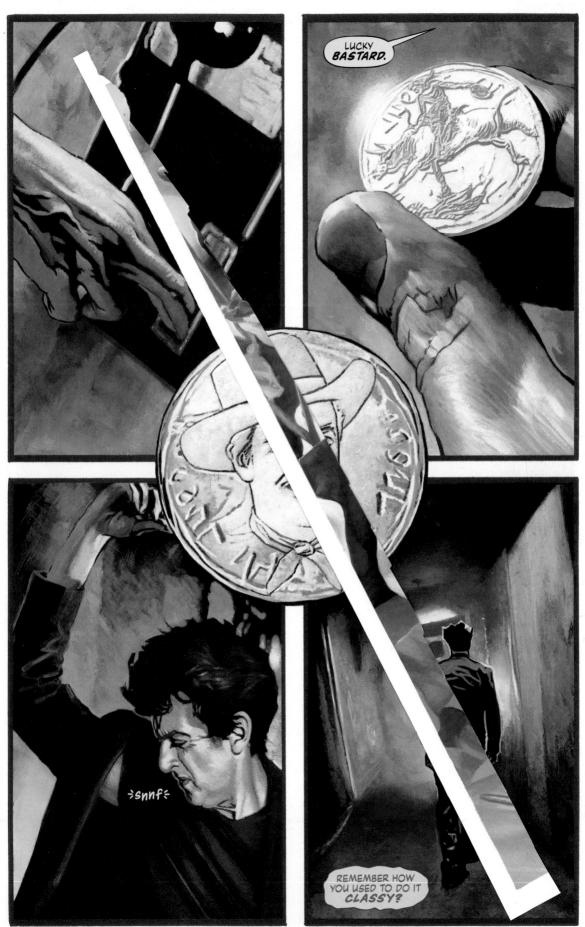

LUCKY **BASTARD**.

≟snnf≟

REMEMBER HOW YOU USED TO DO IT **CLASSY?**

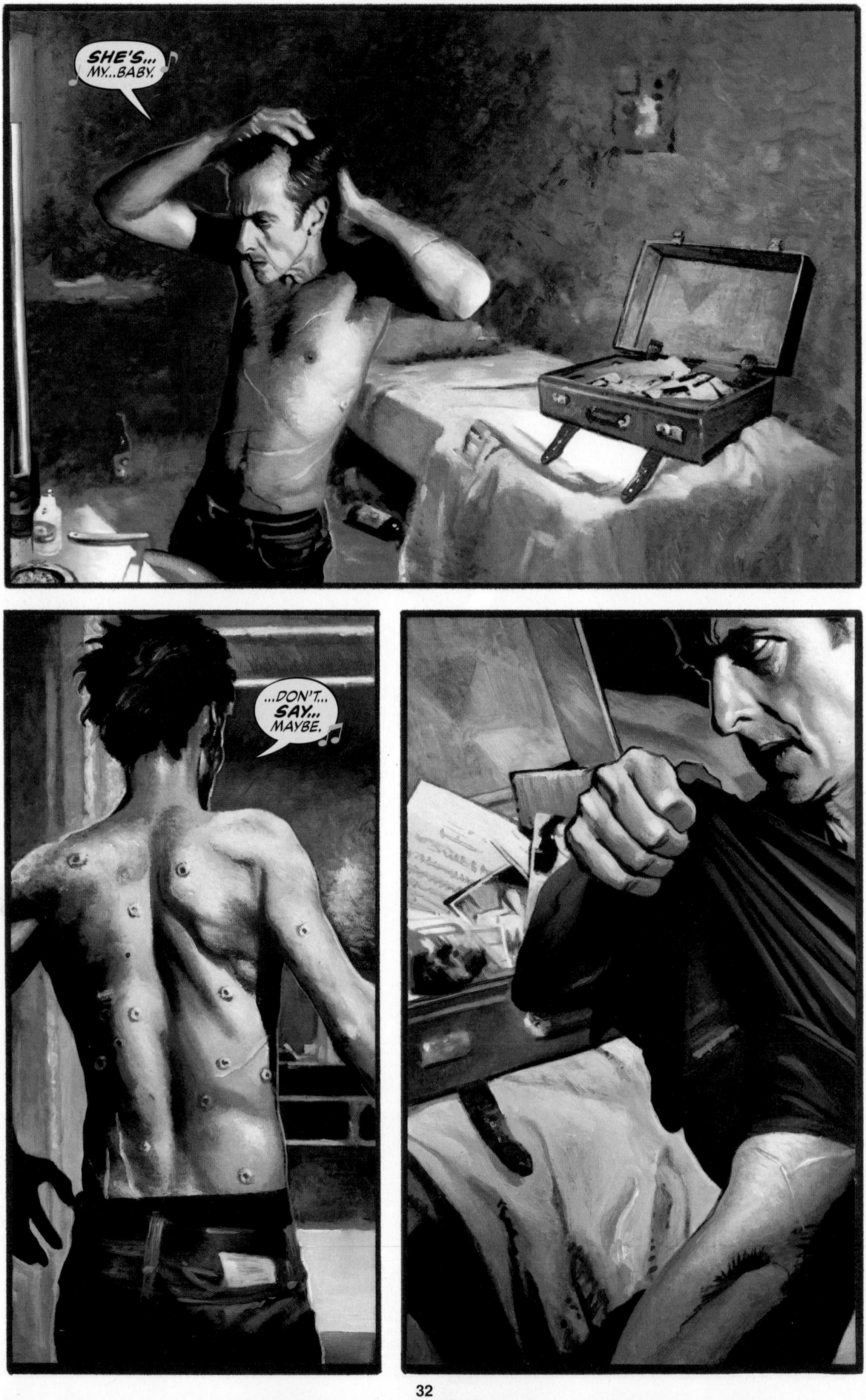
SHE'S... MY...BABY.
...DON'T... SAY... MAYBE.

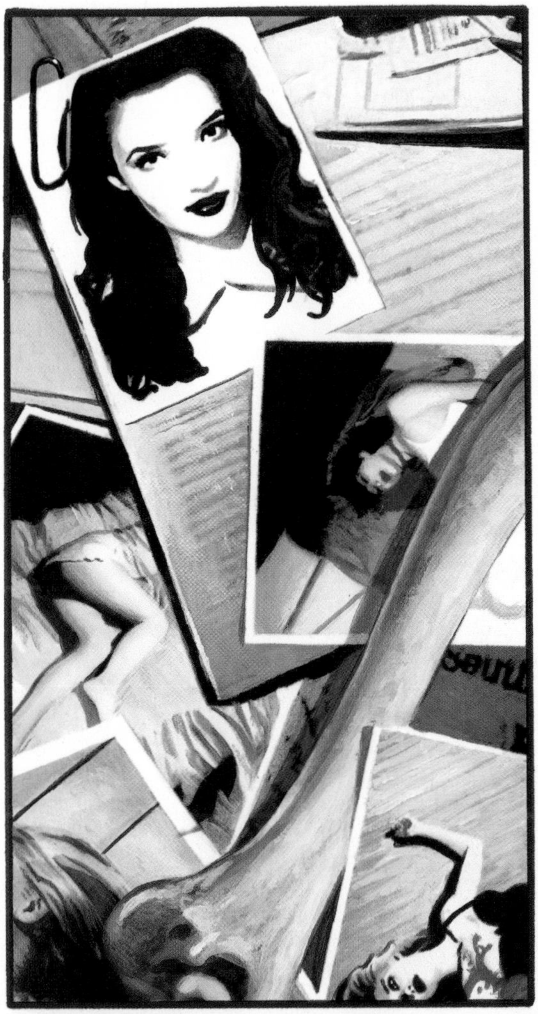

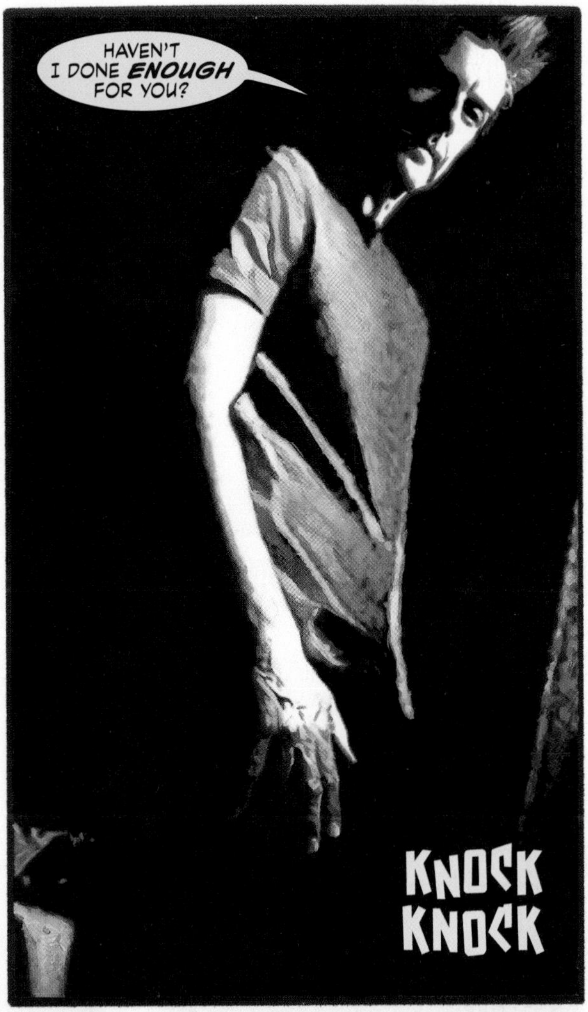
HAVEN'T I DONE ENOUGH FOR YOU?
KNOCK KNOCK

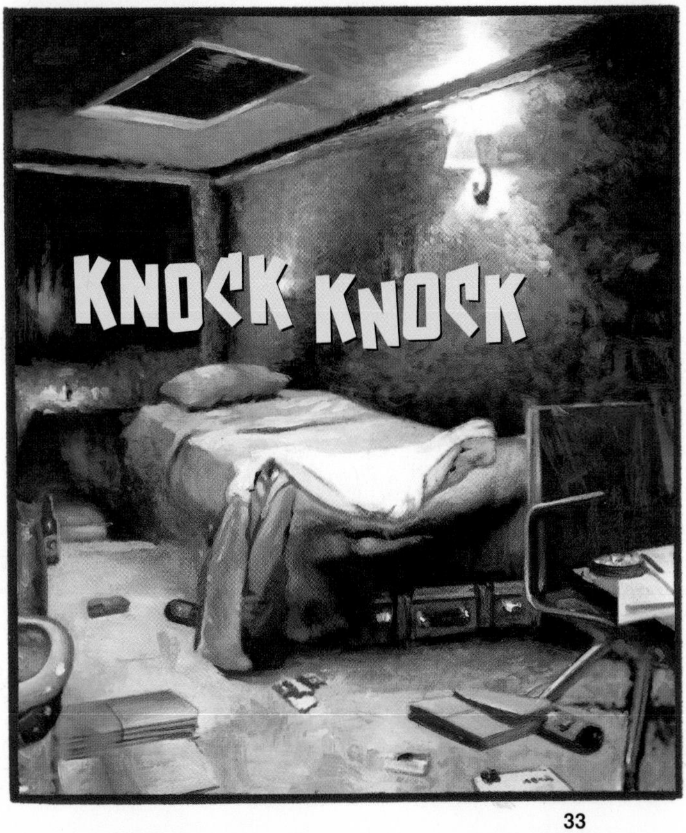
KNOCK KNOCK

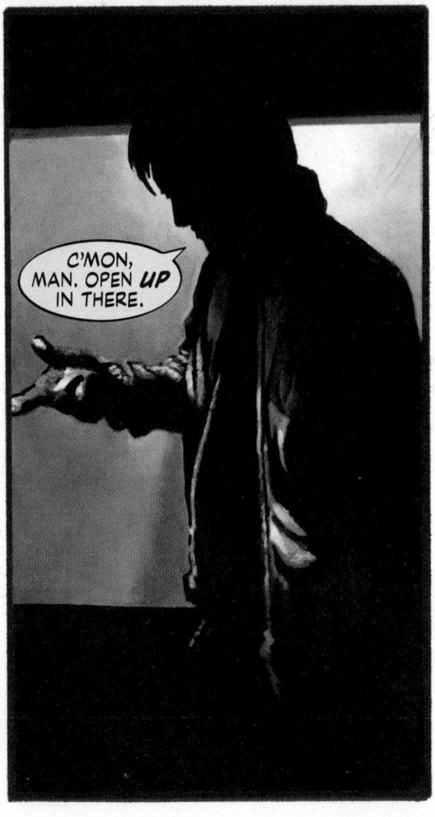
C'MON, MAN. OPEN UP IN THERE.

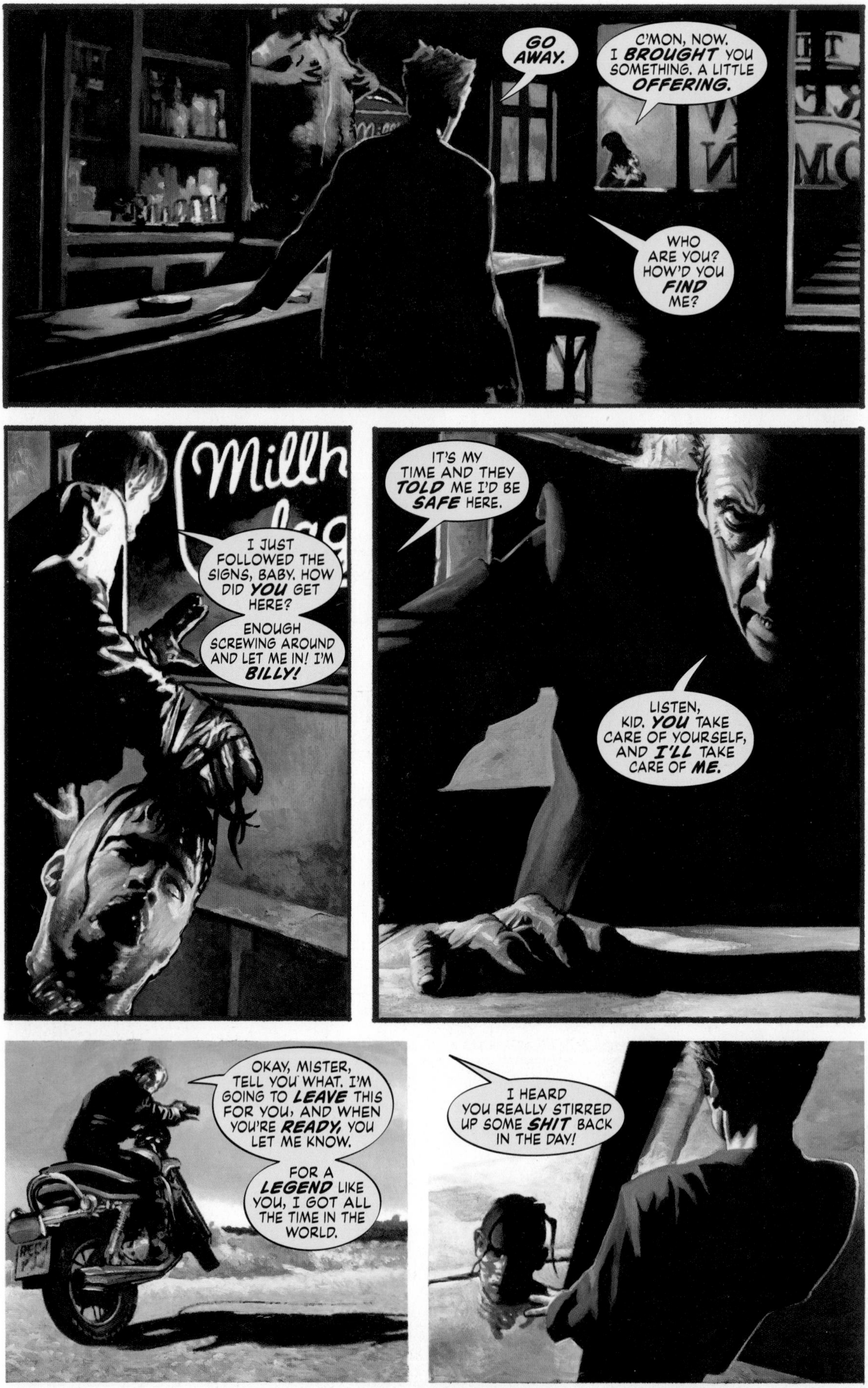
GO AWAY.
C'MON, NOW. I BROUGHT YOU SOMETHING. A LITTLE OFFERING.
WHO ARE YOU? HOW'D YOU FIND ME?
Millh
I JUST FOLLOWED THE SIGNS, BABY. HOW DID YOU GET HERE?
ENOUGH SCREWING AROUND AND LET ME IN! I'M BILLY!
IT'S MY TIME AND THEY TOLD ME I'D BE SAFE HERE.
LISTEN, KID. YOU TAKE CARE OF YOURSELF, AND I'LL TAKE CARE OF ME.
OKAY, MISTER, TELL YOU WHAT. I'M GOING TO LEAVE THIS FOR YOU, AND WHEN YOU'RE READY, YOU LET ME KNOW.
FOR A LEGEND LIKE YOU, I GOT ALL THE TIME IN THE WORLD.
I HEARD YOU REALLY STIRRED UP SOME SHIT BACK IN THE DAY!

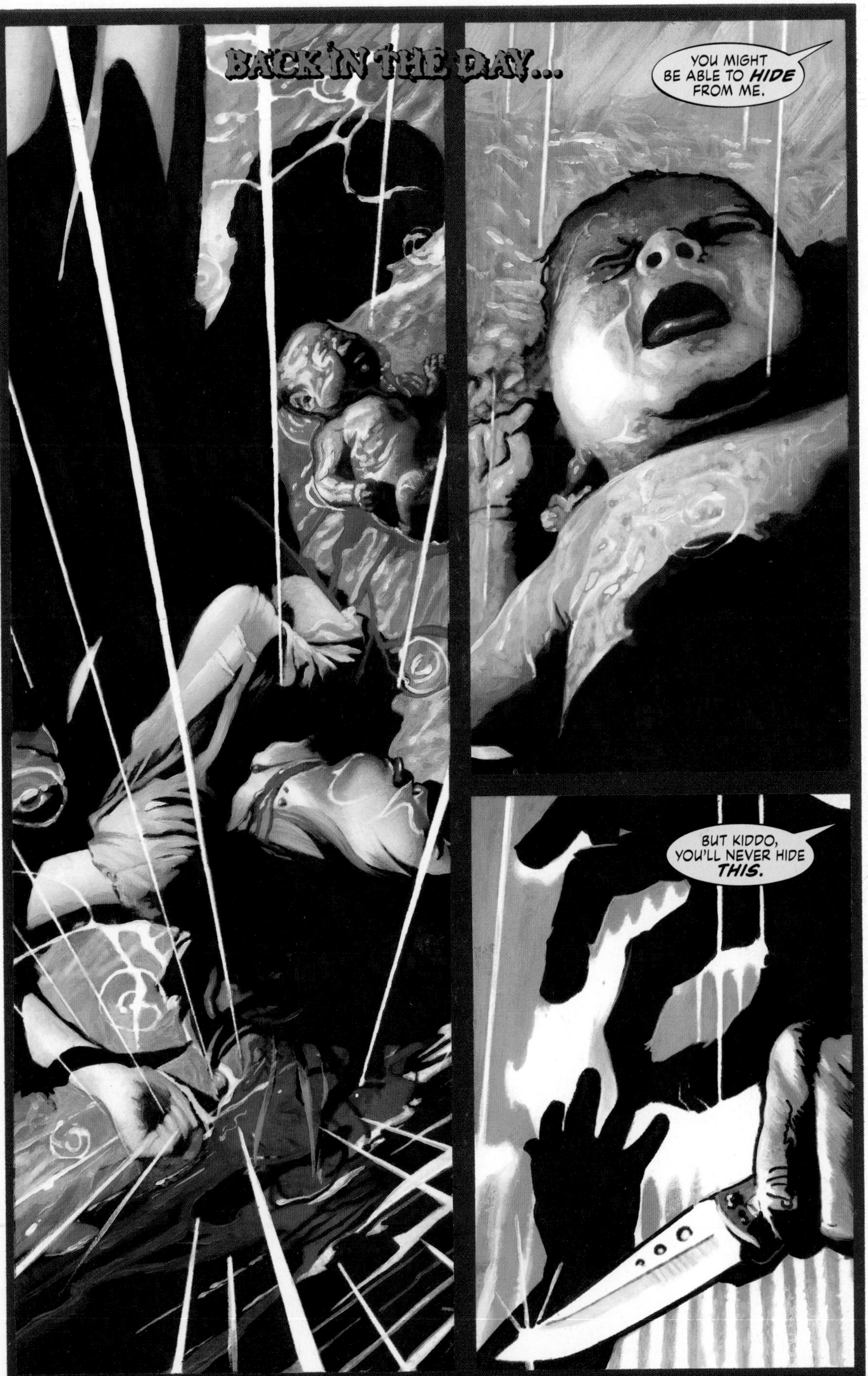
BACK IN THE DAY...
YOU MIGHT BE ABLE TO HIDE FROM ME.
BUT KIDDO, YOU'LL NEVER HIDE THIS.

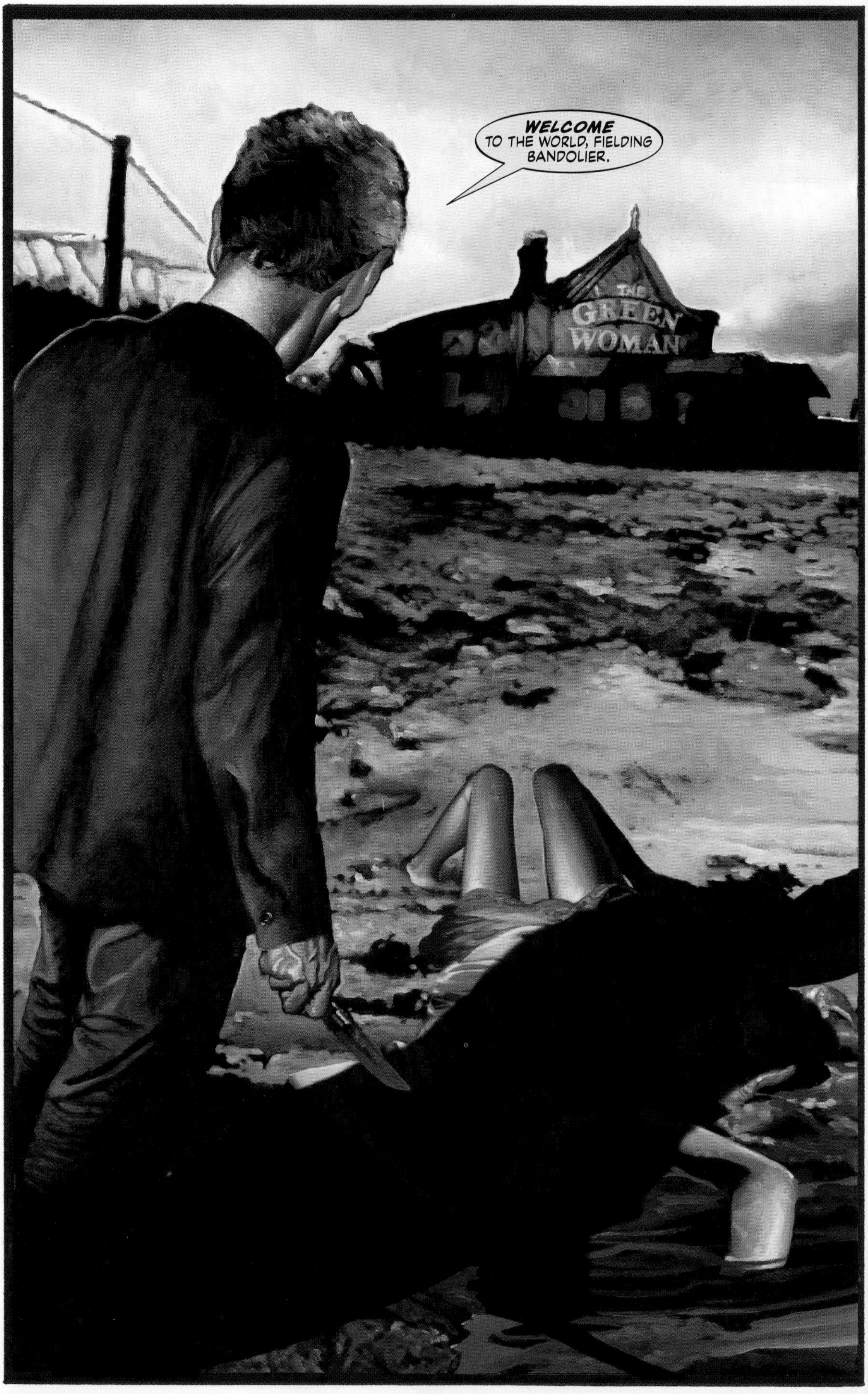
WELCOME TO THE WORLD, FIELDING BANDOLIER.
THE GREEN WOMAN

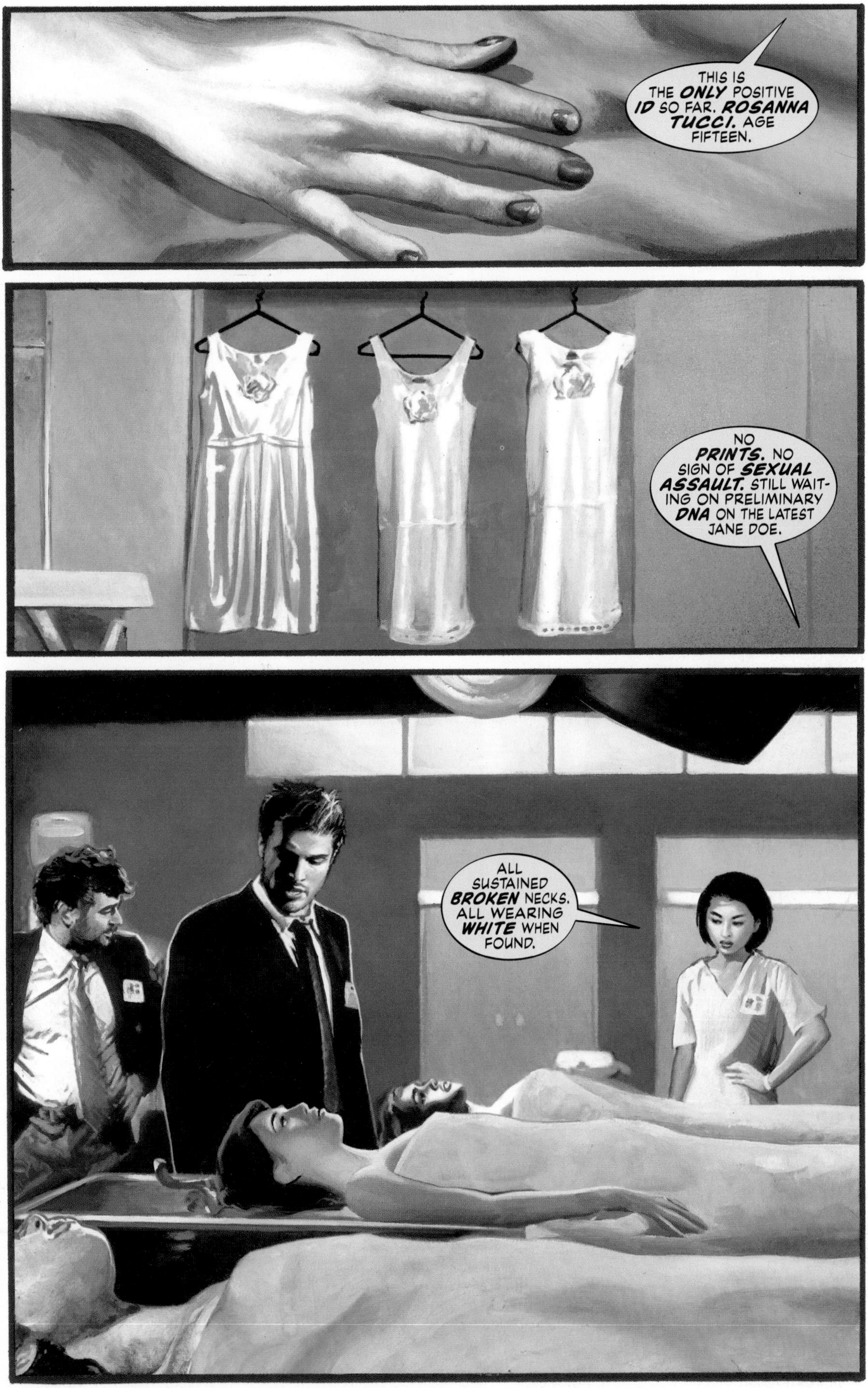
THIS IS THE ONLY POSITIVE ID SO FAR. ROSANNA TUCCI. AGE FIFTEEN.
NO PRINTS. NO SIGN OF SEXUAL ASSAULT. STILL WAITING ON PRELIMINARY DNA ON THE LATEST JANE DOE.
ALL SUSTAINED BROKEN NECKS. ALL WEARING WHITE WHEN FOUND.

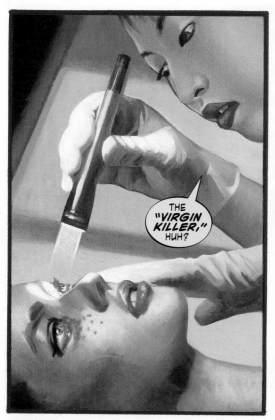

THE *"VIRGIN KILLER,"* HUH?

YOU CAN THANK *THE POST* FOR THAT ONE.

TELL ME, DETECTIVE STEELE, DO YOU SEE ANY *SIGNIFICANCE* TO THE DRESSES?

DON'T GET HIM *STARTED,* DOC.

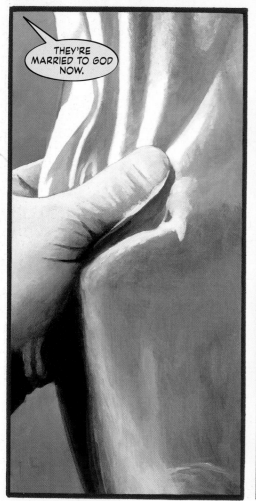

THEY'RE MARRIED TO GOD NOW.

C'MON, ROLLO. WHAT KIND OF *GUINEA* ARE YOU, ANYWAY?

I WAS BORN IN POUGHKEEPSIE. WHATA'YOU *WANT* FROM ME? I HAD TO EXPLAIN TO EVERY TEACHER IN GRADE SCHOOL HOW TO *SPELL* MY NAME.

WELL, I LIVED ON *CARMINE STREET* FOR TEN YEARS AND *REAL* ITALIANS ARE VERY SPECIFIC ABOUT THIS KIND OF STUFF.

38

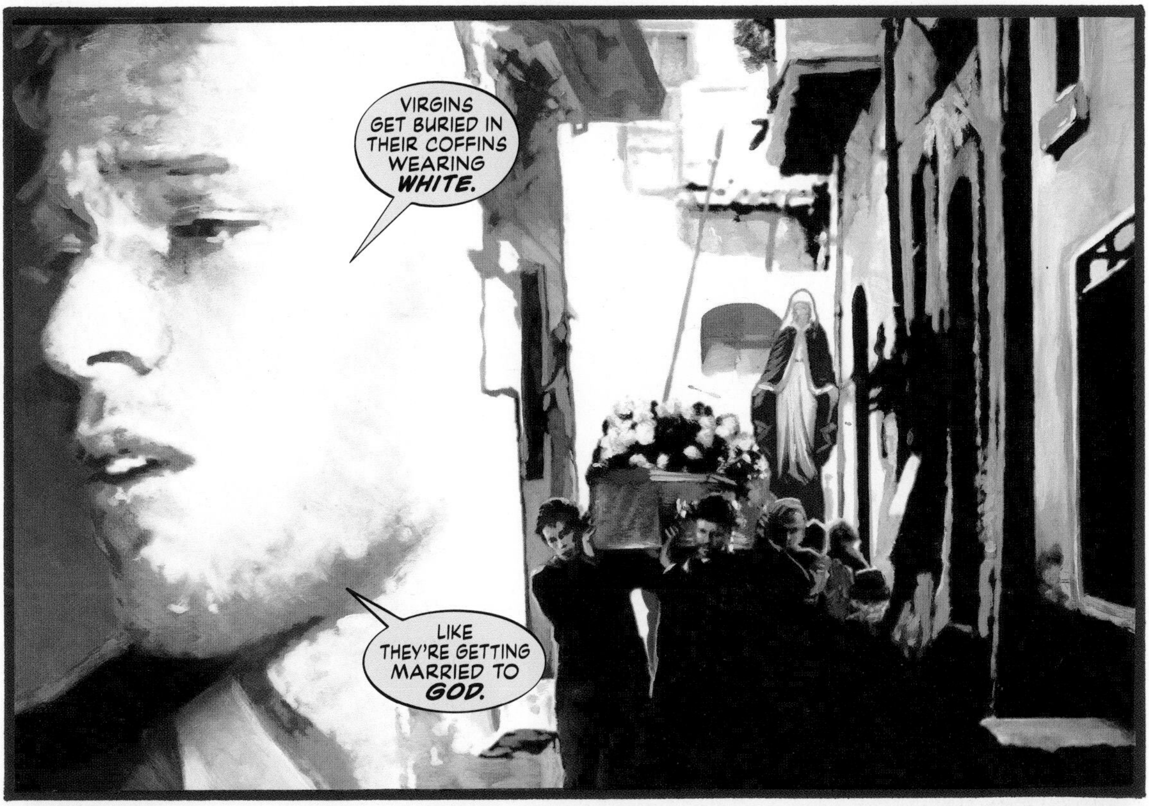
VIRGINS GET BURIED IN THEIR COFFINS WEARING WHITE.
LIKE THEY'RE GETTING MARRIED TO GOD.

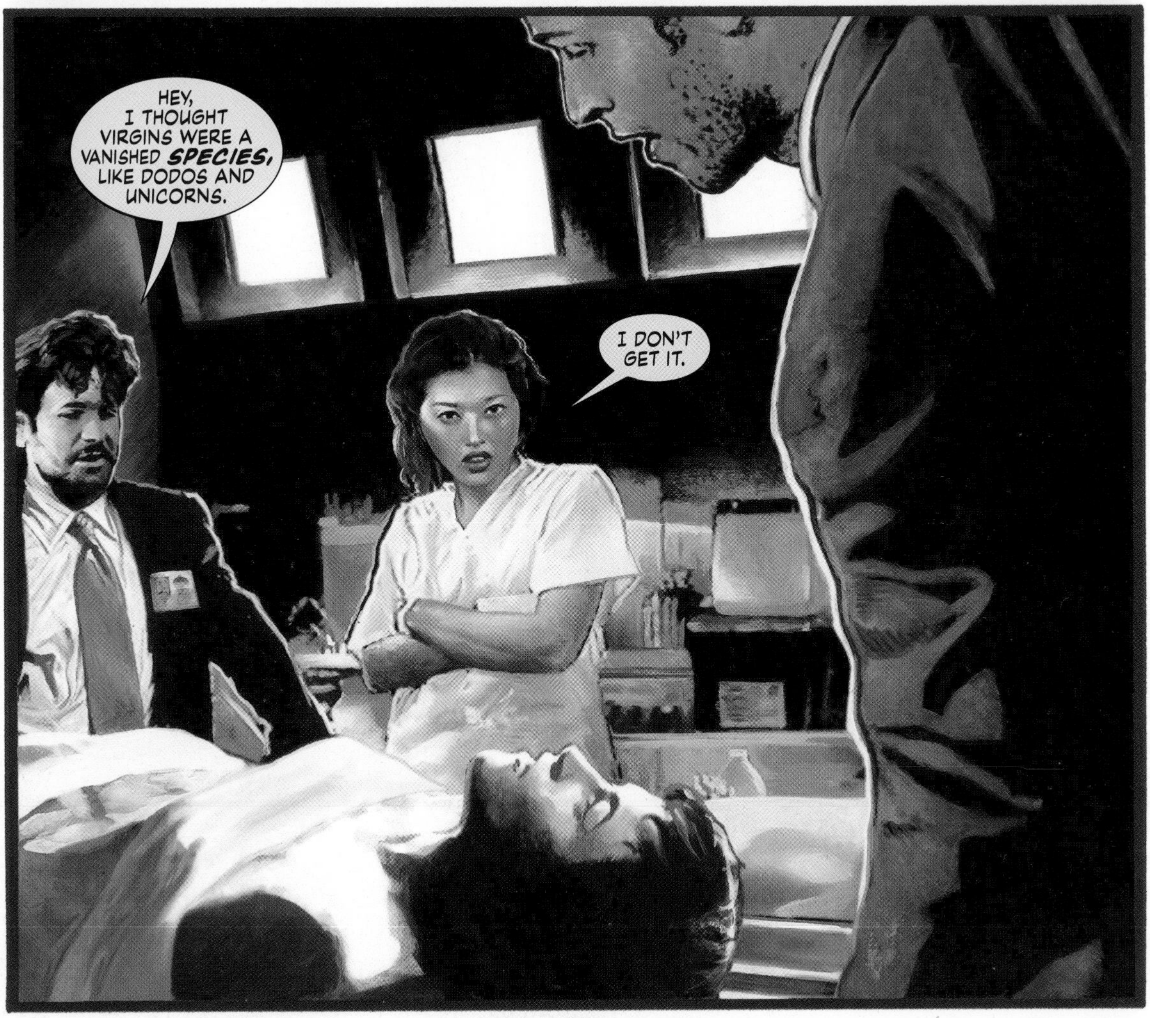
HEY, I THOUGHT VIRGINS WERE A VANISHED SPECIES, LIKE DODOS AND UNICORNS.
I DON'T GET IT.

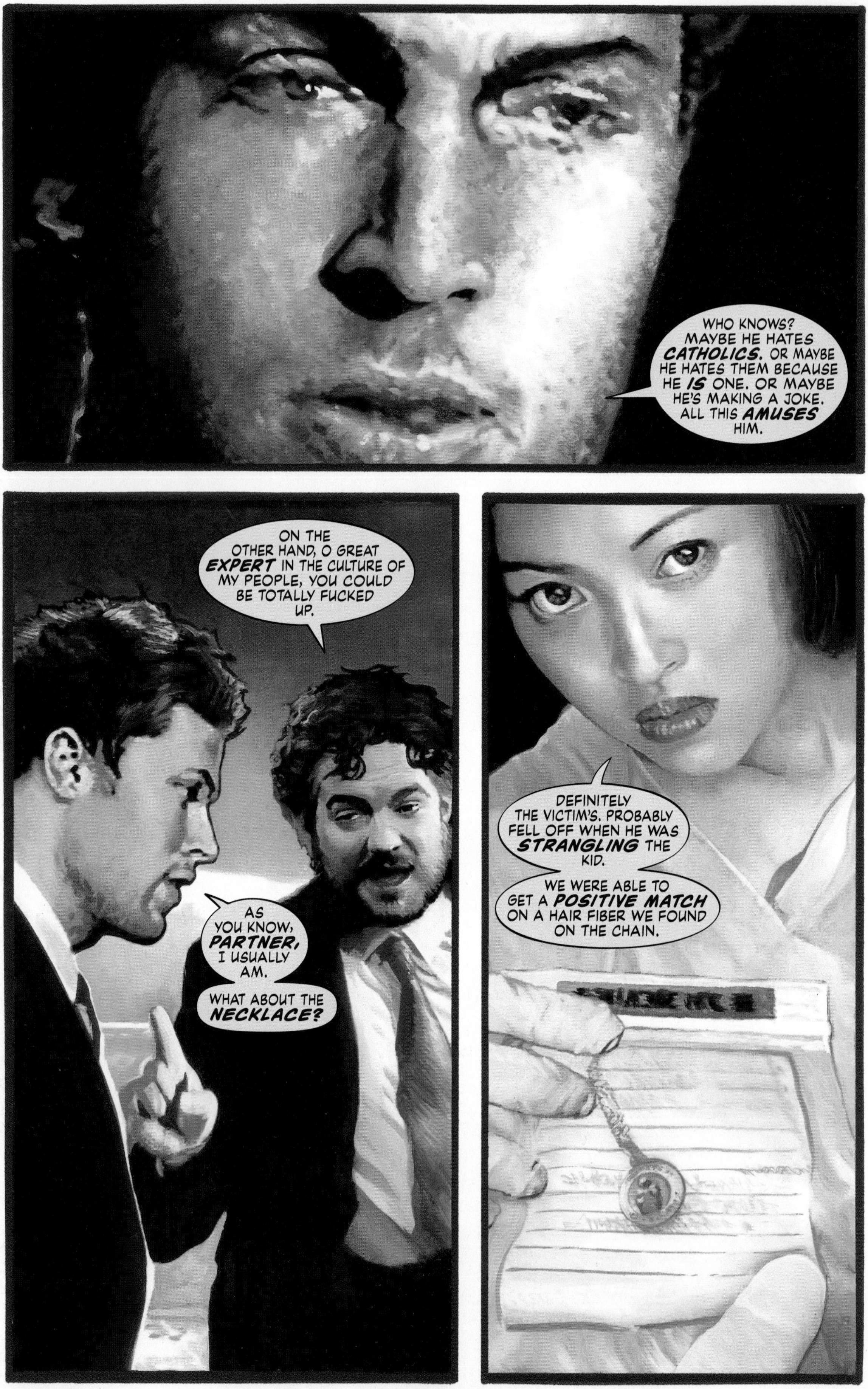
WHO KNOWS? MAYBE HE HATES CATHOLICS. OR MAYBE HE HATES THEM BECAUSE HE IS ONE. OR MAYBE HE'S MAKING A JOKE. ALL THIS AMUSES HIM.
ON THE OTHER HAND, O GREAT EXPERT IN THE CULTURE OF MY PEOPLE, YOU COULD BE TOTALLY FUCKED UP.
AS YOU KNOW, PARTNER, I USUALLY AM.
WHAT ABOUT THE NECKLACE?
DEFINITELY THE VICTIM'S. PROBABLY FELL OFF WHEN HE WAS STRANGLING THE KID.
WE WERE ABLE TO GET A POSITIVE MATCH ON A HAIR FIBER WE FOUND ON THE CHAIN.

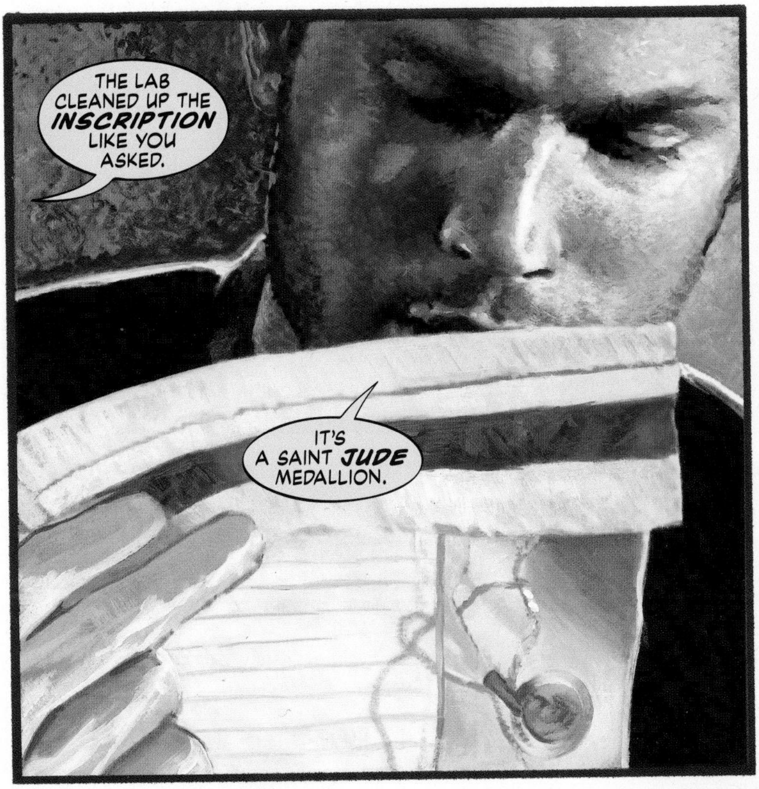
THE LAB CLEANED UP THE INSCRIPTION LIKE YOU ASKED.
IT'S A SAINT JUDE MEDALLION.

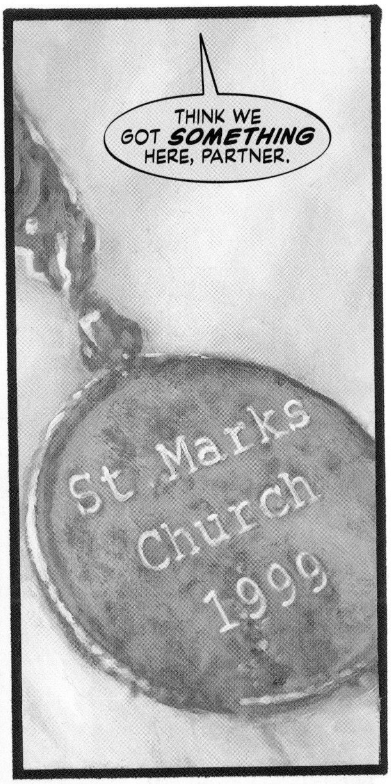
THINK WE GOT SOMETHING HERE, PARTNER.
St Marks Church 1999

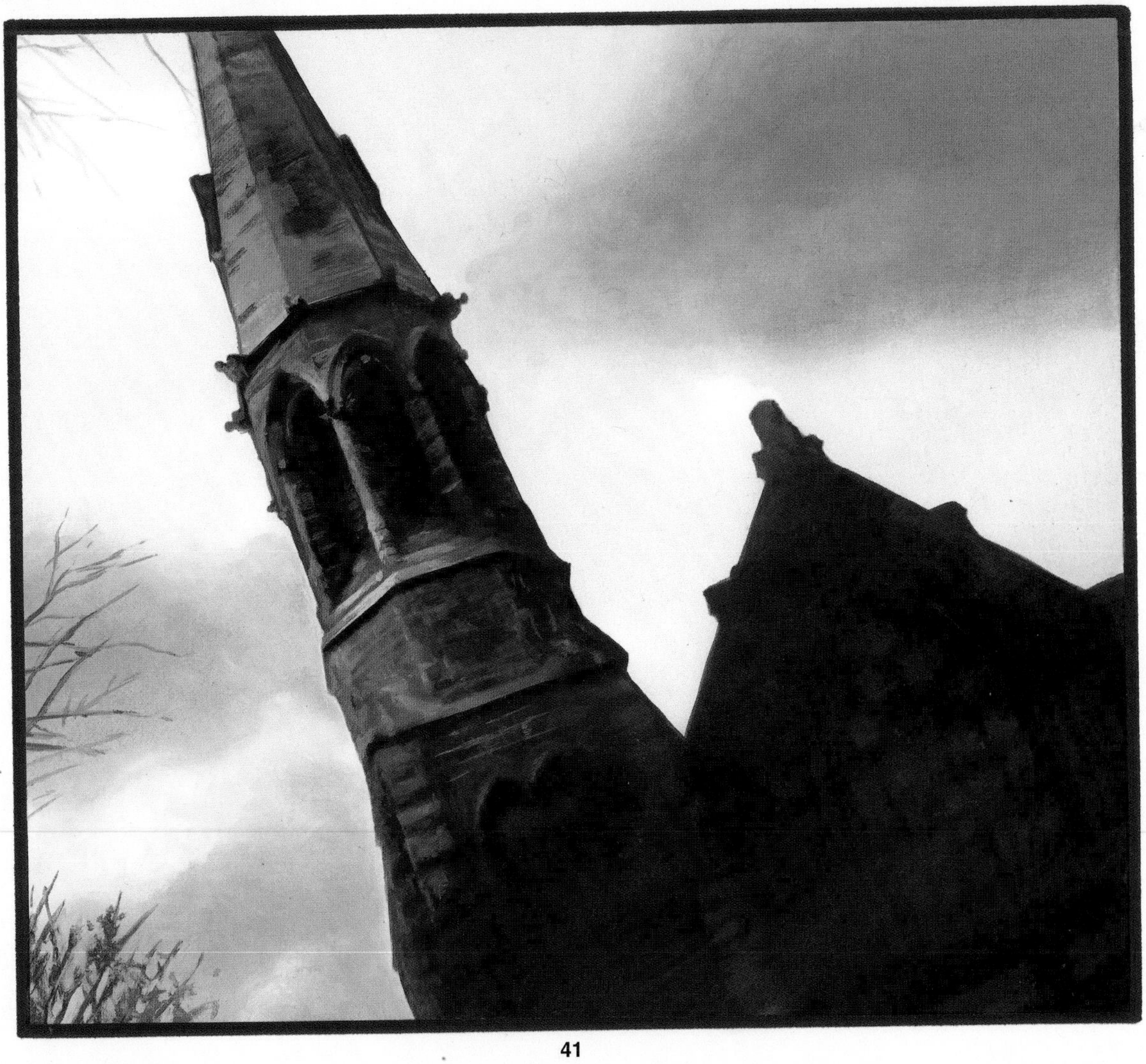

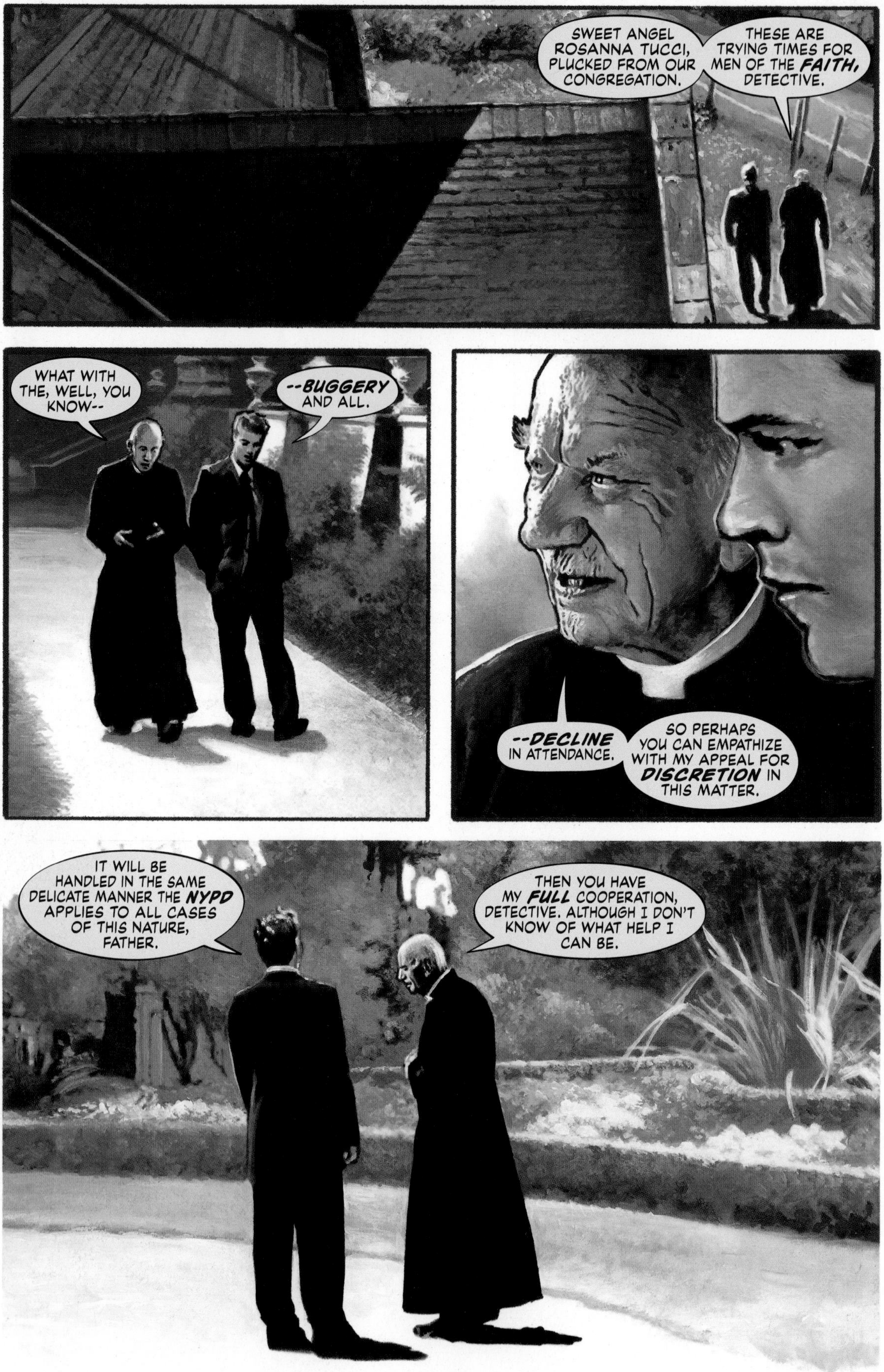
SWEET ANGEL ROSANNA TUCCI, PLUCKED FROM OUR CONGREGATION.
THESE ARE TRYING TIMES FOR MEN OF THE FAITH, DETECTIVE.
WHAT WITH THE, WELL, YOU KNOW--
--BUGGERY AND ALL.
--DECLINE IN ATTENDANCE.
SO PERHAPS YOU CAN EMPATHIZE WITH MY APPEAL FOR DISCRETION IN THIS MATTER.
IT WILL BE HANDLED IN THE SAME DELICATE MANNER THE NYPD APPLIES TO ALL CASES OF THIS NATURE, FATHER.
THEN YOU HAVE MY FULL COOPERATION, DETECTIVE. ALTHOUGH I DON'T KNOW OF WHAT HELP I CAN BE.

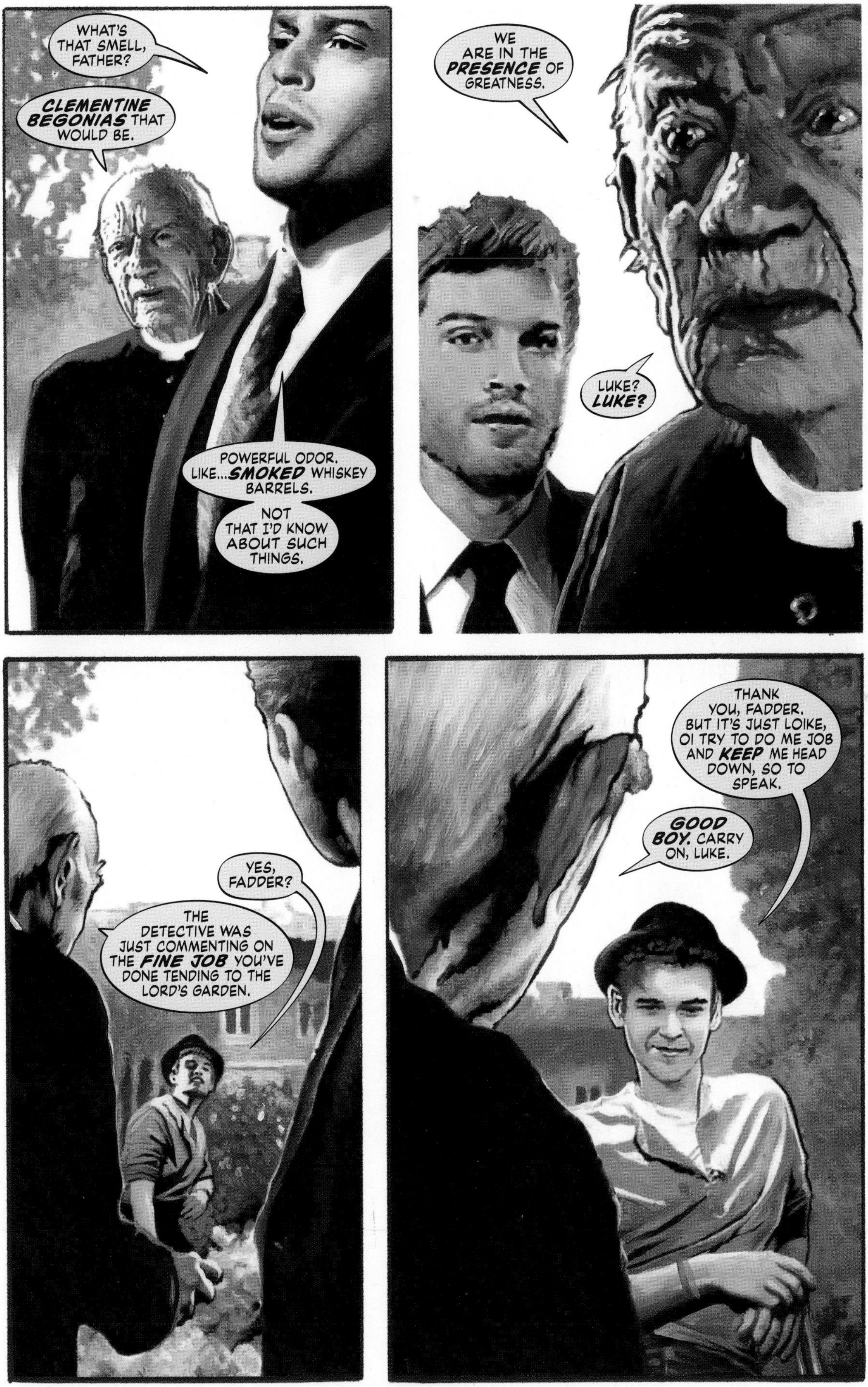
WHAT'S THAT SMELL, FATHER?
CLEMENTINE BEGONIAS THAT WOULD BE.
POWERFUL ODOR. LIKE...SMOKED WHISKEY BARRELS.
NOT THAT I'D KNOW ABOUT SUCH THINGS.
WE ARE IN THE PRESENCE OF GREATNESS.
LUKE? LUKE?
YES, FADDER?
THE DETECTIVE WAS JUST COMMENTING ON THE FINE JOB YOU'VE DONE TENDING TO THE LORD'S GARDEN.
THANK YOU, FADDER. BUT IT'S JUST LOIKE, OI TRY TO DO ME JOB AND KEEP ME HEAD DOWN, SO TO SPEAK.
GOOD BOY. CARRY ON, LUKE.

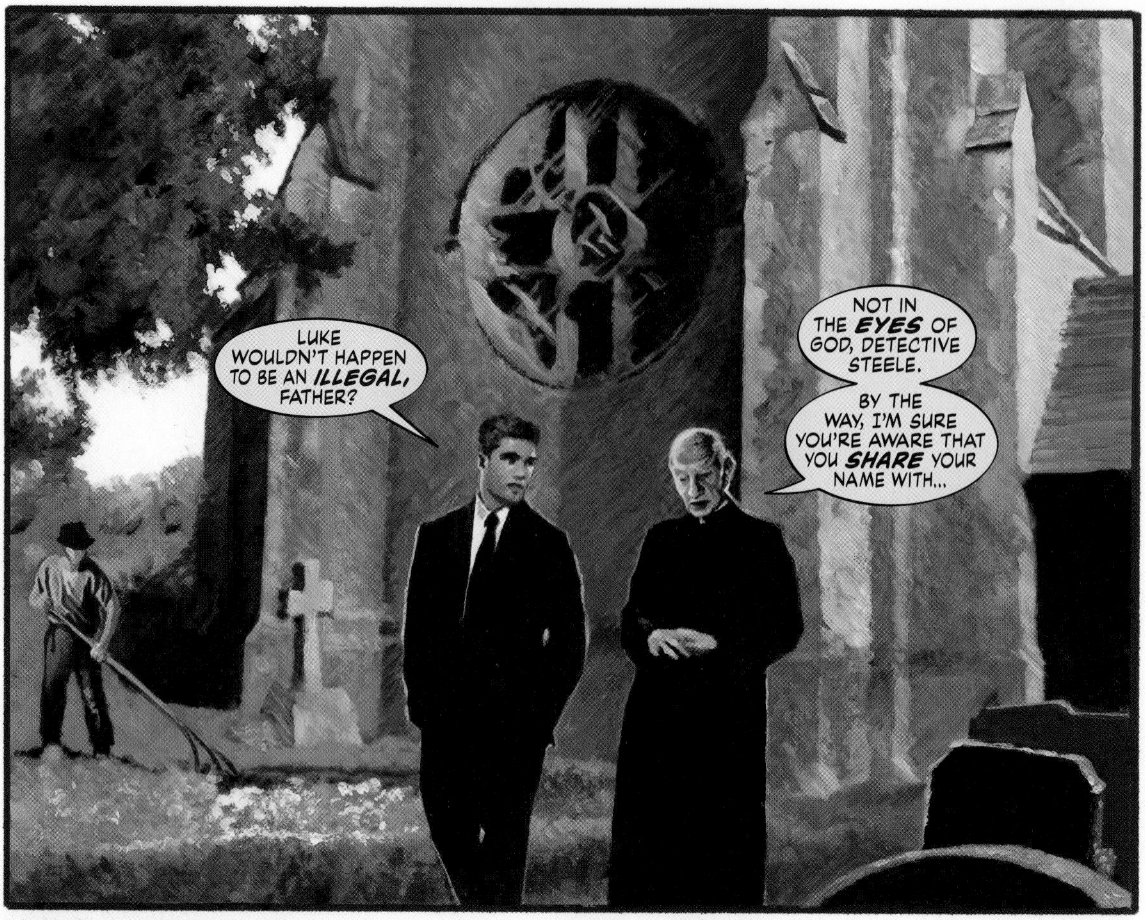
LUKE WOULDN'T HAPPEN TO BE AN ILLEGAL, FATHER?
NOT IN THE EYES OF GOD, DETECTIVE STEELE.
BY THE WAY, I'M SURE YOU'RE AWARE THAT YOU SHARE YOUR NAME WITH...

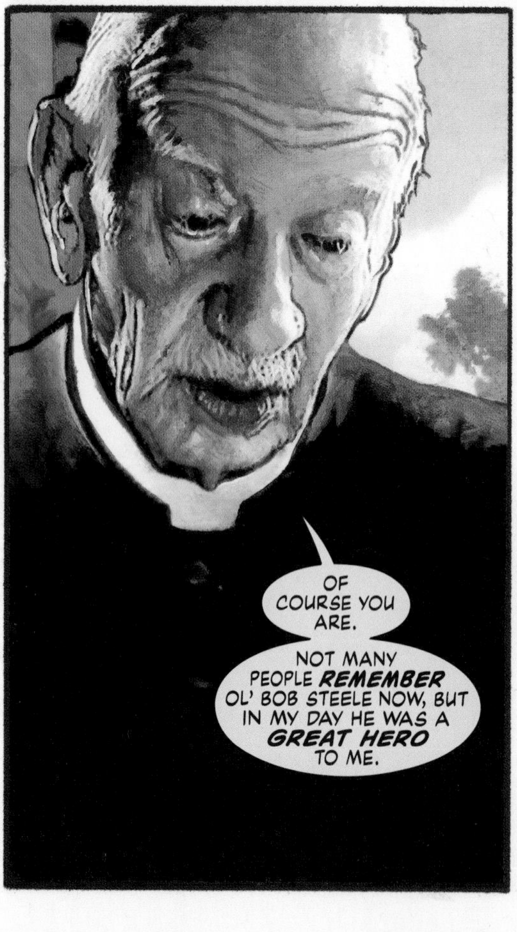
OF COURSE YOU ARE.
NOT MANY PEOPLE REMEMBER OL' BOB STEELE NOW, BUT IN MY DAY HE WAS A GREAT HERO TO ME.

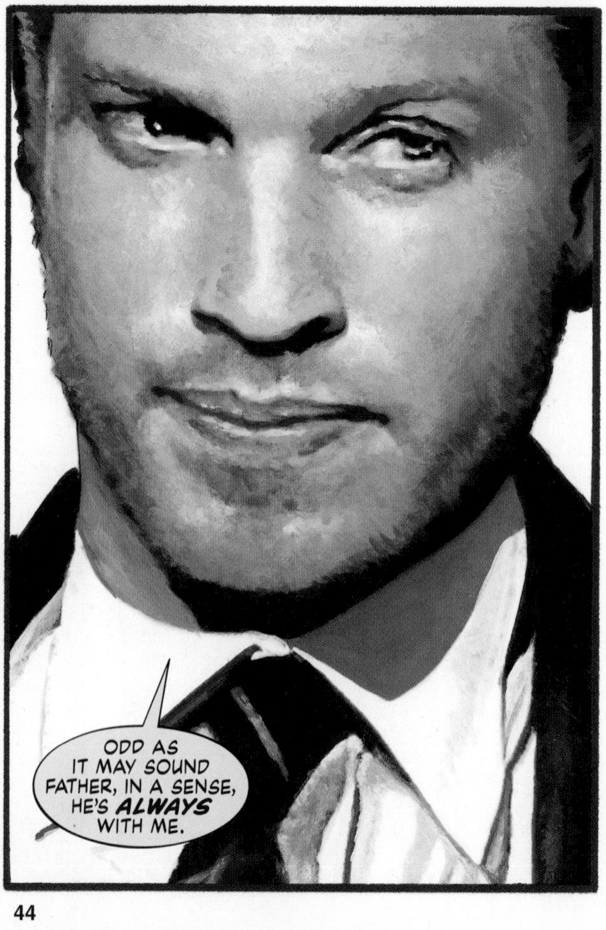
ODD AS IT MAY SOUND FATHER, IN A SENSE, HE'S ALWAYS WITH ME.

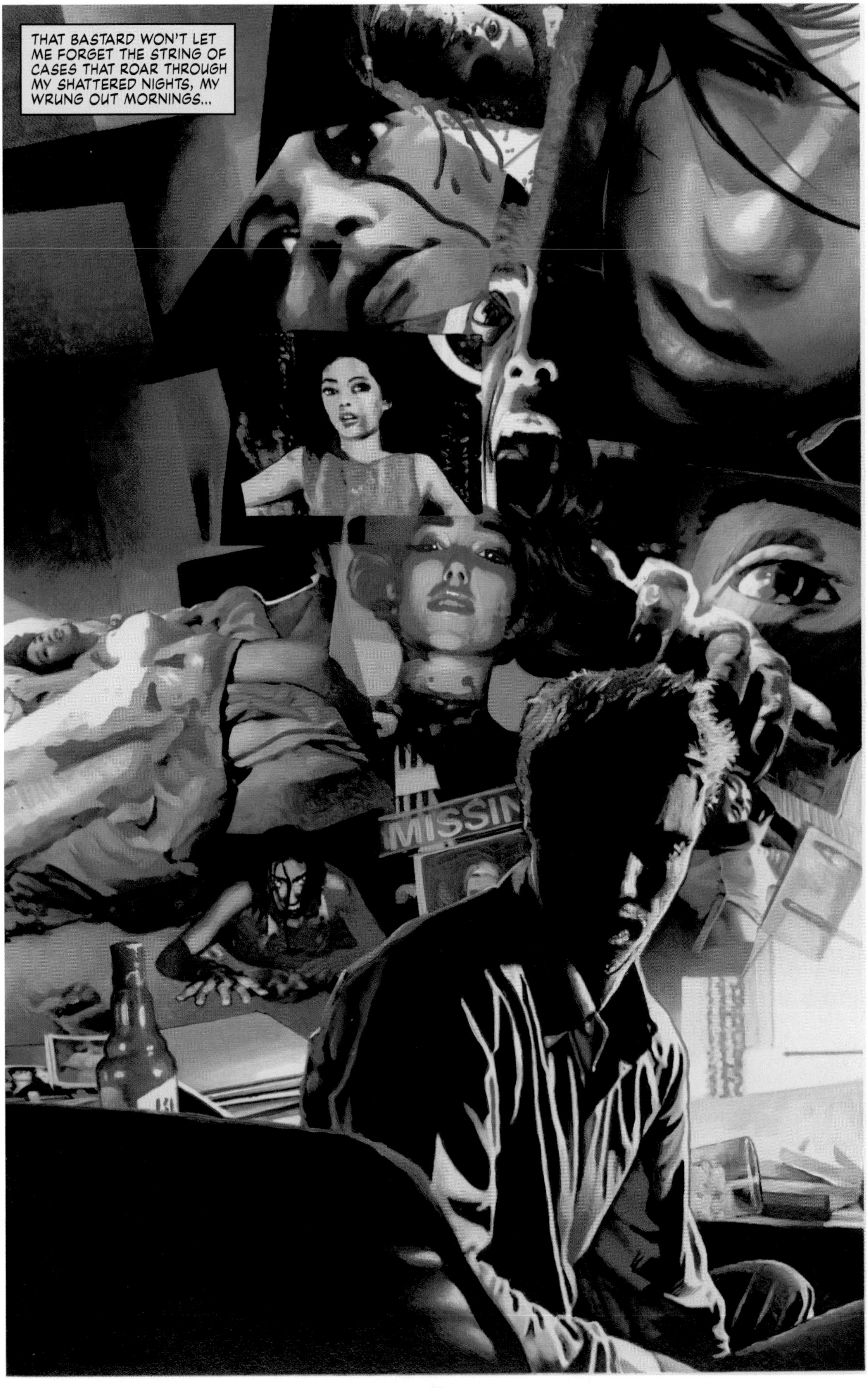
THAT BASTARD WON'T LET ME FORGET THE STRING OF CASES THAT ROAR THROUGH MY SHATTERED NIGHTS, MY WRUNG OUT MORNINGS...
MISSIN

LOOK AT THAT WOMAN. MY GOD, LOOK AT HER.

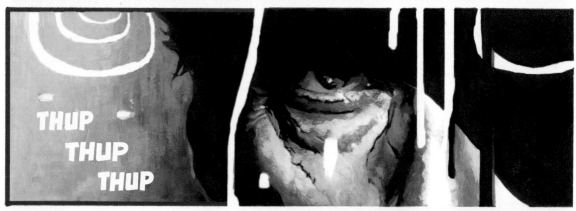

THUP

THUP

THUP

In the distant World beating behind all our thoughts...

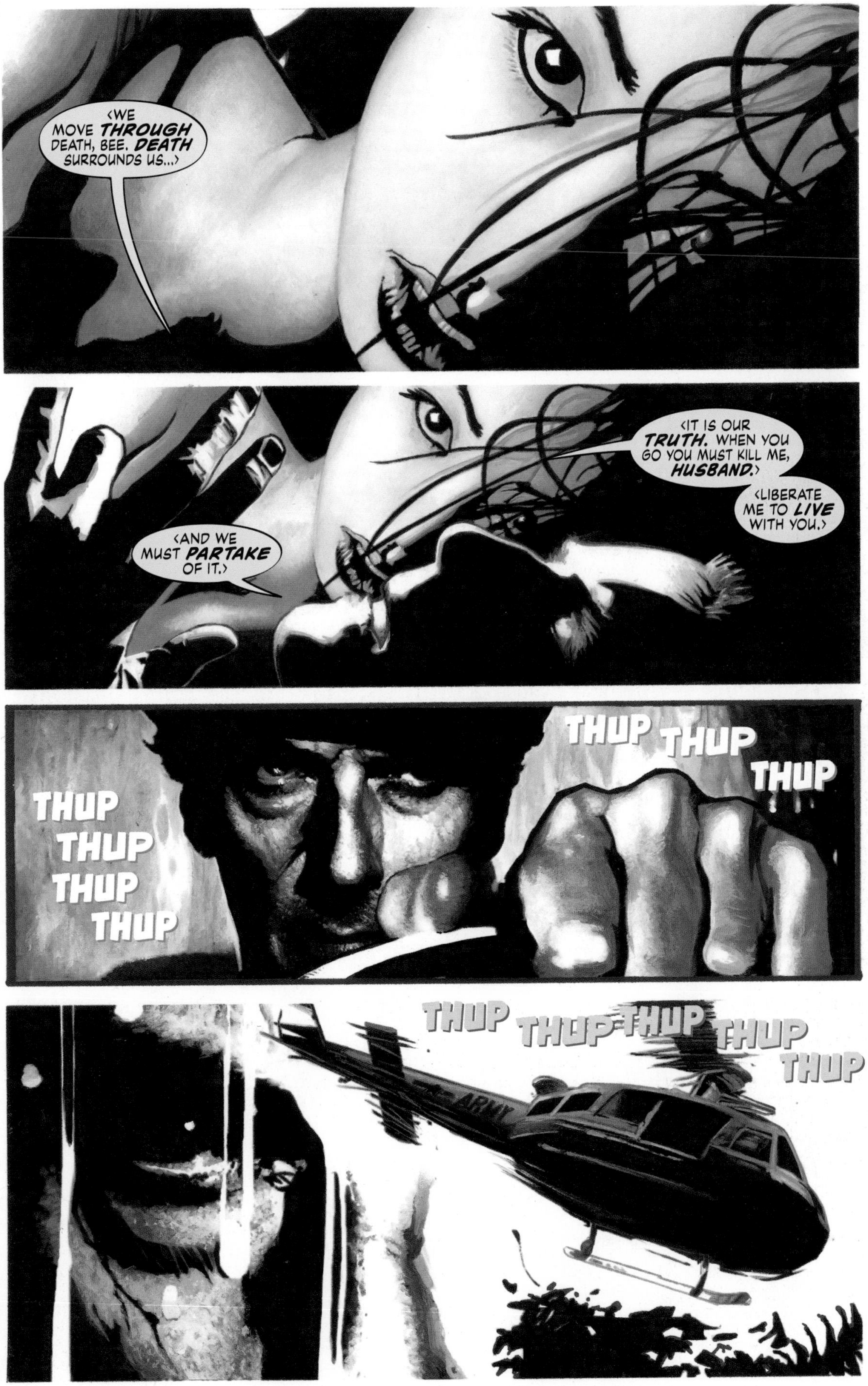
‹WE MOVE THROUGH DEATH, BEE. DEATH SURROUNDS US...›
‹IT IS OUR TRUTH. WHEN YOU GO YOU MUST KILL ME, HUSBAND.›
‹LIBERATE ME TO LIVE WITH YOU.›
‹AND WE MUST PARTAKE OF IT.›
THUP THUP THUP
THUP THUP THUP THUP
THUP THUP THUP THUP THUP
ARMY

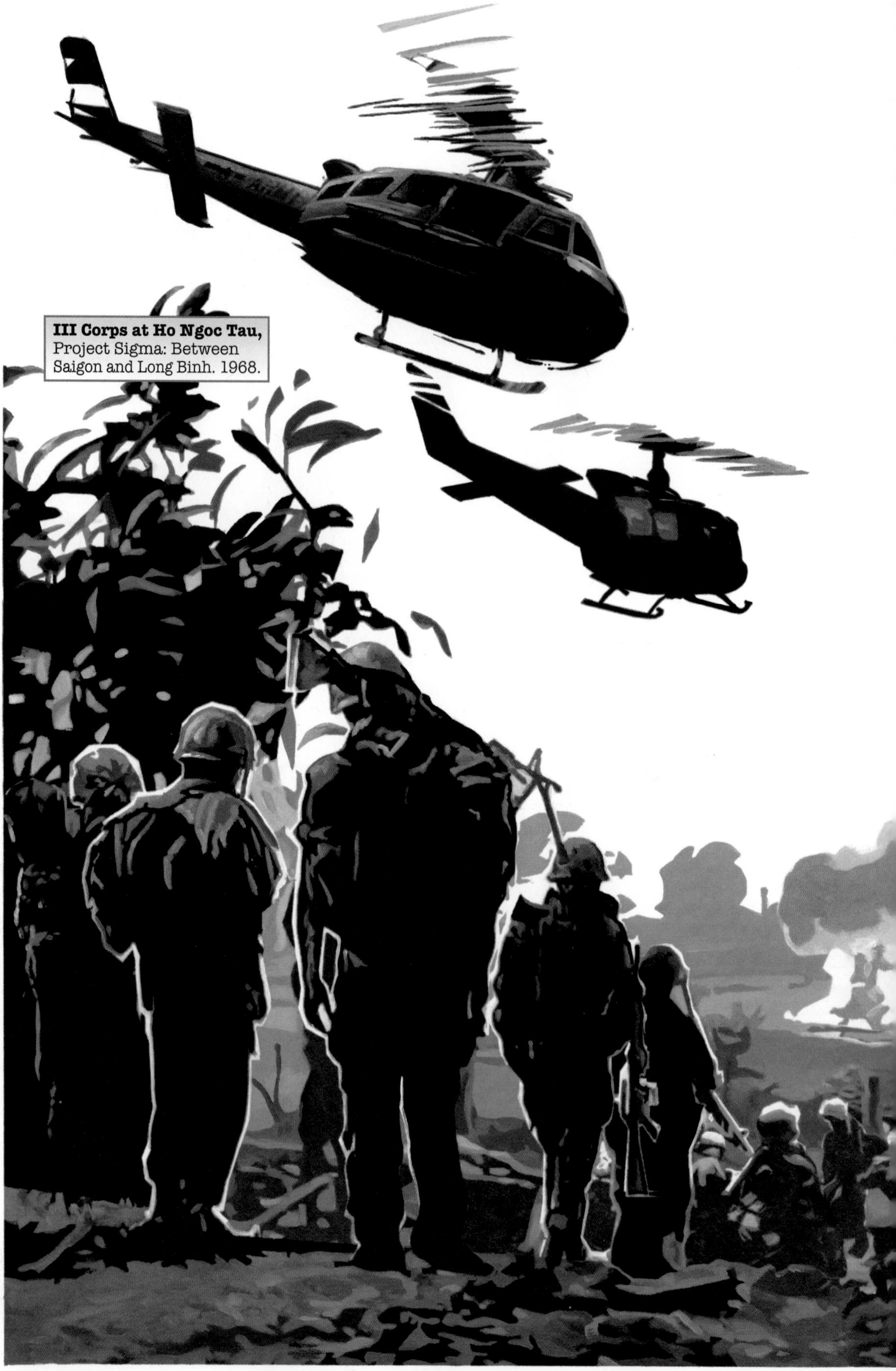
III Corps at Ho Ngoc Tau,
Project Sigma: Between
Saigon and Long Binh. 1968.

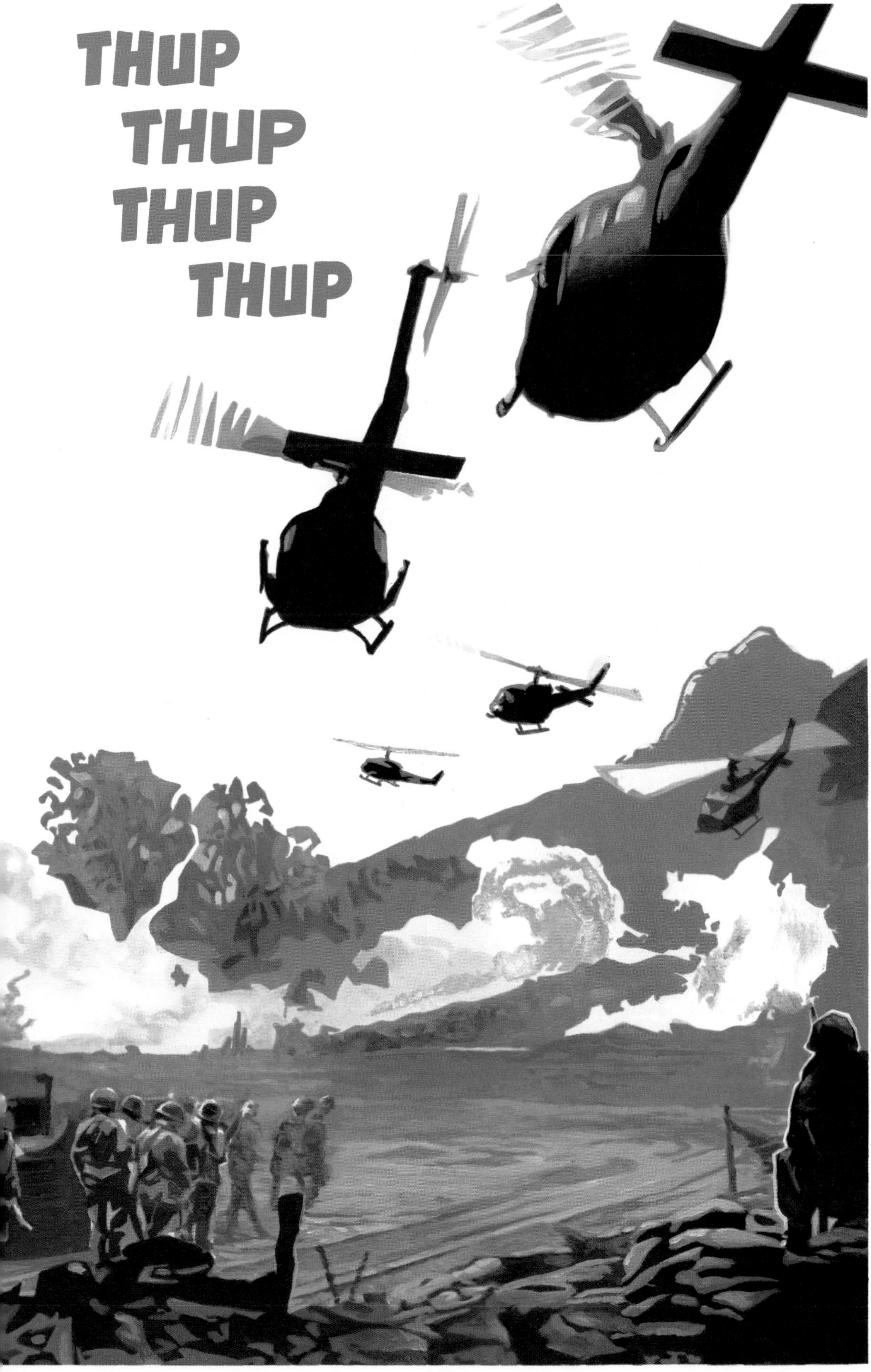
THUP
THUP
THUP
THUP

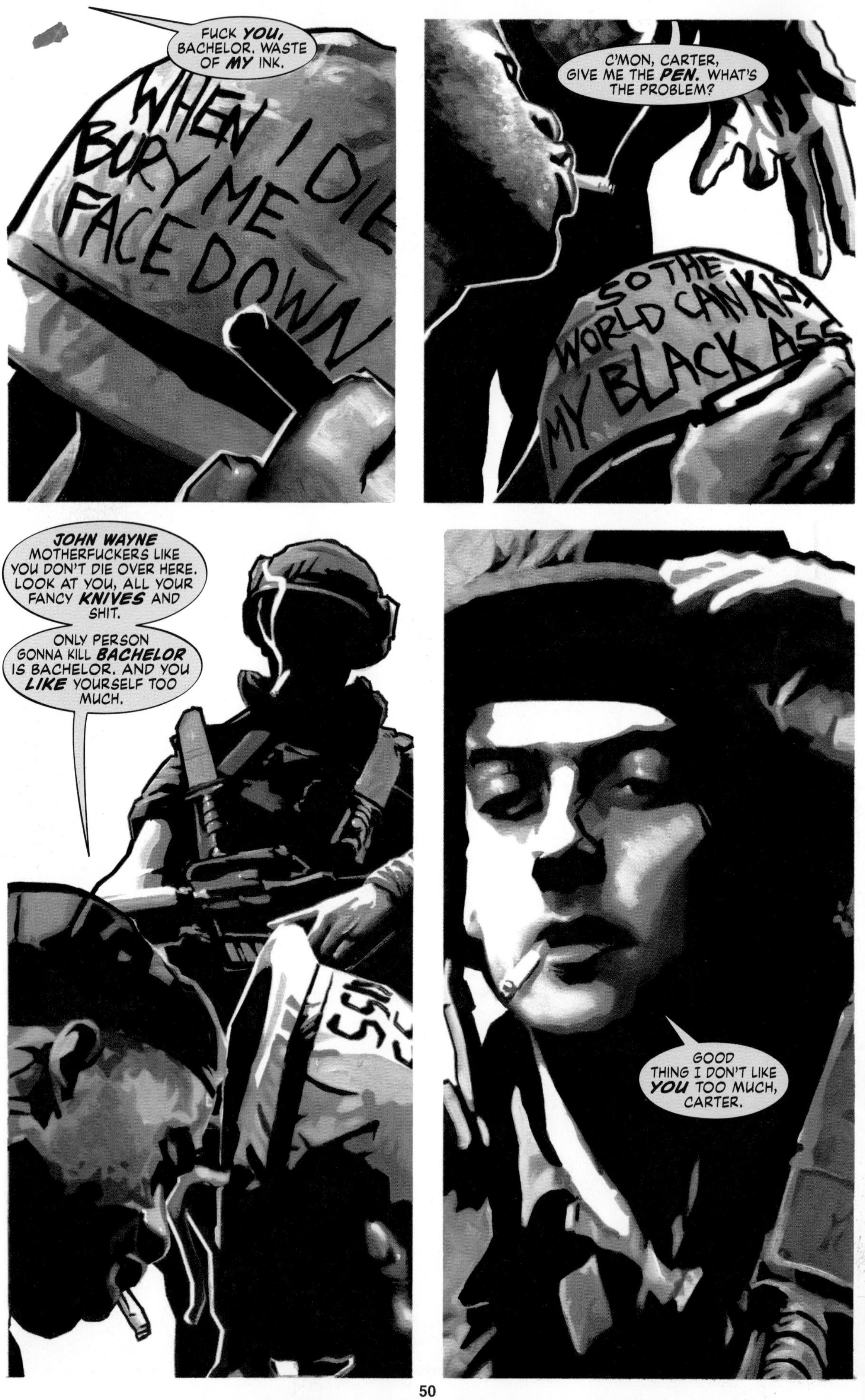
FUCK YOU, BACHELOR. WASTE OF MY INK.
WHEN I DIE BURY ME FACE DOWN
C'MON, CARTER, GIVE ME THE PEN. WHAT'S THE PROBLEM?
SO THE WORLD CAN KISS MY BLACK ASS
JOHN WAYNE MOTHERFUCKERS LIKE YOU DON'T DIE OVER HERE. LOOK AT YOU, ALL YOUR FANCY KNIVES AND SHIT.
ONLY PERSON GONNA KILL BACHELOR IS BACHELOR. AND YOU LIKE YOURSELF TOO MUCH.
GOOD THING I DON'T LIKE YOU TOO MUCH, CARTER.

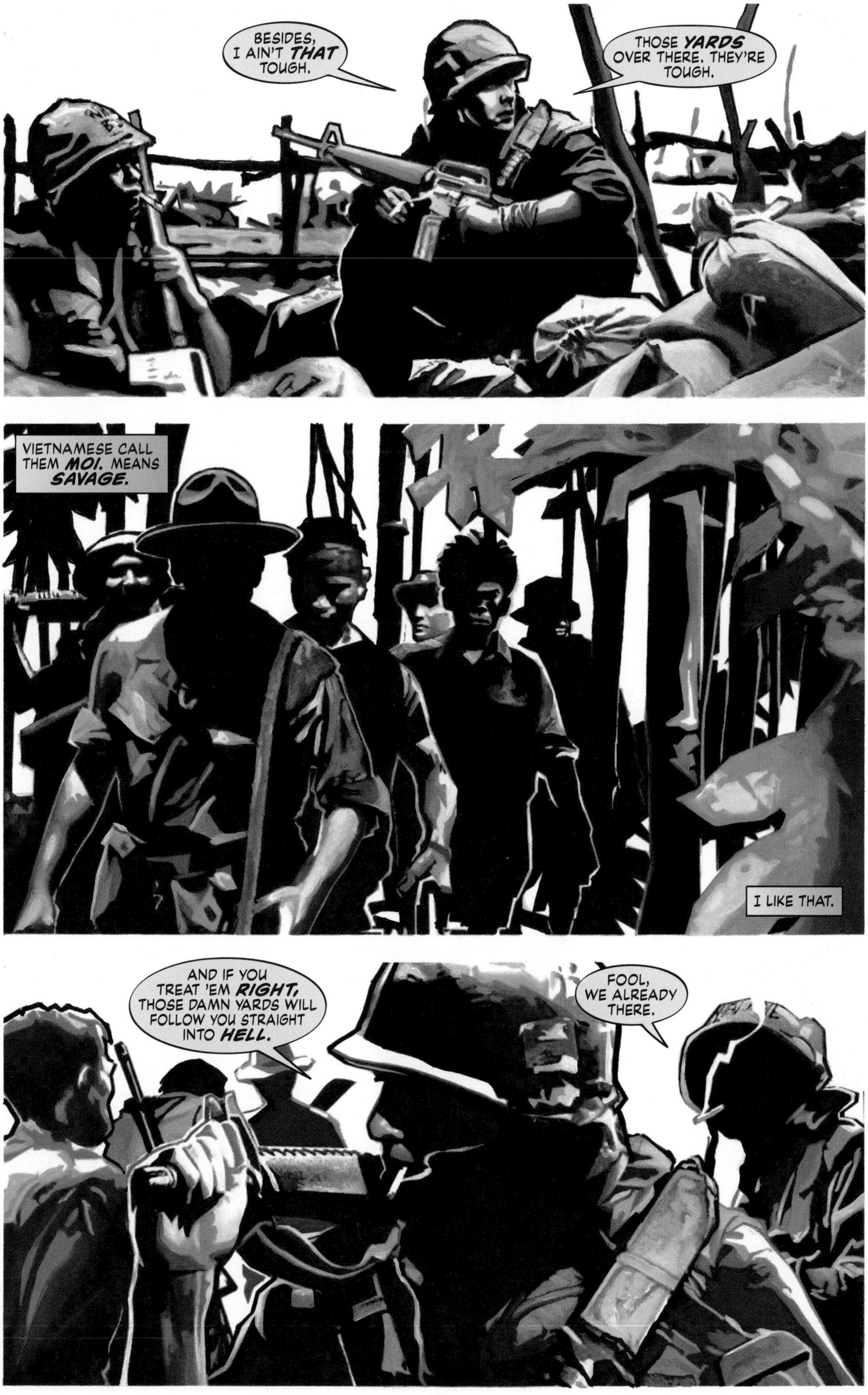
BESIDES, I AIN'T *THAT* TOUGH.
THOSE *YARDS* OVER THERE. THEY'RE TOUGH.
VIETNAMESE CALL THEM *MOI.* MEANS *SAVAGE.*
I LIKE THAT.
AND IF YOU TREAT 'EM *RIGHT,* THOSE DAMN YARDS WILL FOLLOW YOU STRAIGHT INTO *HELL.*
FOOL, WE ALREADY THERE.

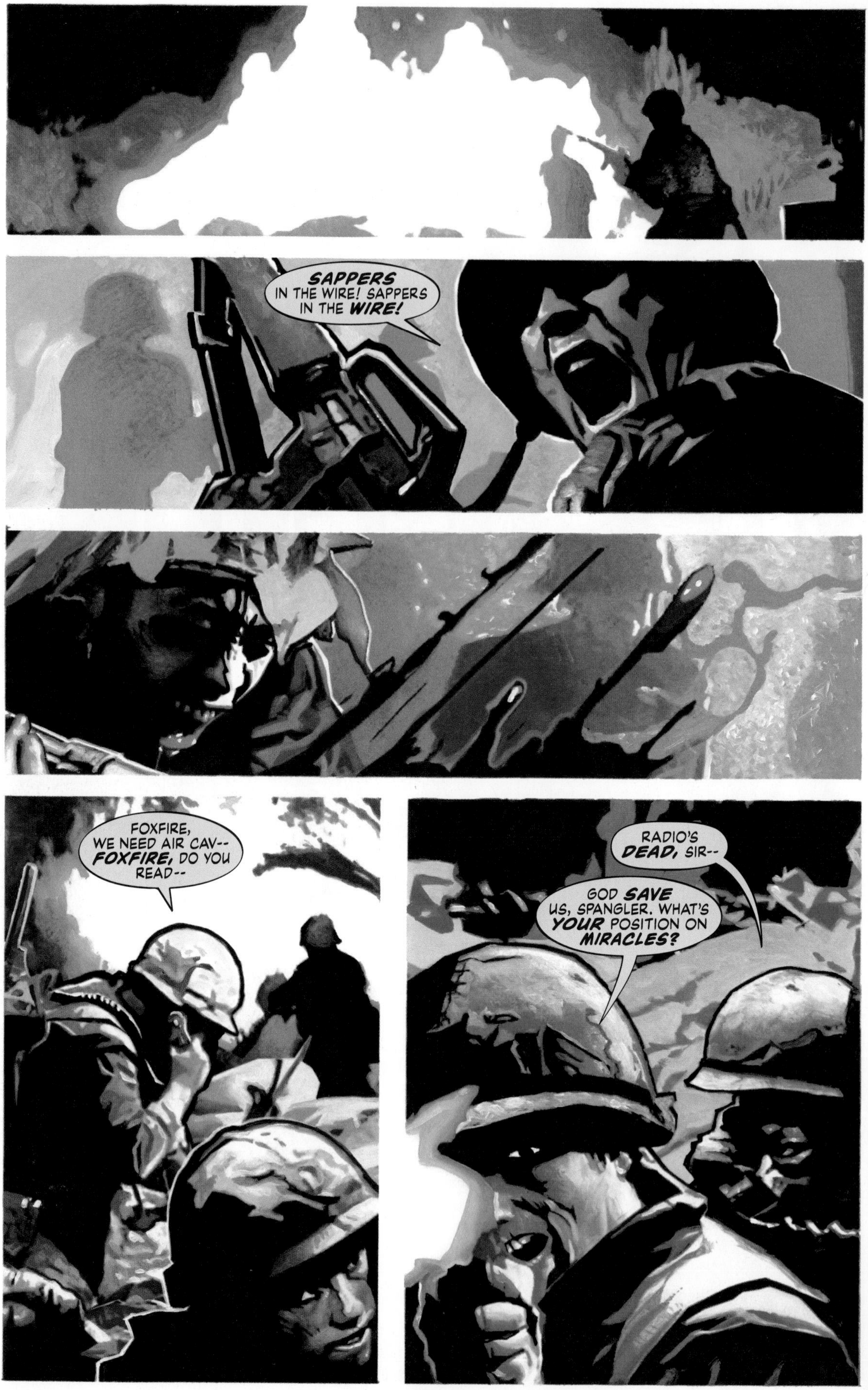
SAPPERS IN THE WIRE! SAPPERS IN THE WIRE!
FOXFIRE, WE NEED AIR CAV-- FOXFIRE, DO YOU READ--
RADIO'S DEAD, SIR--
GOD SAVE US, SPANGLER. WHAT'S YOUR POSITION ON MIRACLES?

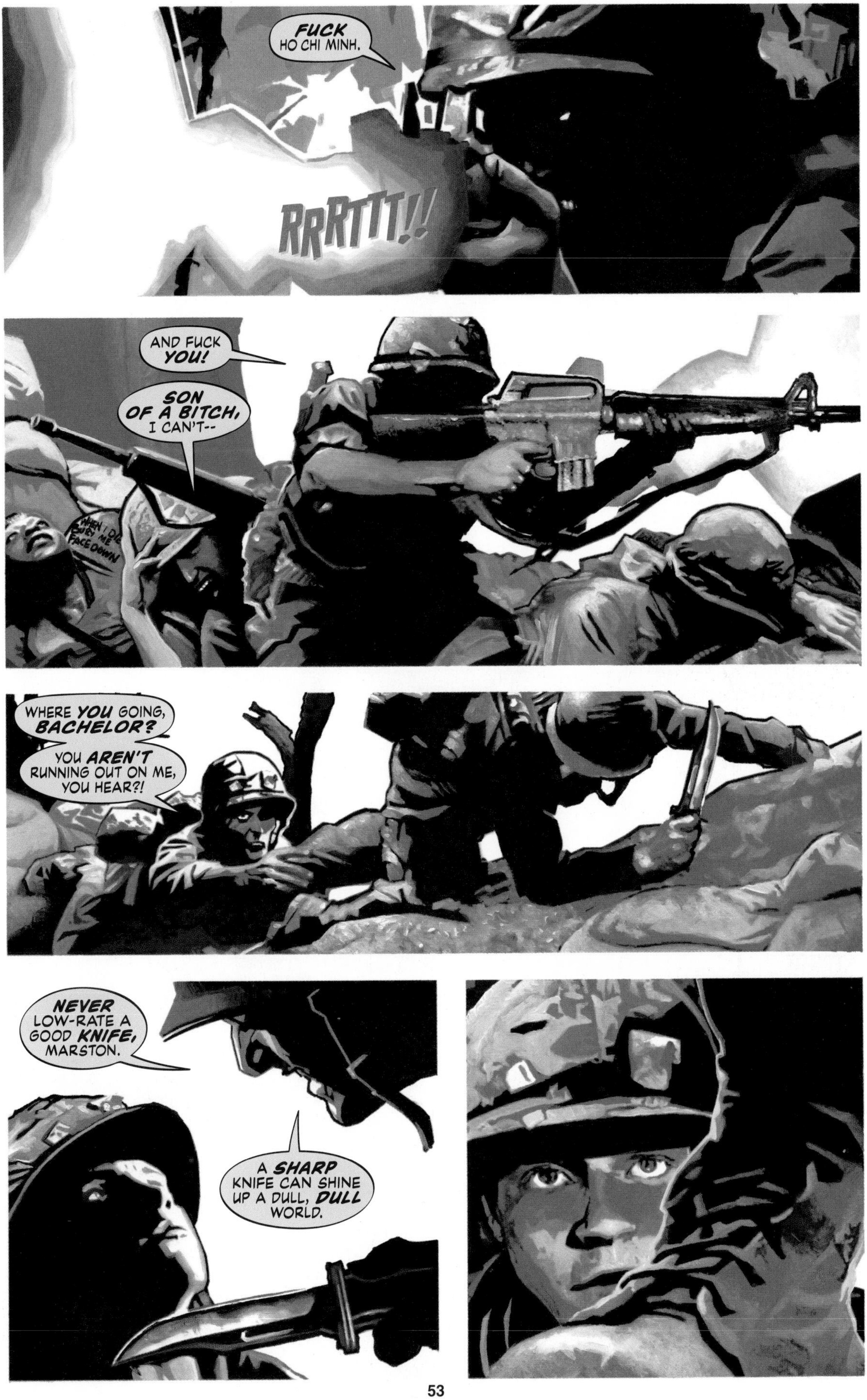
FUCK HO CHI MINH.
RRRTTT!!
AND FUCK YOU!
SON OF A BITCH, I CAN'T--
WHEN I DIE BURY ME FACE DOWN
WHERE YOU GOING, BACHELOR?
YOU AREN'T RUNNING OUT ON ME, YOU HEAR?!
NEVER LOW-RATE A GOOD KNIFE, MARSTON.
A SHARP KNIFE CAN SHINE UP A DULL, DULL WORLD.

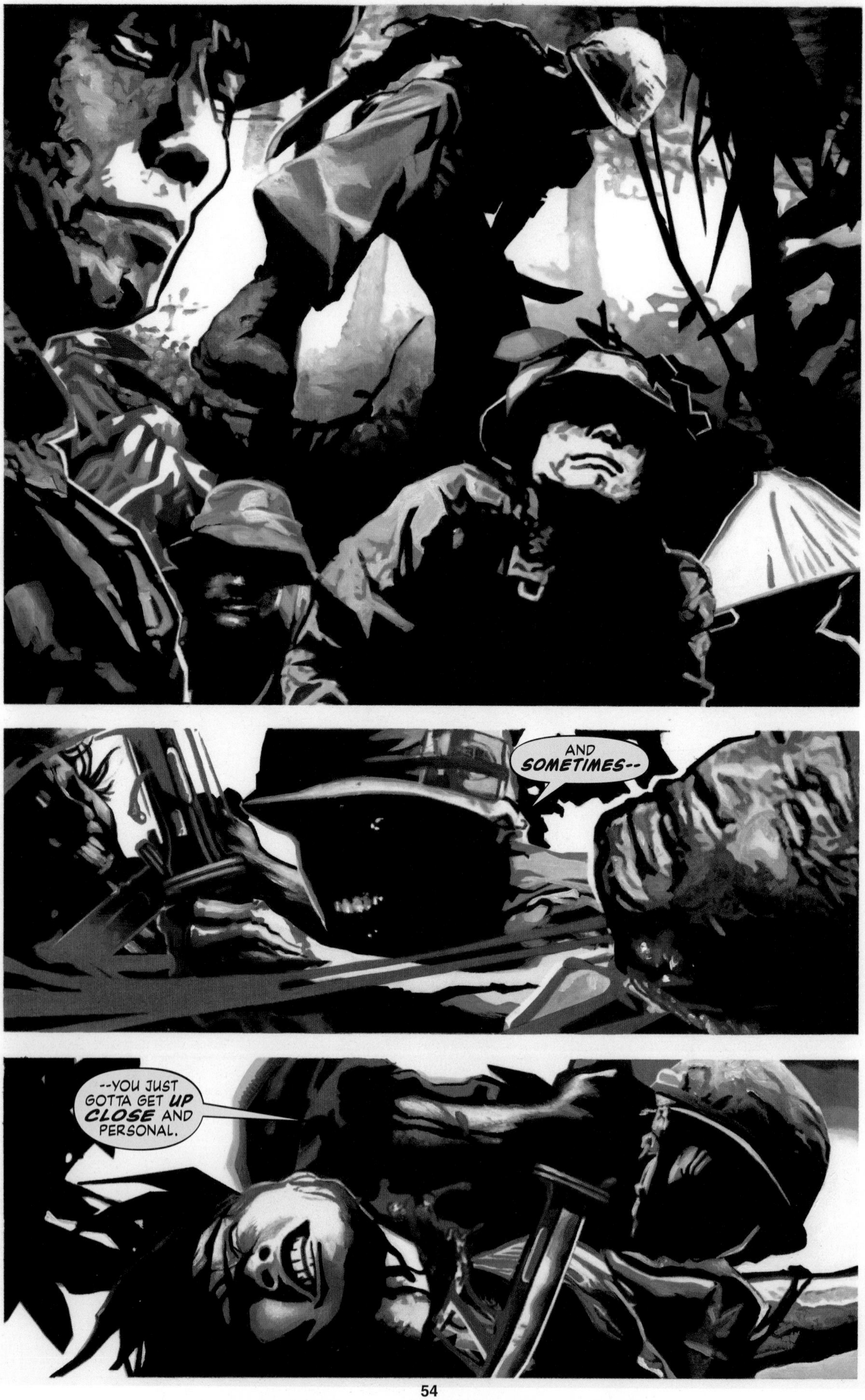
AND SOMETIMES--
--YOU JUST GOTTA GET UP CLOSE AND PERSONAL.

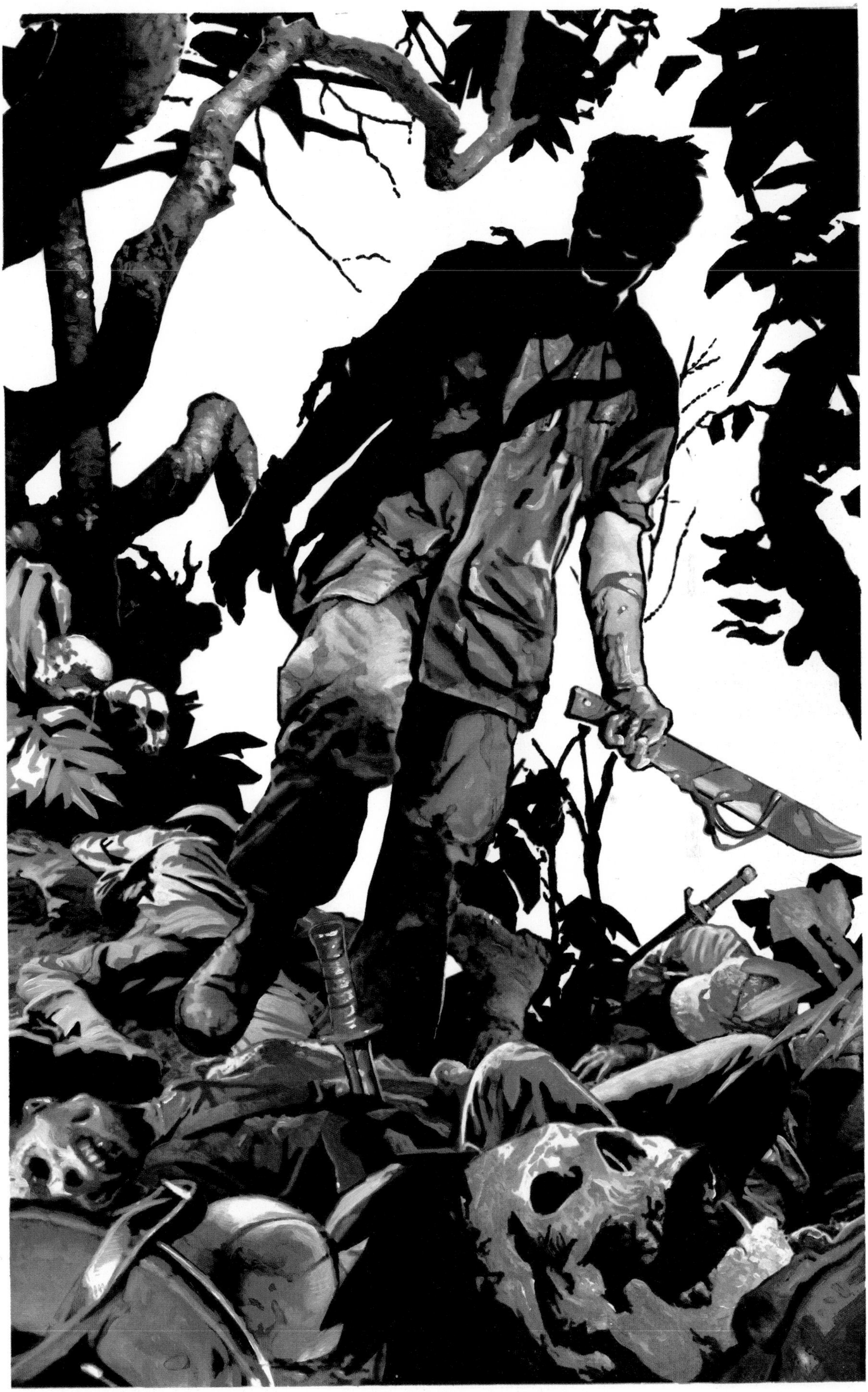

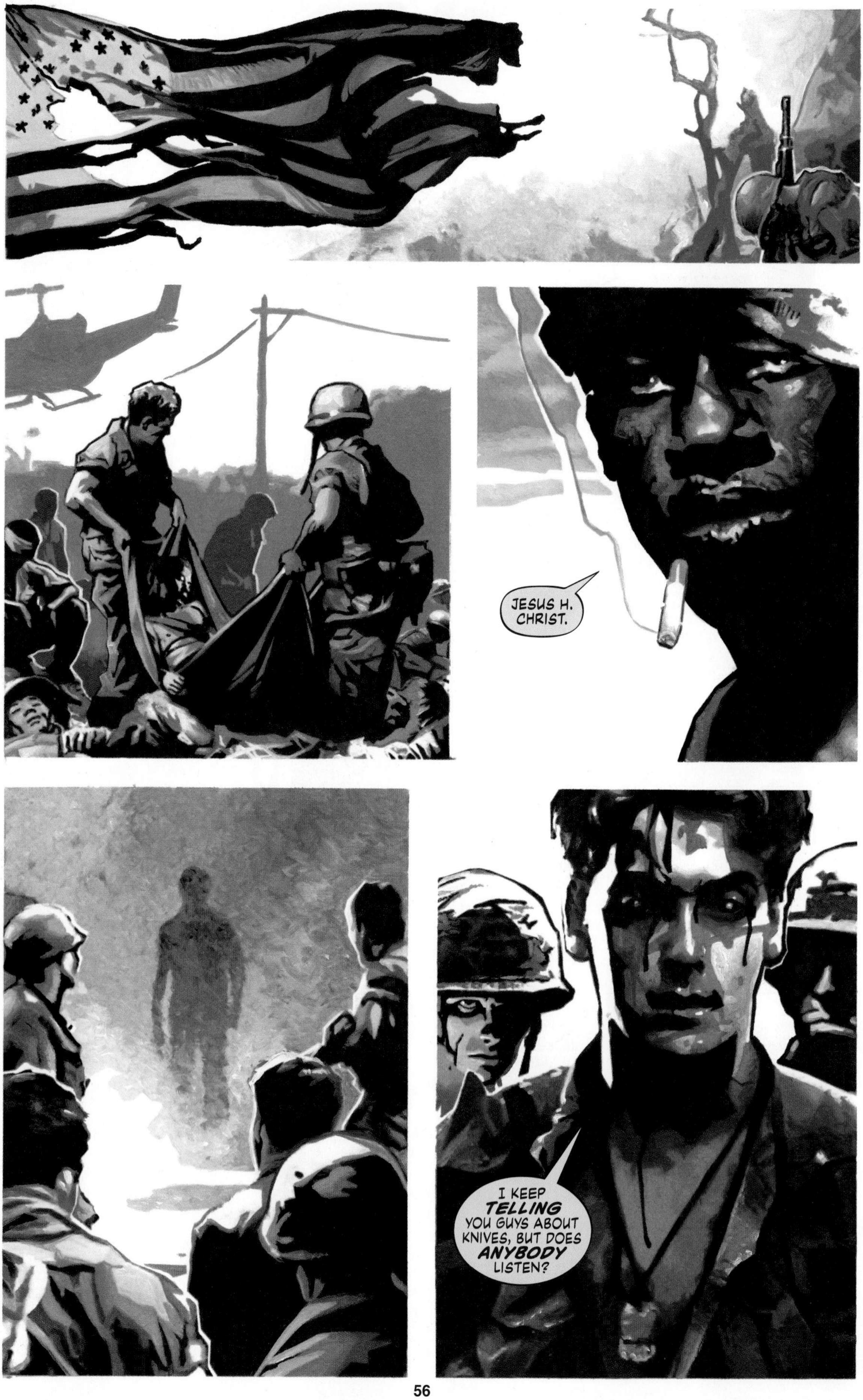
JESUS H. CHRIST.
I KEEP TELLING YOU GUYS ABOUT KNIVES, BUT DOES ANYBODY LISTEN?

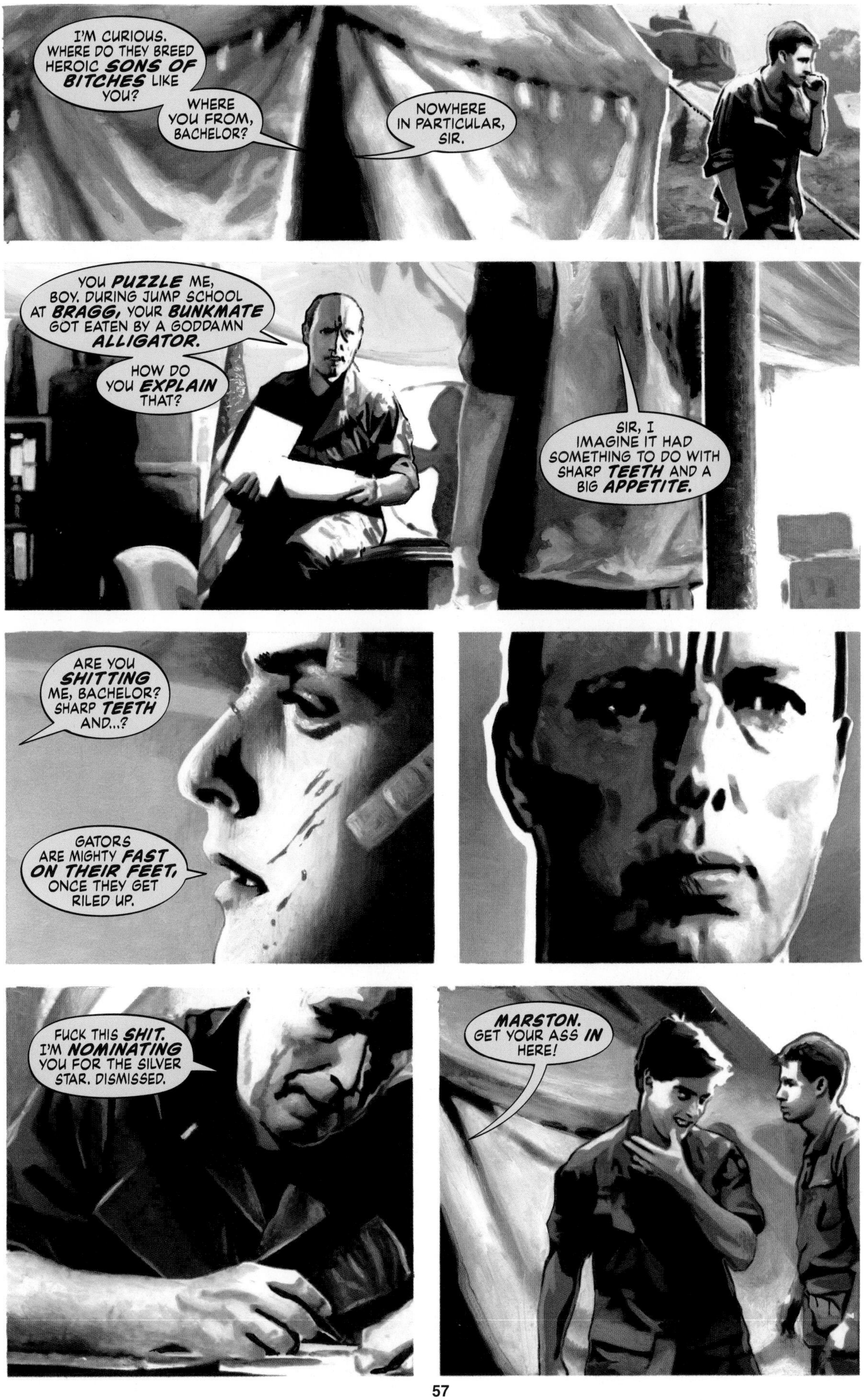
I'M CURIOUS. WHERE DO THEY BREED HEROIC SONS OF BITCHES LIKE YOU?
WHERE YOU FROM, BACHELOR?
NOWHERE IN PARTICULAR, SIR.
YOU PUZZLE ME, BOY. DURING JUMP SCHOOL AT BRAGG, YOUR BUNKMATE GOT EATEN BY A GODDAMN ALLIGATOR.
HOW DO YOU EXPLAIN THAT?
SIR, I IMAGINE IT HAD SOMETHING TO DO WITH SHARP TEETH AND A BIG APPETITE.
ARE YOU SHITTING ME, BACHELOR? SHARP TEETH AND...?
GATORS ARE MIGHTY FAST ON THEIR FEET, ONCE THEY GET RILED UP.
FUCK THIS SHIT. I'M NOMINATING YOU FOR THE SILVER STAR. DISMISSED.
MARSTON. GET YOUR ASS IN HERE!

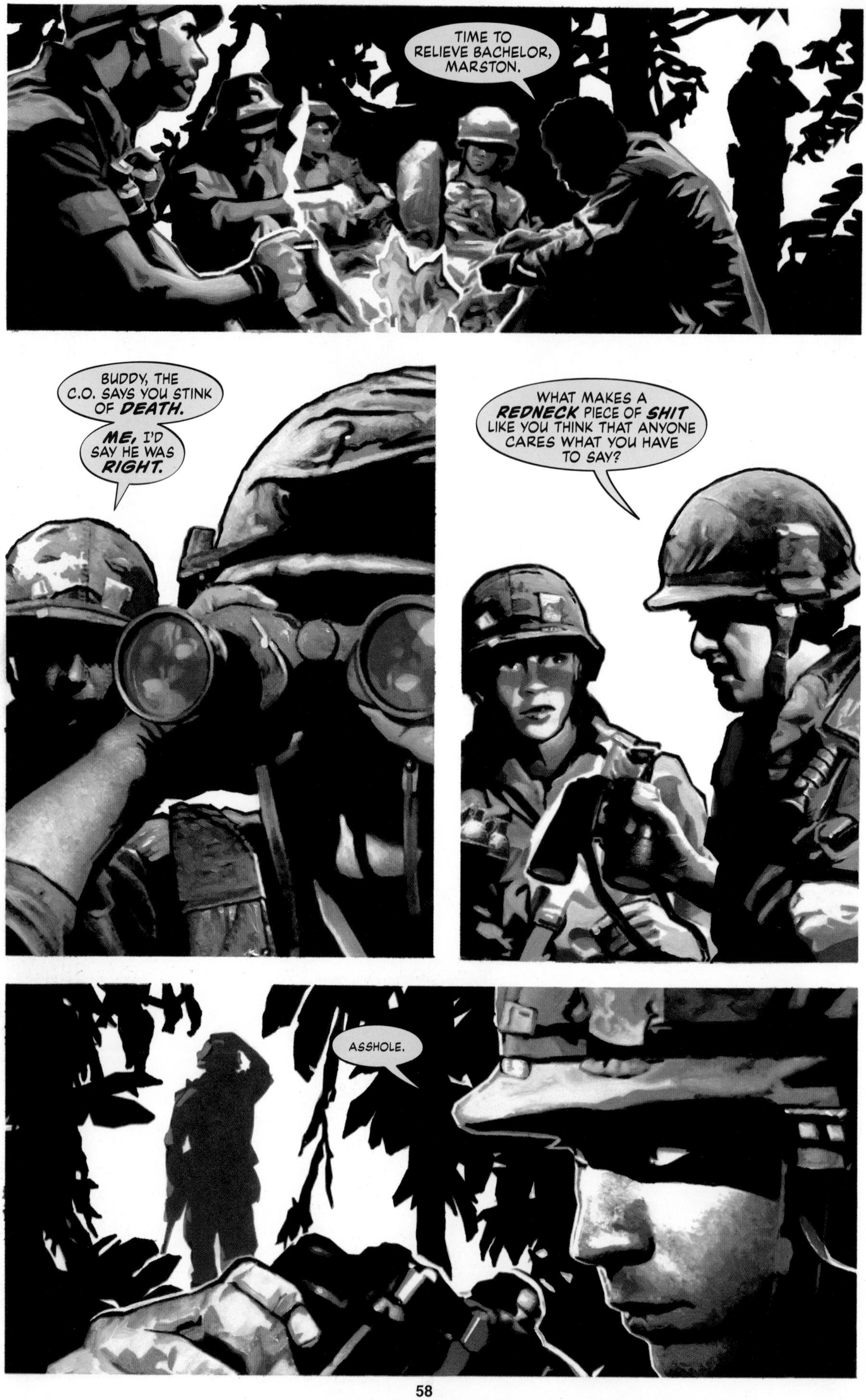
TIME TO RELIEVE BACHELOR, MARSTON.
BUDDY, THE C.O. SAYS YOU STINK OF DEATH.
ME, I'D SAY HE WAS RIGHT.
WHAT MAKES A REDNECK PIECE OF SHIT LIKE YOU THINK THAT ANYONE CARES WHAT YOU HAVE TO SAY?
ASSHOLE.

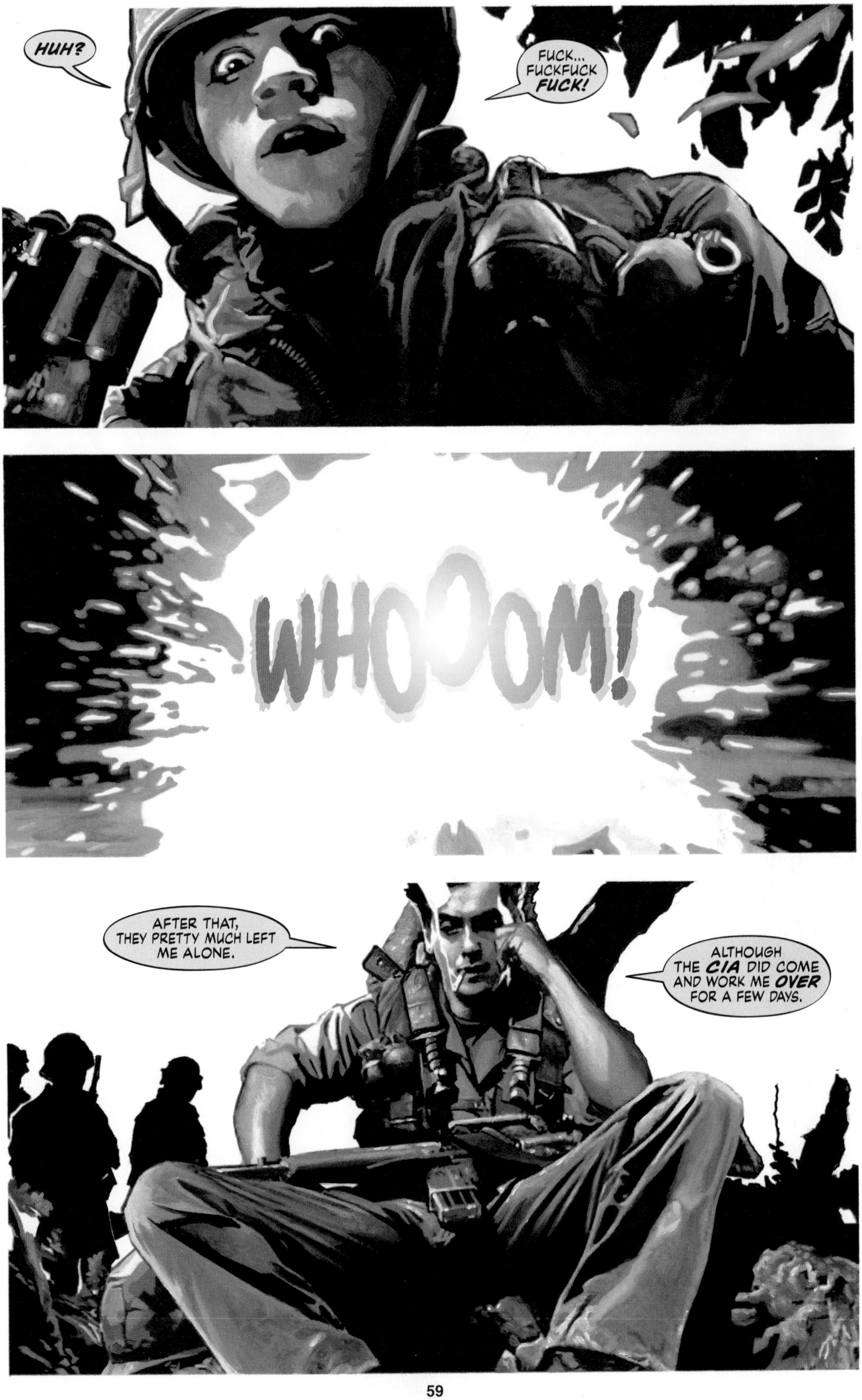
HUH?
FUCK... FUCKFUCK FUCK!
WHOOOOM!
AFTER THAT, THEY PRETTY MUCH LEFT ME ALONE.
ALTHOUGH THE CIA DID COME AND WORK ME OVER FOR A FEW DAYS.

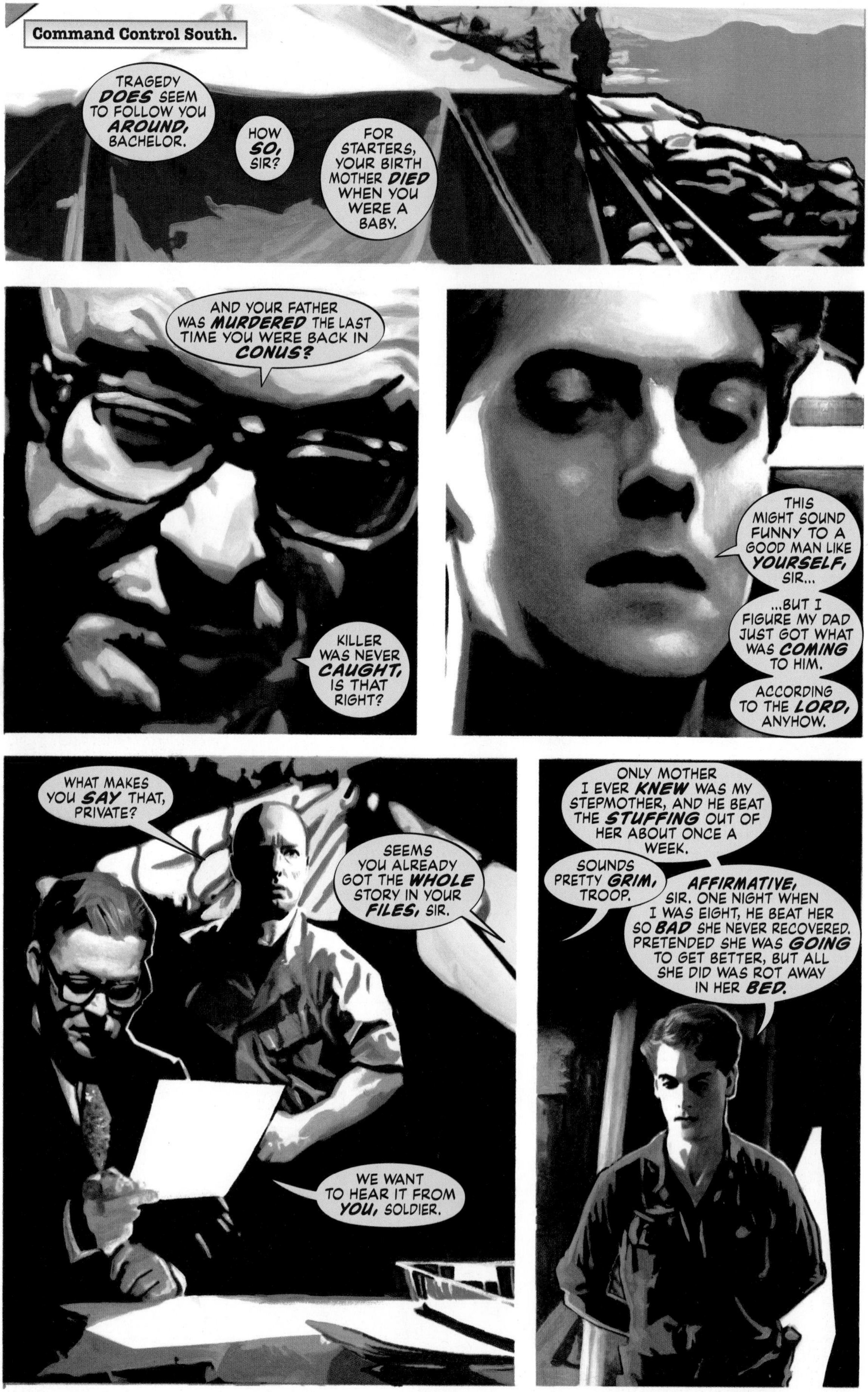

Command Control South.
TRAGEDY DOES SEEM TO FOLLOW YOU AROUND, BACHELOR.
HOW SO, SIR?
FOR STARTERS, YOUR BIRTH MOTHER DIED WHEN YOU WERE A BABY.
AND YOUR FATHER WAS MURDERED THE LAST TIME YOU WERE BACK IN CONUS?
KILLER WAS NEVER CAUGHT, IS THAT RIGHT?
THIS MIGHT SOUND FUNNY TO A GOOD MAN LIKE YOURSELF, SIR...
...BUT I FIGURE MY DAD JUST GOT WHAT WAS COMING TO HIM.
ACCORDING TO THE LORD, ANYHOW.
WHAT MAKES YOU SAY THAT, PRIVATE?
SEEMS YOU ALREADY GOT THE WHOLE STORY IN YOUR FILES, SIR.
WE WANT TO HEAR IT FROM YOU, SOLDIER.
ONLY MOTHER I EVER KNEW WAS MY STEPMOTHER, AND HE BEAT THE STUFFING OUT OF HER ABOUT ONCE A WEEK.
SOUNDS PRETTY GRIM, TROOP.
AFFIRMATIVE, SIR. ONE NIGHT WHEN I WAS EIGHT, HE BEAT HER SO BAD SHE NEVER RECOVERED. PRETENDED SHE WAS GOING TO GET BETTER, BUT ALL SHE DID WAS ROT AWAY IN HER BED.

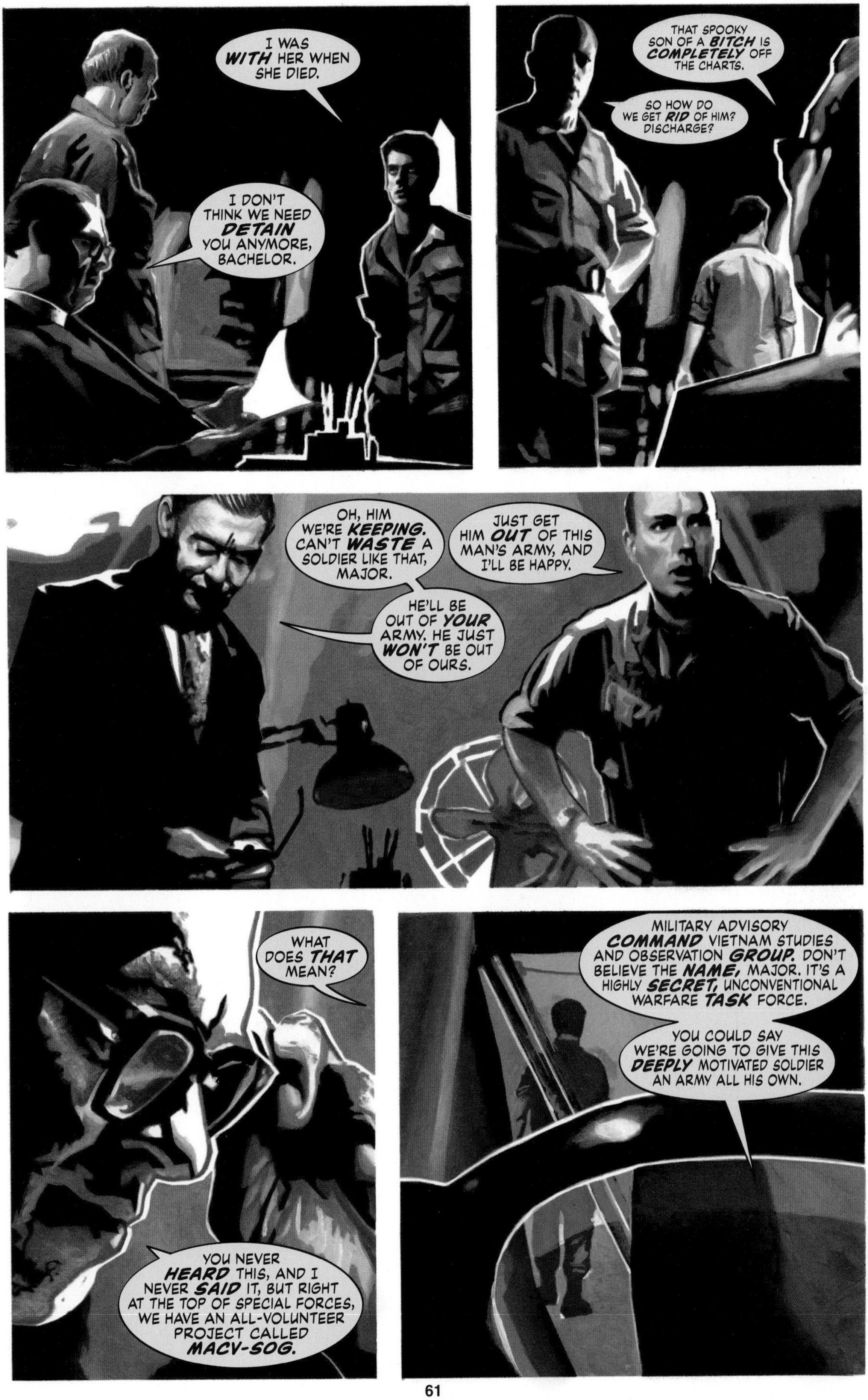
I WAS WITH HER WHEN SHE DIED.
I DON'T THINK WE NEED DETAIN YOU ANYMORE, BACHELOR.
THAT SPOOKY SON OF A BITCH IS COMPLETELY OFF THE CHARTS.
SO HOW DO WE GET RID OF HIM? DISCHARGE?
OH, HIM WE'RE KEEPING. CAN'T WASTE A SOLDIER LIKE THAT, MAJOR.
JUST GET HIM OUT OF THIS MAN'S ARMY, AND I'LL BE HAPPY.
HE'LL BE OUT OF YOUR ARMY. HE JUST WON'T BE OUT OF OURS.
WHAT DOES THAT MEAN?
YOU NEVER HEARD THIS, AND I NEVER SAID IT, BUT RIGHT AT THE TOP OF SPECIAL FORCES, WE HAVE AN ALL-VOLUNTEER PROJECT CALLED MACV-SOG.
MILITARY ADVISORY COMMAND VIETNAM STUDIES AND OBSERVATION GROUP. DON'T BELIEVE THE NAME, MAJOR. IT'S A HIGHLY SECRET, UNCONVENTIONAL WARFARE TASK FORCE.
YOU COULD SAY WE'RE GOING TO GIVE THIS DEEPLY MOTIVATED SOLDIER AN ARMY ALL HIS OWN.

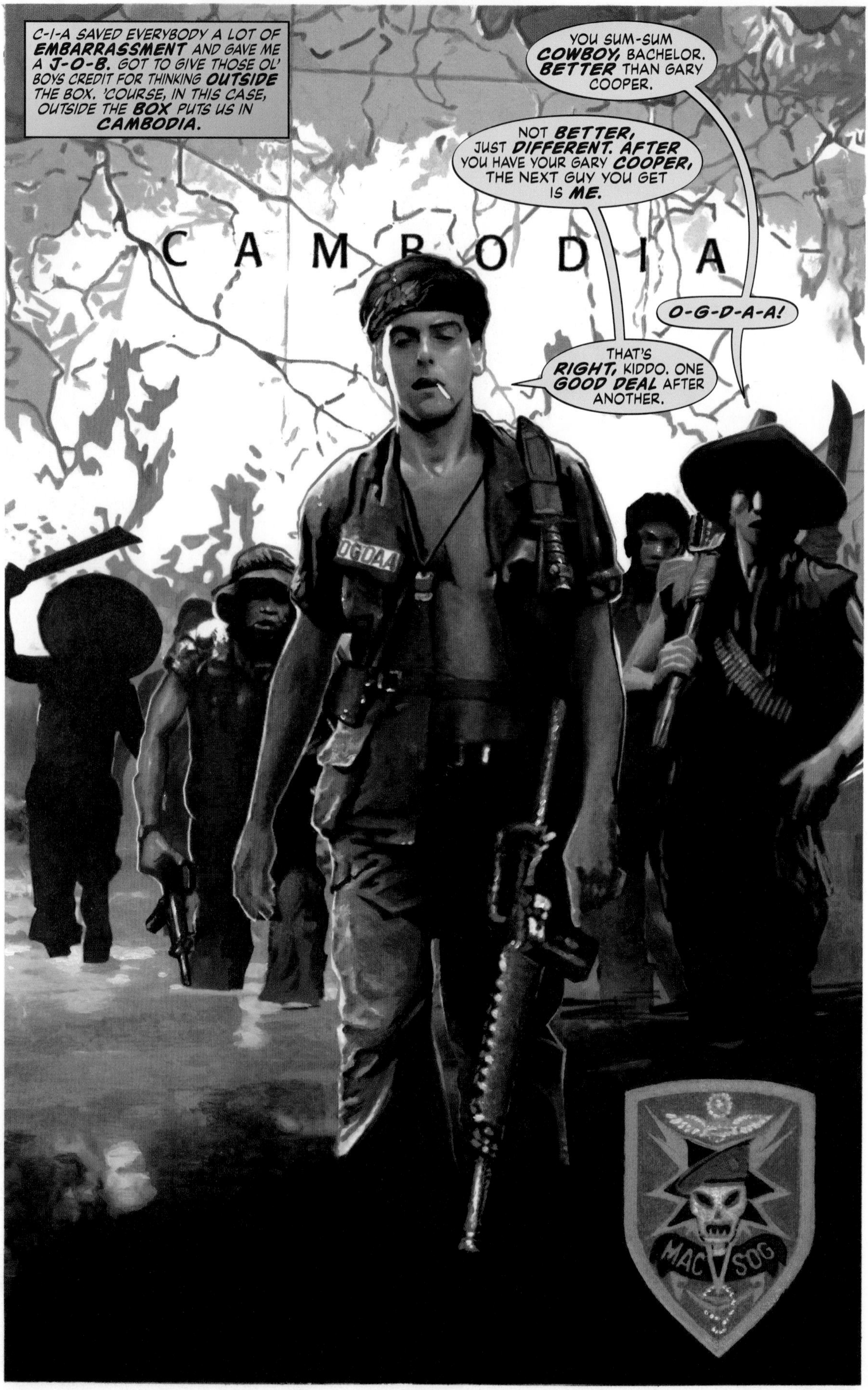
C-I-A SAVED EVERYBODY A LOT OF EMBARRASSMENT AND GAVE ME A J-O-B. GOT TO GIVE THOSE OL' BOYS CREDIT FOR THINKING OUTSIDE THE BOX. 'COURSE, IN THIS CASE, OUTSIDE THE BOX PUTS US IN CAMBODIA.
YOU SUM-SUM COWBOY, BACHELOR. BETTER THAN GARY COOPER.
NOT BETTER, JUST DIFFERENT. AFTER YOU HAVE YOUR GARY COOPER, THE NEXT GUY YOU GET IS ME.
CAMBODIA
O-G-D-A-A!
THAT'S RIGHT, KIDDO. ONE GOOD DEAL AFTER ANOTHER.
OGDAA
MAC SOG

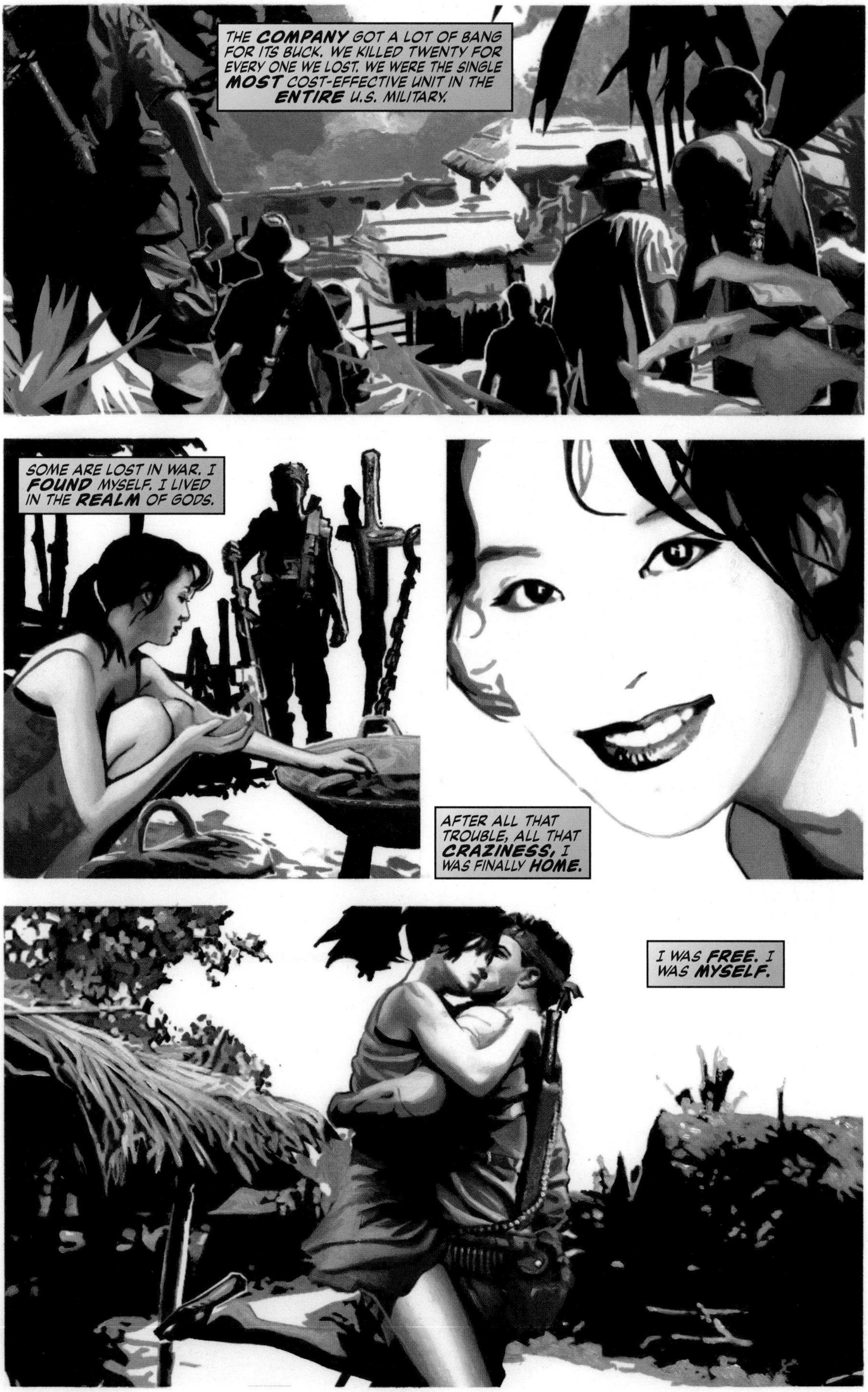
THE COMPANY GOT A LOT OF BANG FOR ITS BUCK. WE KILLED TWENTY FOR EVERY ONE WE LOST. WE WERE THE SINGLE MOST COST-EFFECTIVE UNIT IN THE ENTIRE U.S. MILITARY.
SOME ARE LOST IN WAR. I FOUND MYSELF. I LIVED IN THE REALM OF GODS.
AFTER ALL THAT TROUBLE, ALL THAT CRAZINESS, I WAS FINALLY HOME.
I WAS FREE. I WAS MYSELF.

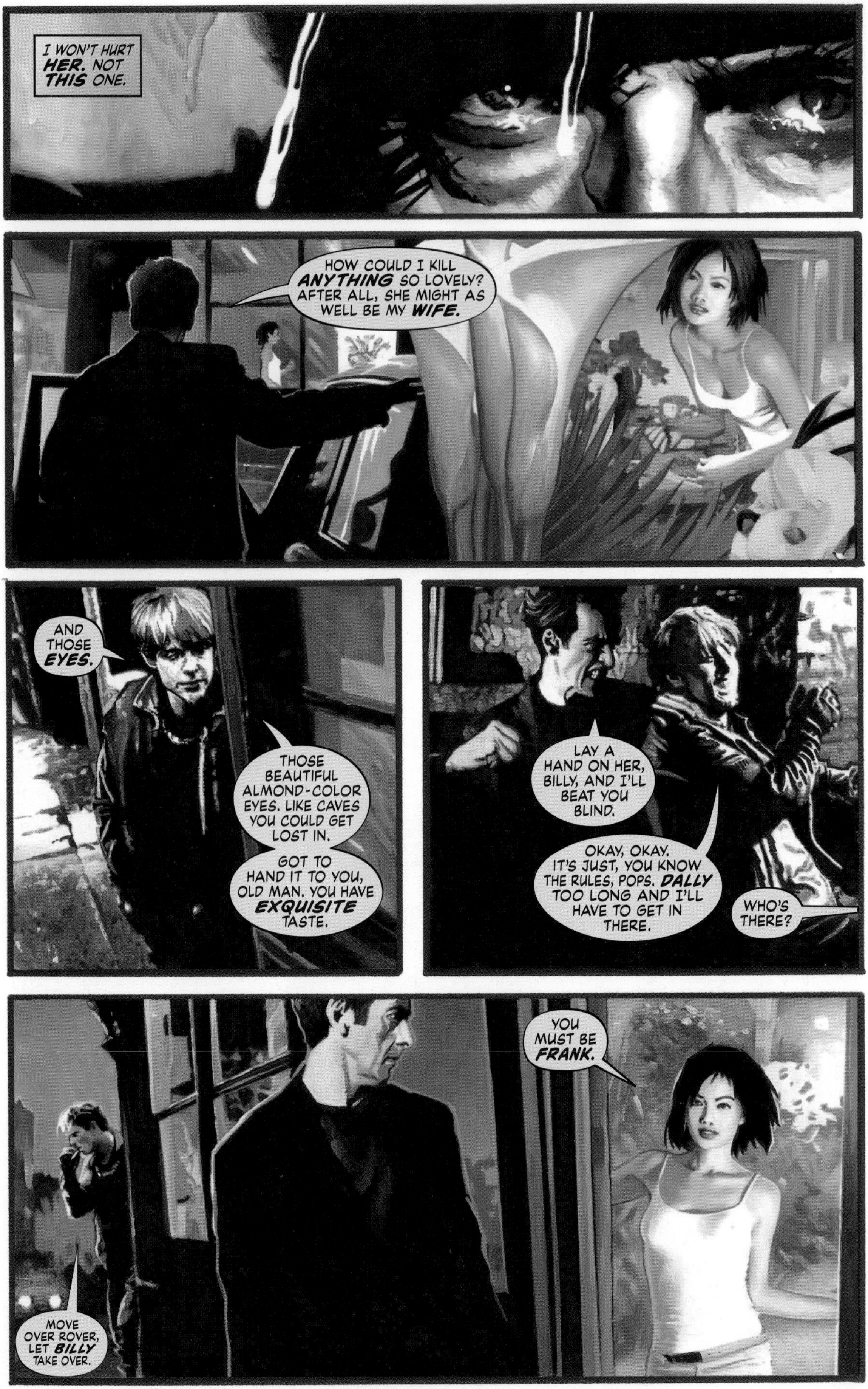
I WON'T HURT HER. NOT THIS ONE.
HOW COULD I KILL ANYTHING SO LOVELY? AFTER ALL, SHE MIGHT AS WELL BE MY WIFE.
AND THOSE EYES.
THOSE BEAUTIFUL ALMOND-COLOR EYES. LIKE CAVES YOU COULD GET LOST IN.
GOT TO HAND IT TO YOU, OLD MAN. YOU HAVE EXQUISITE TASTE.
LAY A HAND ON HER, BILLY, AND I'LL BEAT YOU BLIND.
OKAY, OKAY. IT'S JUST, YOU KNOW THE RULES, POPS. DALLY TOO LONG AND I'LL HAVE TO GET IN THERE.
WHO'S THERE?
YOU MUST BE FRANK.
MOVE OVER ROVER, LET BILLY TAKE OVER.

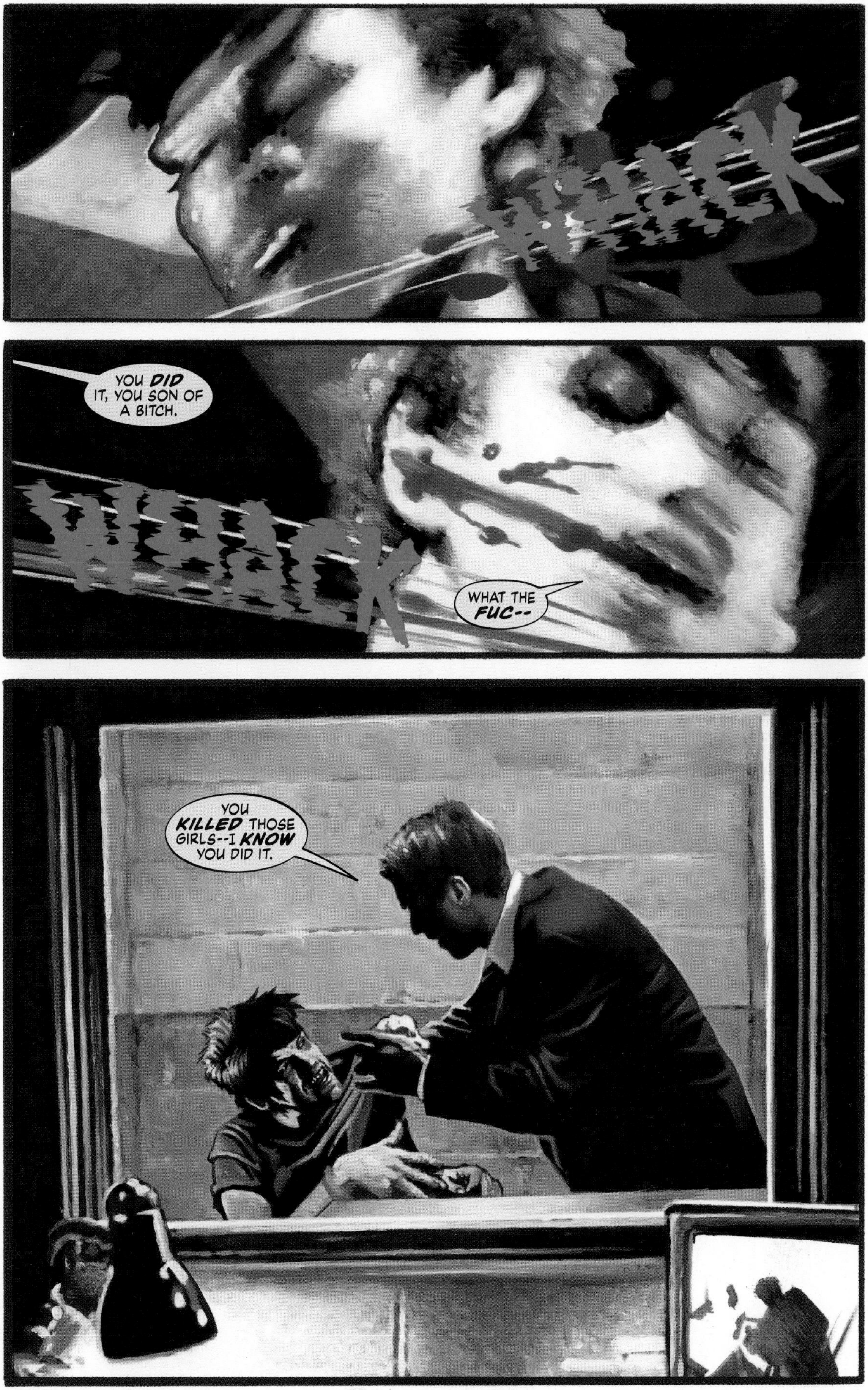
WHACK
YOU **DID** IT, YOU SON OF A BITCH.
WHACK
WHAT THE **FUC--**
YOU **KILLED** THOSE GIRLS--I **KNOW** YOU DID IT.

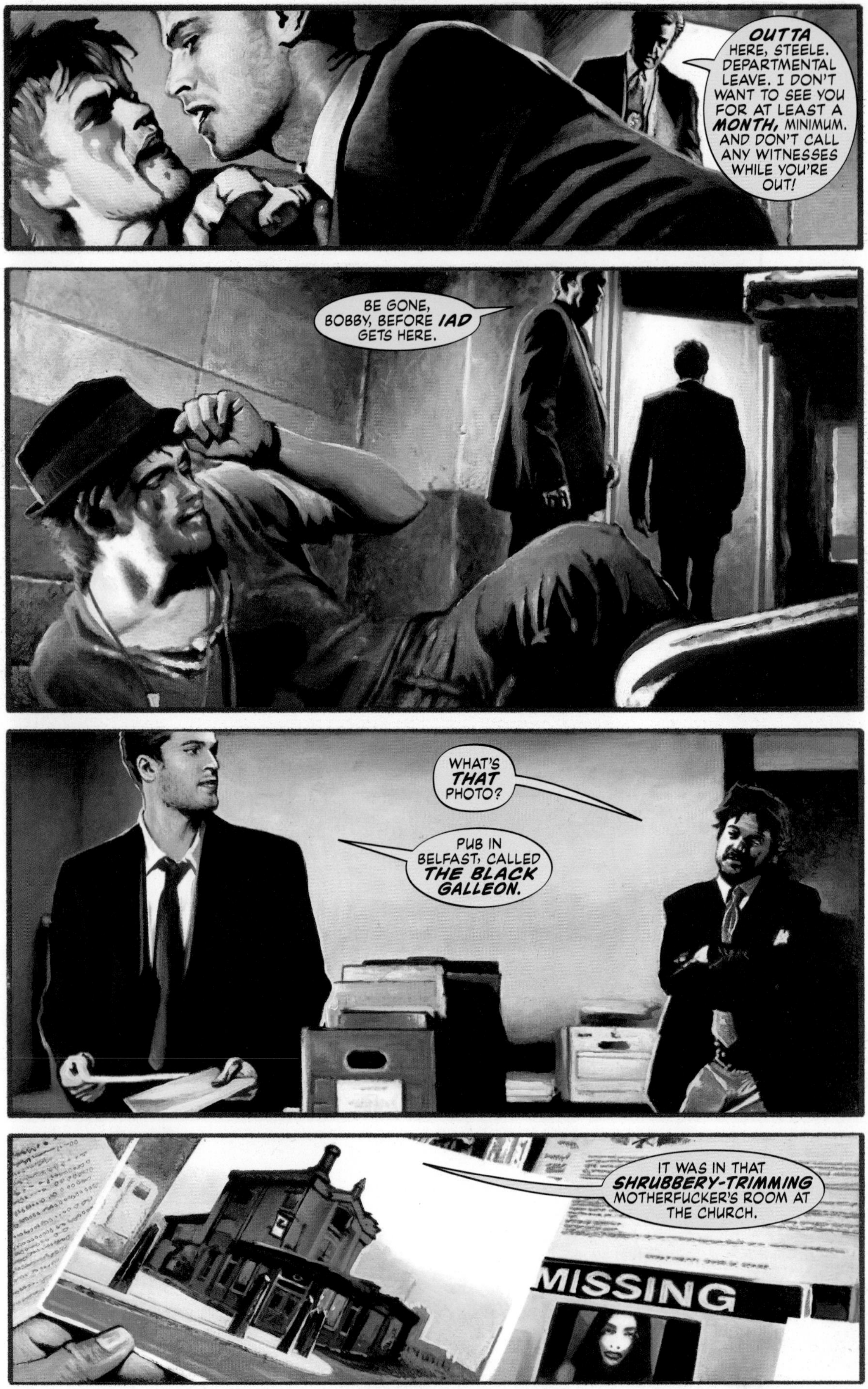
OUTTA HERE, STEELE. DEPARTMENTAL LEAVE. I DON'T WANT TO SEE YOU FOR AT LEAST A MONTH, MINIMUM. AND DON'T CALL ANY WITNESSES WHILE YOU'RE OUT!
BE GONE, BOBBY, BEFORE IAD GETS HERE.
WHAT'S THAT PHOTO?
PUB IN BELFAST, CALLED THE BLACK GALLEON.
IT WAS IN THAT SHRUBBERY-TRIMMING MOTHERFUCKER'S ROOM AT THE CHURCH.
MISSING

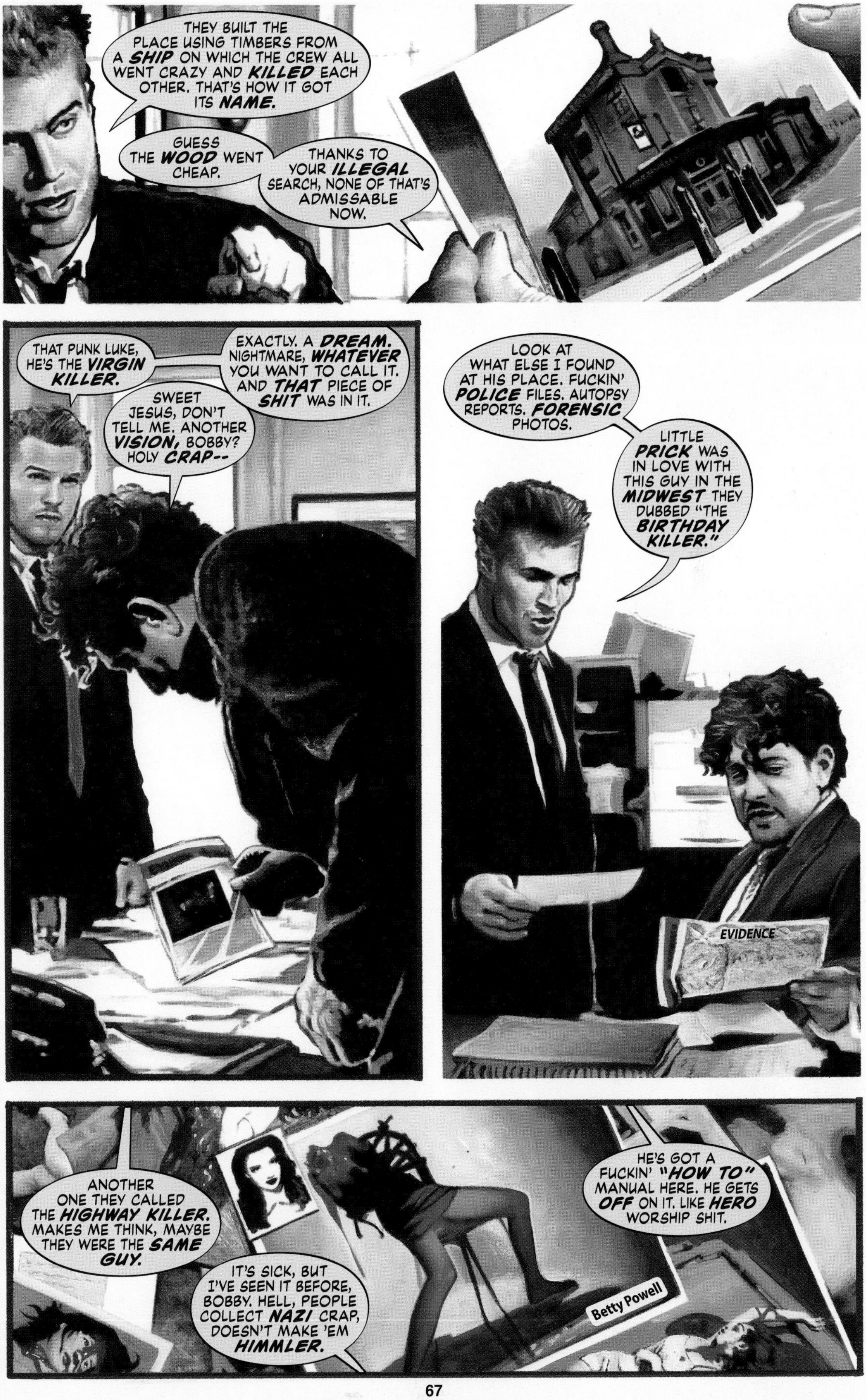
THEY BUILT THE PLACE USING TIMBERS FROM A SHIP ON WHICH THE CREW ALL WENT CRAZY AND KILLED EACH OTHER. THAT'S HOW IT GOT ITS NAME.
GUESS THE WOOD WENT CHEAP.
THANKS TO YOUR ILLEGAL SEARCH, NONE OF THAT'S ADMISSABLE NOW.
THAT PUNK LUKE, HE'S THE VIRGIN KILLER.
SWEET JESUS, DON'T TELL ME. ANOTHER VISION, BOBBY? HOLY CRAP--
EXACTLY. A DREAM. NIGHTMARE, WHATEVER YOU WANT TO CALL IT. AND THAT PIECE OF SHIT WAS IN IT.
LOOK AT WHAT ELSE I FOUND AT HIS PLACE. FUCKIN' POLICE FILES. AUTOPSY REPORTS. FORENSIC PHOTOS.
LITTLE PRICK WAS IN LOVE WITH THIS GUY IN THE MIDWEST THEY DUBBED "THE BIRTHDAY KILLER."
EVIDENCE
ANOTHER ONE THEY CALLED THE HIGHWAY KILLER. MAKES ME THINK, MAYBE THEY WERE THE SAME GUY.
IT'S SICK, BUT I'VE SEEN IT BEFORE, BOBBY. HELL, PEOPLE COLLECT NAZI CRAP, DOESN'T MAKE 'EM HIMMLER.
HE'S GOT A FUCKIN' "HOW TO" MANUAL HERE. HE GETS OFF ON IT. LIKE HERO WORSHIP SHIT.
Betty Powell

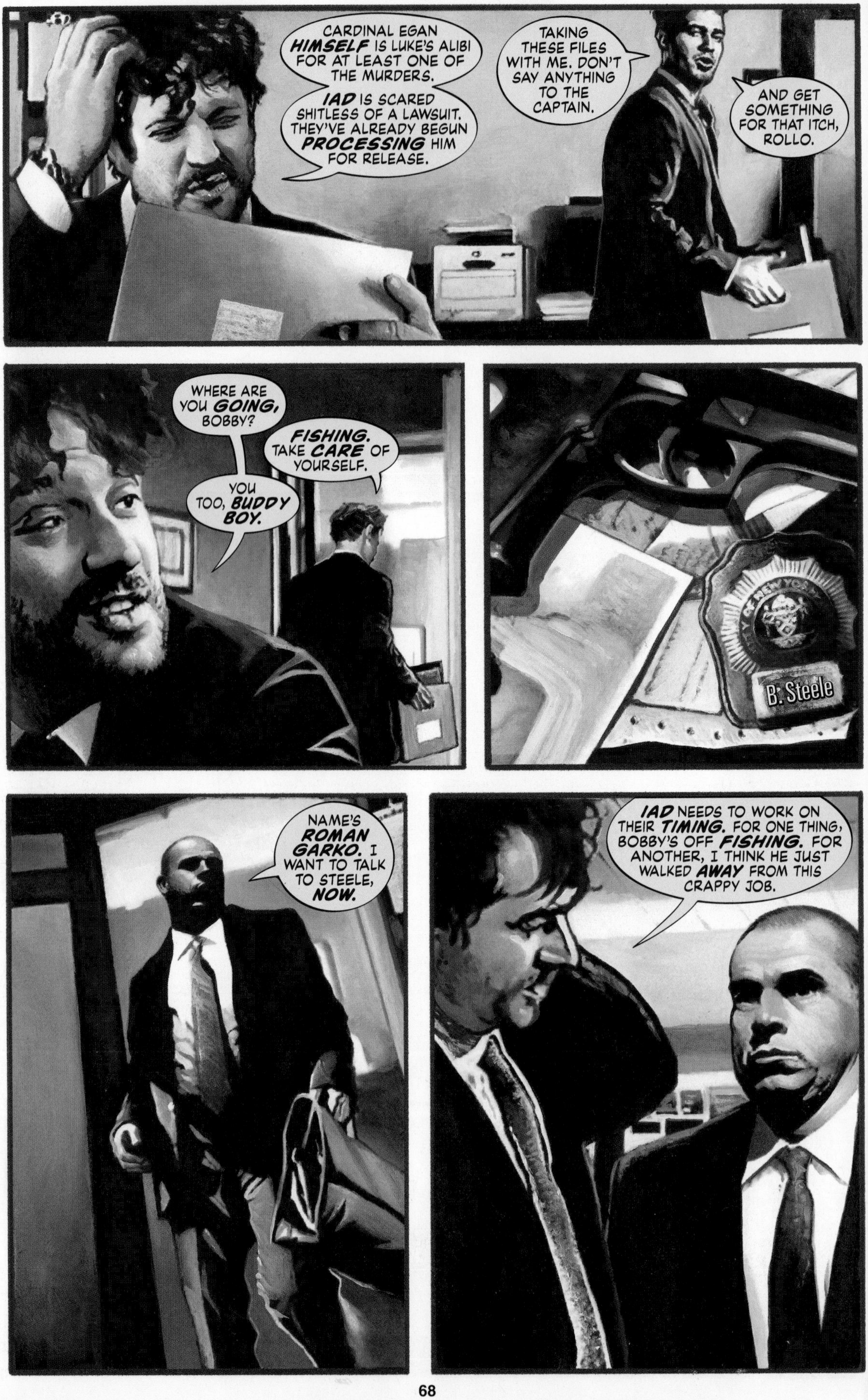
CARDINAL EGAN HIMSELF IS LUKE'S ALIBI FOR AT LEAST ONE OF THE MURDERS.
IAD IS SCARED SHITLESS OF A LAWSUIT. THEY'VE ALREADY BEGUN PROCESSING HIM FOR RELEASE.
TAKING THESE FILES WITH ME. DON'T SAY ANYTHING TO THE CAPTAIN.
AND GET SOMETHING FOR THAT ITCH, ROLLO.
WHERE ARE YOU GOING, BOBBY?
FISHING. TAKE CARE OF YOURSELF.
YOU TOO, BUDDY BOY.
B. Steele
NAME'S ROMAN GARKO. I WANT TO TALK TO STEELE, NOW.
IAD NEEDS TO WORK ON THEIR TIMING. FOR ONE THING, BOBBY'S OFF FISHING. FOR ANOTHER, I THINK HE JUST WALKED AWAY FROM THIS CRAPPY JOB.

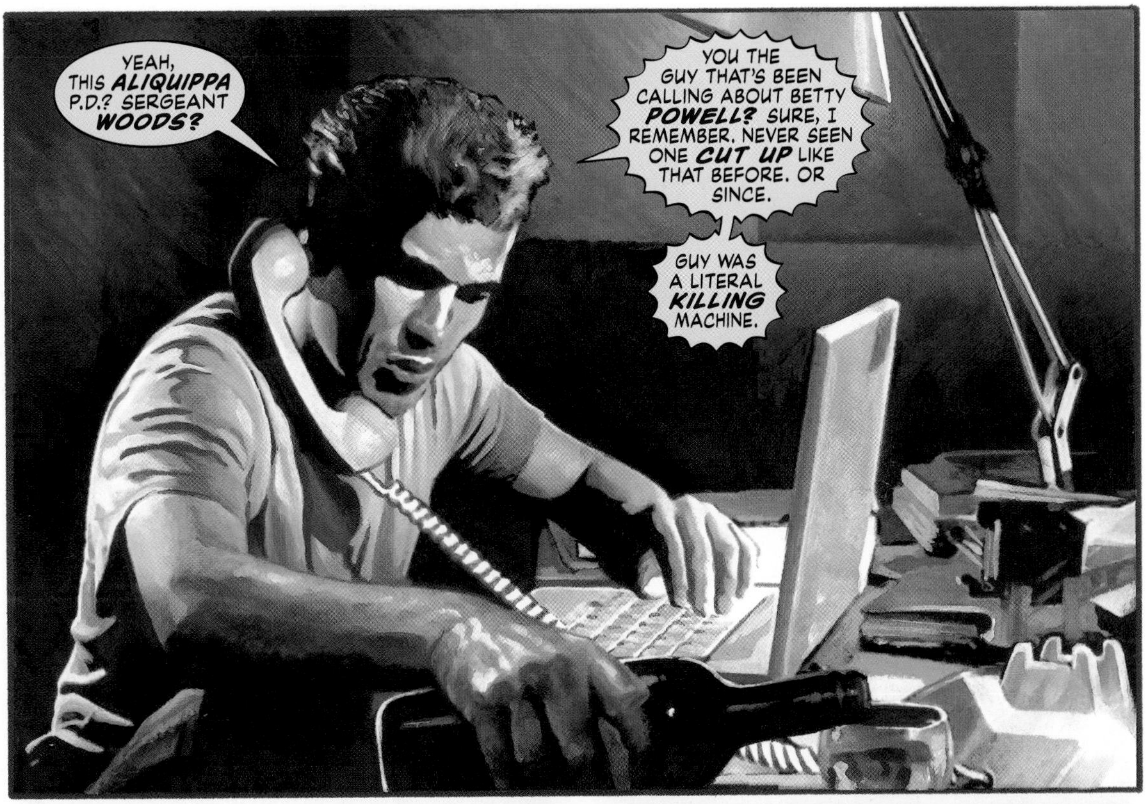
YEAH, THIS ALIQUIPPA P.D.? SERGEANT WOODS?
YOU THE GUY THAT'S BEEN CALLING ABOUT BETTY POWELL? SURE, I REMEMBER. NEVER SEEN ONE CUT UP LIKE THAT BEFORE. OR SINCE.
GUY WAS A LITERAL KILLING MACHINE.

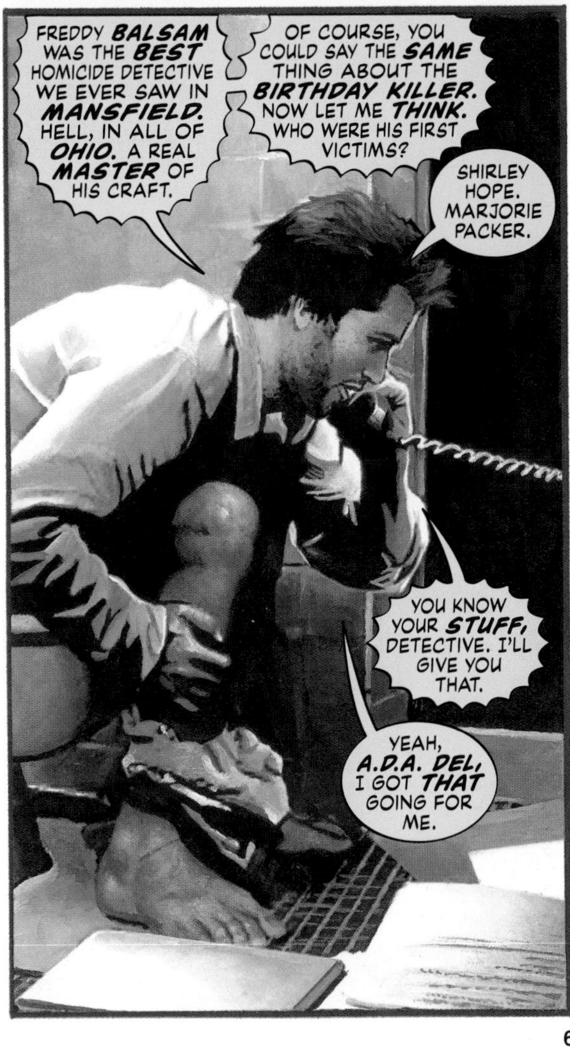
FREDDY BALSAM WAS THE BEST HOMICIDE DETECTIVE WE EVER SAW IN MANSFIELD. HELL, IN ALL OF OHIO. A REAL MASTER OF HIS CRAFT.
OF COURSE, YOU COULD SAY THE SAME THING ABOUT THE BIRTHDAY KILLER. NOW LET ME THINK. WHO WERE HIS FIRST VICTIMS?
SHIRLEY HOPE. MARJORIE PACKER.
YOU KNOW YOUR STUFF, DETECTIVE. I'LL GIVE YOU THAT.
YEAH, A.D.A. DEL, I GOT THAT GOING FOR ME.

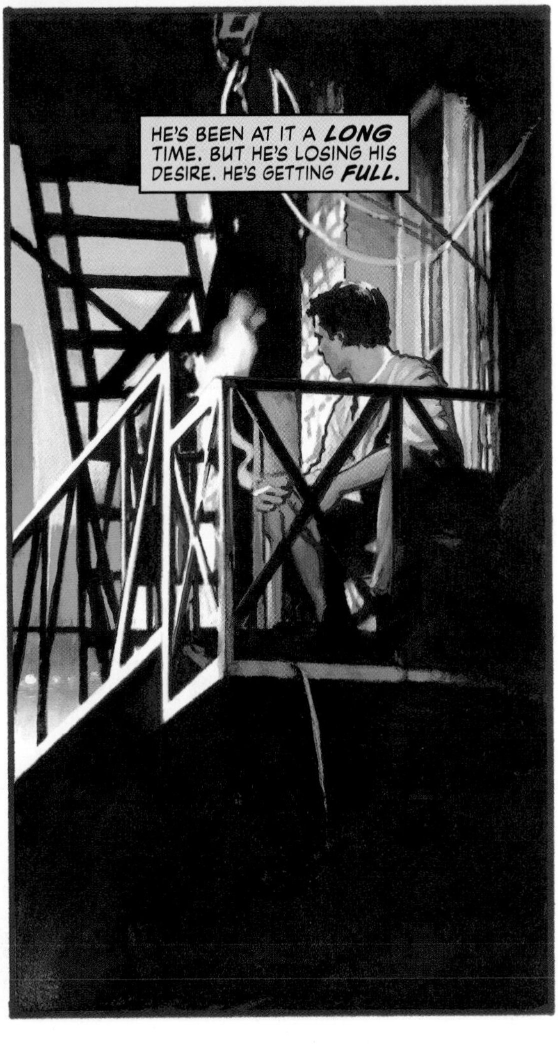
HE'S BEEN AT IT A LONG TIME. BUT HE'S LOSING HIS DESIRE. HE'S GETTING FULL.

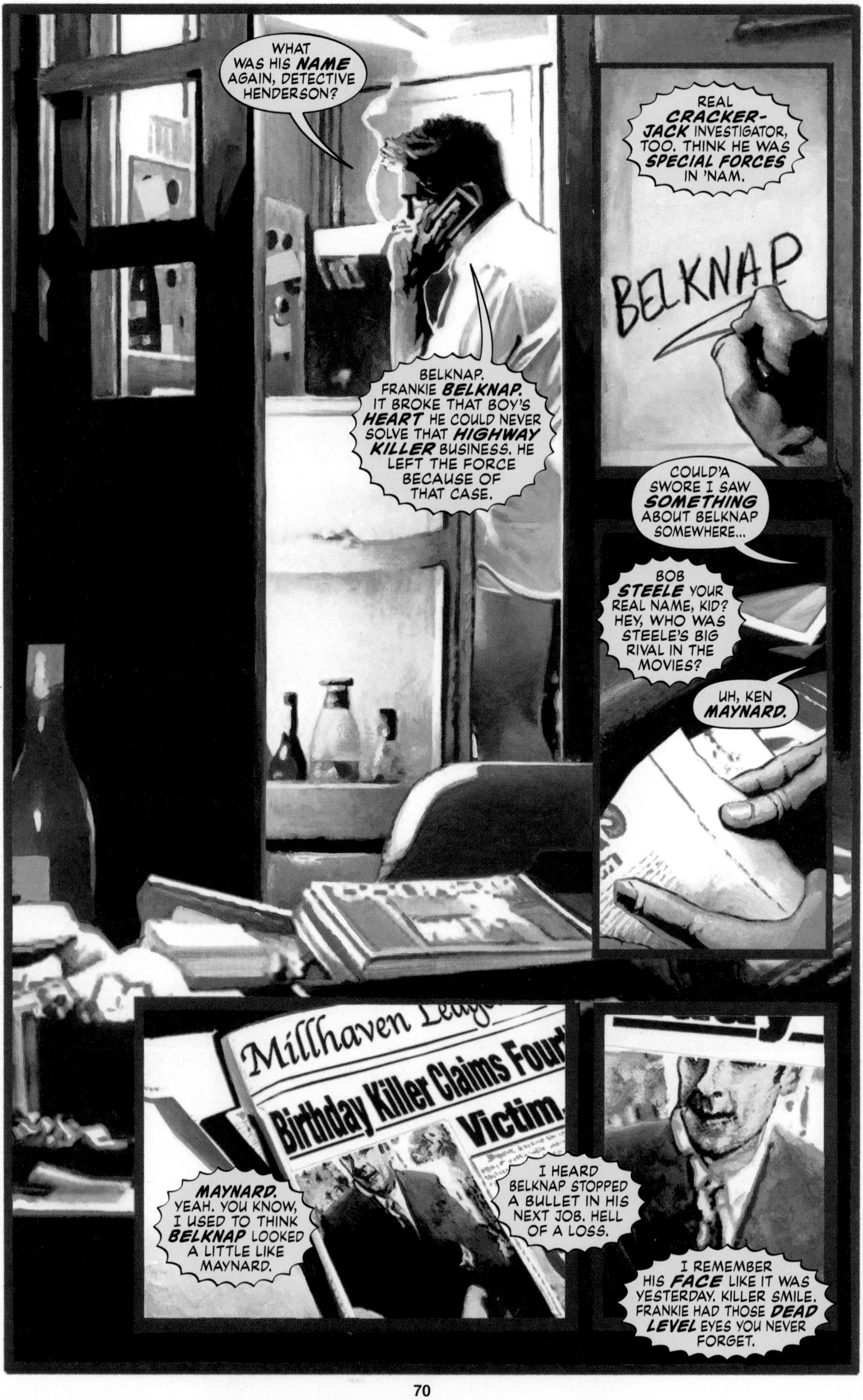
WHAT WAS HIS NAME AGAIN, DETECTIVE HENDERSON?
BELKNAP. FRANKIE BELKNAP. IT BROKE THAT BOY'S HEART HE COULD NEVER SOLVE THAT HIGHWAY KILLER BUSINESS. HE LEFT THE FORCE BECAUSE OF THAT CASE.
REAL CRACKER-JACK INVESTIGATOR, TOO. THINK HE WAS SPECIAL FORCES IN 'NAM.
BELKNAP
COULD'A SWORE I SAW SOMETHING ABOUT BELKNAP SOMEWHERE...
BOB STEELE YOUR REAL NAME, KID? HEY, WHO WAS STEELE'S BIG RIVAL IN THE MOVIES?
UH, KEN MAYNARD.
Millhaven Leag
Birthday Killer Claims Fourt
Victim.
MAYNARD. YEAH. YOU KNOW, I USED TO THINK BELKNAP LOOKED A LITTLE LIKE MAYNARD.
I HEARD BELKNAP STOPPED A BULLET IN HIS NEXT JOB. HELL OF A LOSS.
I REMEMBER HIS FACE LIKE IT WAS YESTERDAY. KILLER SMILE. FRANKIE HAD THOSE DEAD LEVEL EYES YOU NEVER FORGET.

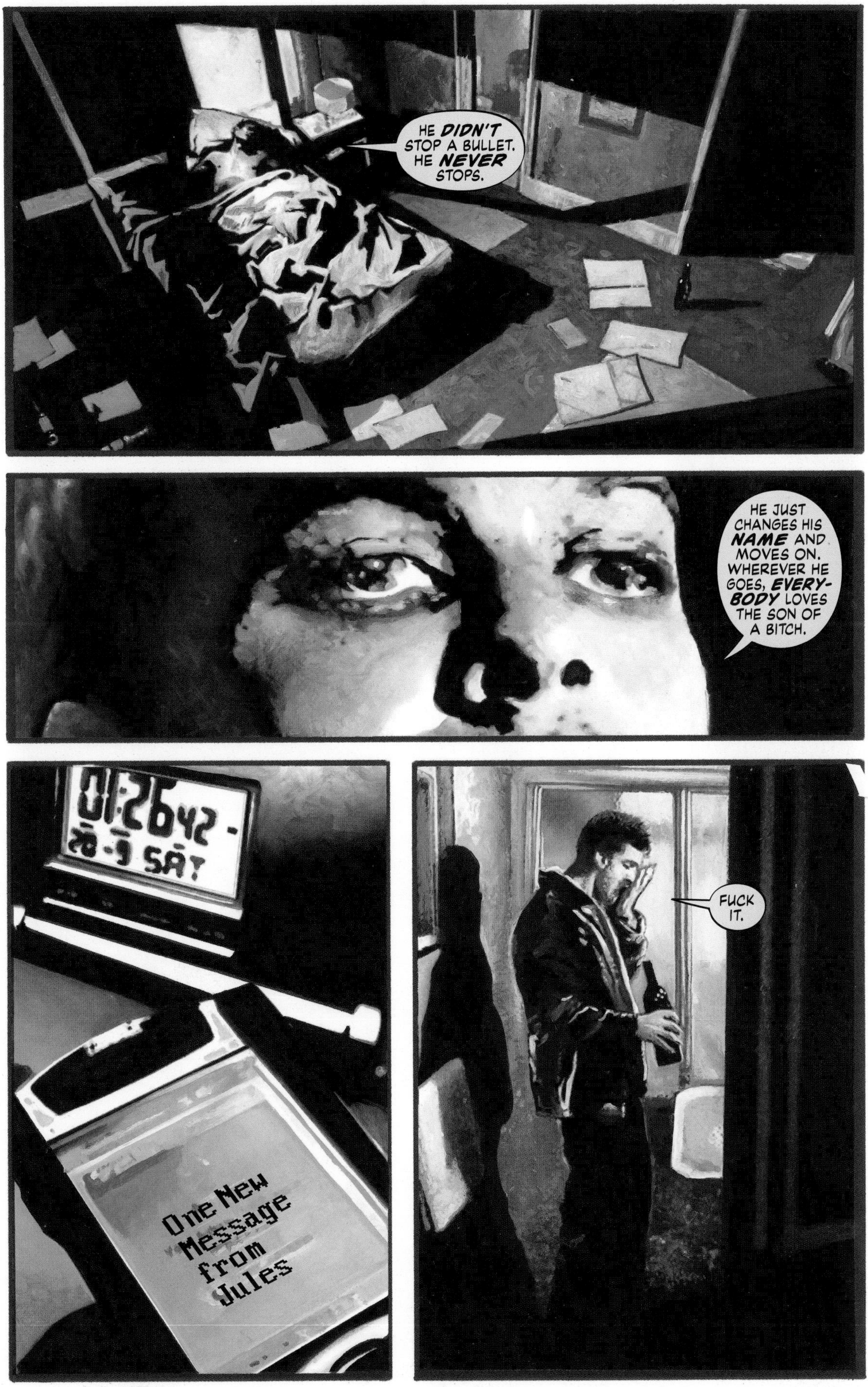
HE *DIDN'T* STOP A BULLET. HE *NEVER* STOPS.
HE JUST CHANGES HIS *NAME* AND MOVES ON. WHEREVER HE GOES, *EVERY-BODY* LOVES THE SON OF A BITCH.
01:26 42 -
20-9 SAT
One New Message from Jules
FUCK IT.

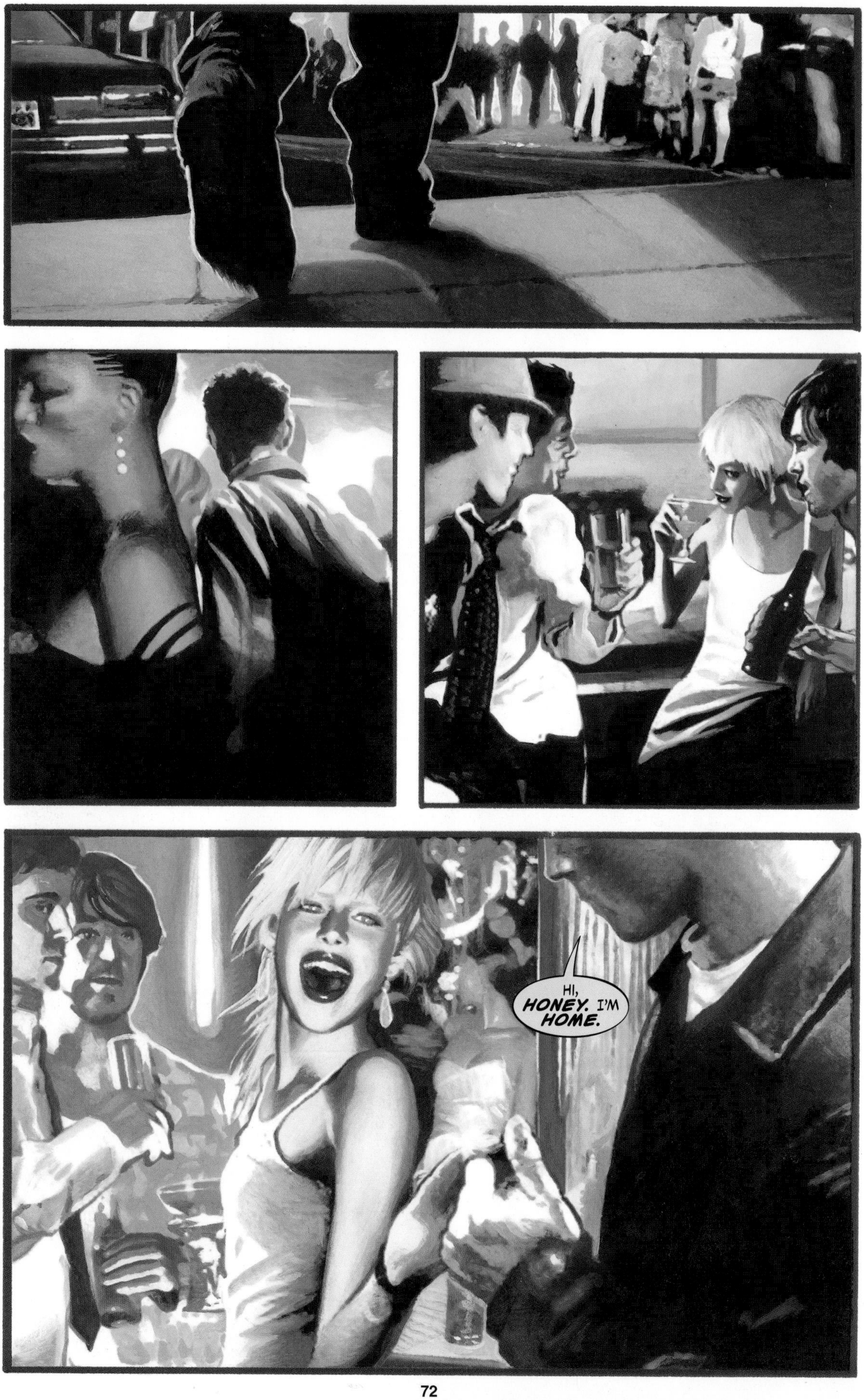
HI, HONEY. I'M HOME.

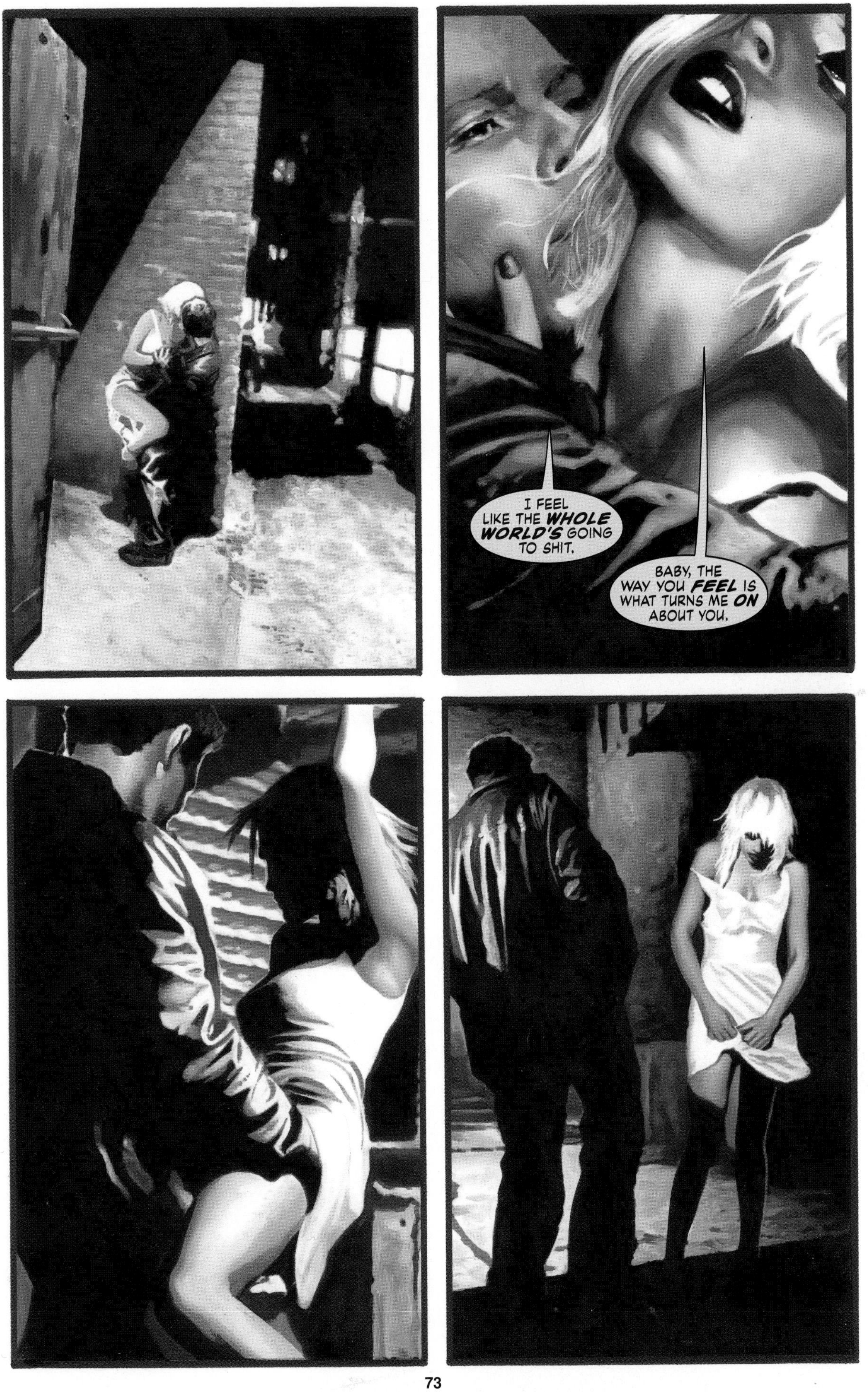
I FEEL LIKE THE WHOLE WORLD'S GOING TO SHIT.
BABY, THE WAY YOU FEEL IS WHAT TURNS ME ON ABOUT YOU.

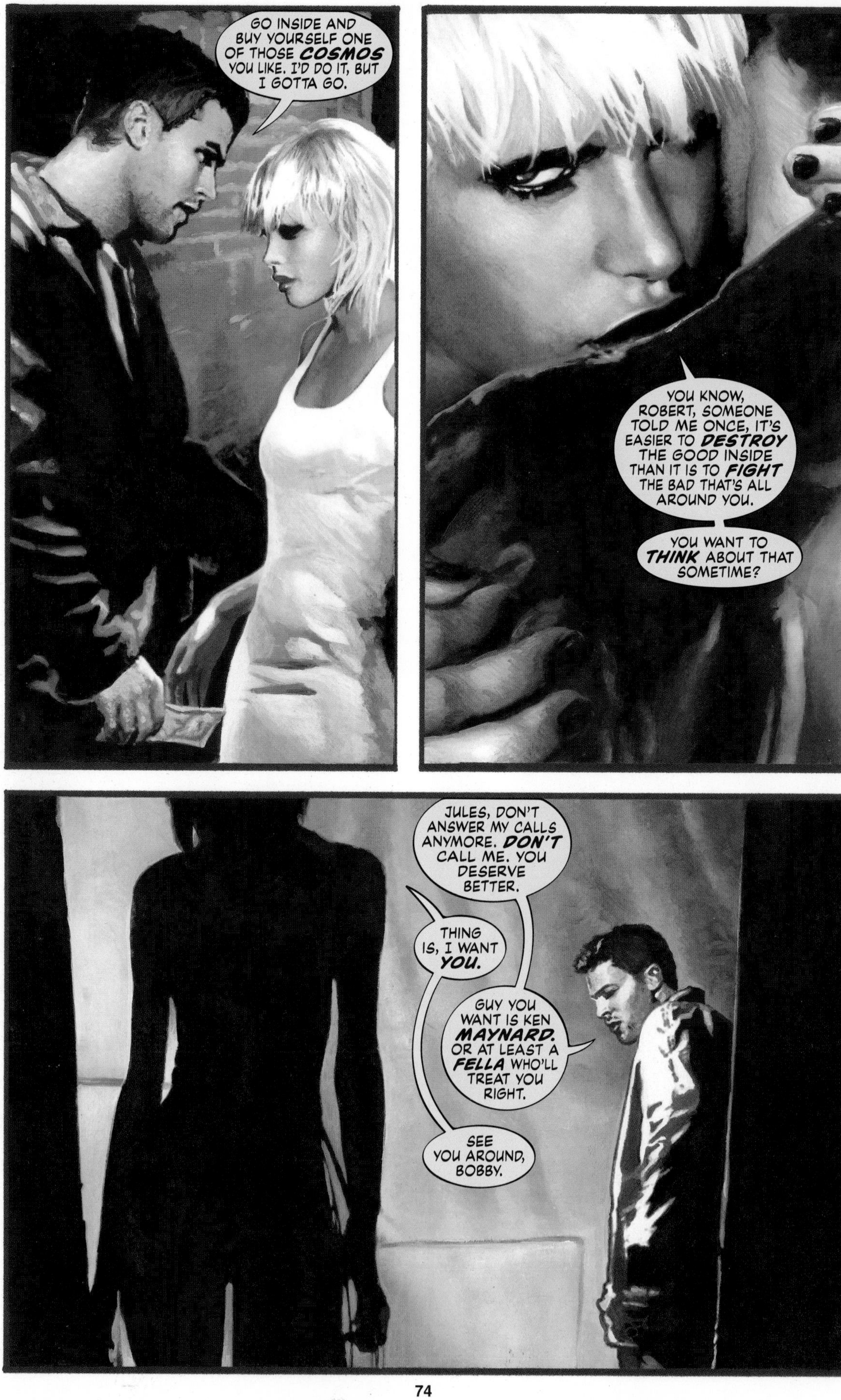
GO INSIDE AND BUY YOURSELF ONE OF THOSE COSMOS YOU LIKE. I'D DO IT, BUT I GOTTA GO.
YOU KNOW, ROBERT, SOMEONE TOLD ME ONCE, IT'S EASIER TO DESTROY THE GOOD INSIDE THAN IT IS TO FIGHT THE BAD THAT'S ALL AROUND YOU.
YOU WANT TO THINK ABOUT THAT SOMETIME?
JULES, DON'T ANSWER MY CALLS ANYMORE. DON'T CALL ME. YOU DESERVE BETTER.
THING IS, I WANT YOU.
GUY YOU WANT IS KEN MAYNARD. OR AT LEAST A FELLA WHO'LL TREAT YOU RIGHT.
SEE YOU AROUND, BOBBY.

RING
RING

BLOARRCH

YOU SITTING *DOWN?*

I AM NOW.

SON OF A *BITCH* HIT AGAIN. SHE'S *FOURTEEN.* WHITE DRESS-- I THINK YOU MIGHT BE RIGHT.

EVEN THOUGH WE HAD HIM UNDER SURVEILLANCE, THE GARDNER, LUKE, HE'S *DISAP-PEARED.*

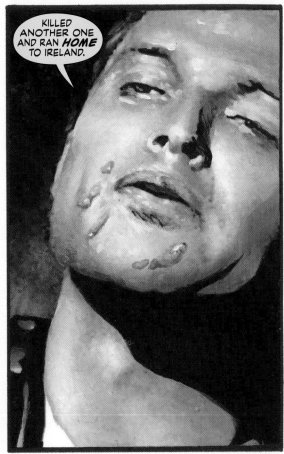

KILLED ANOTHER ONE AND RAN *HOME* TO IRELAND.

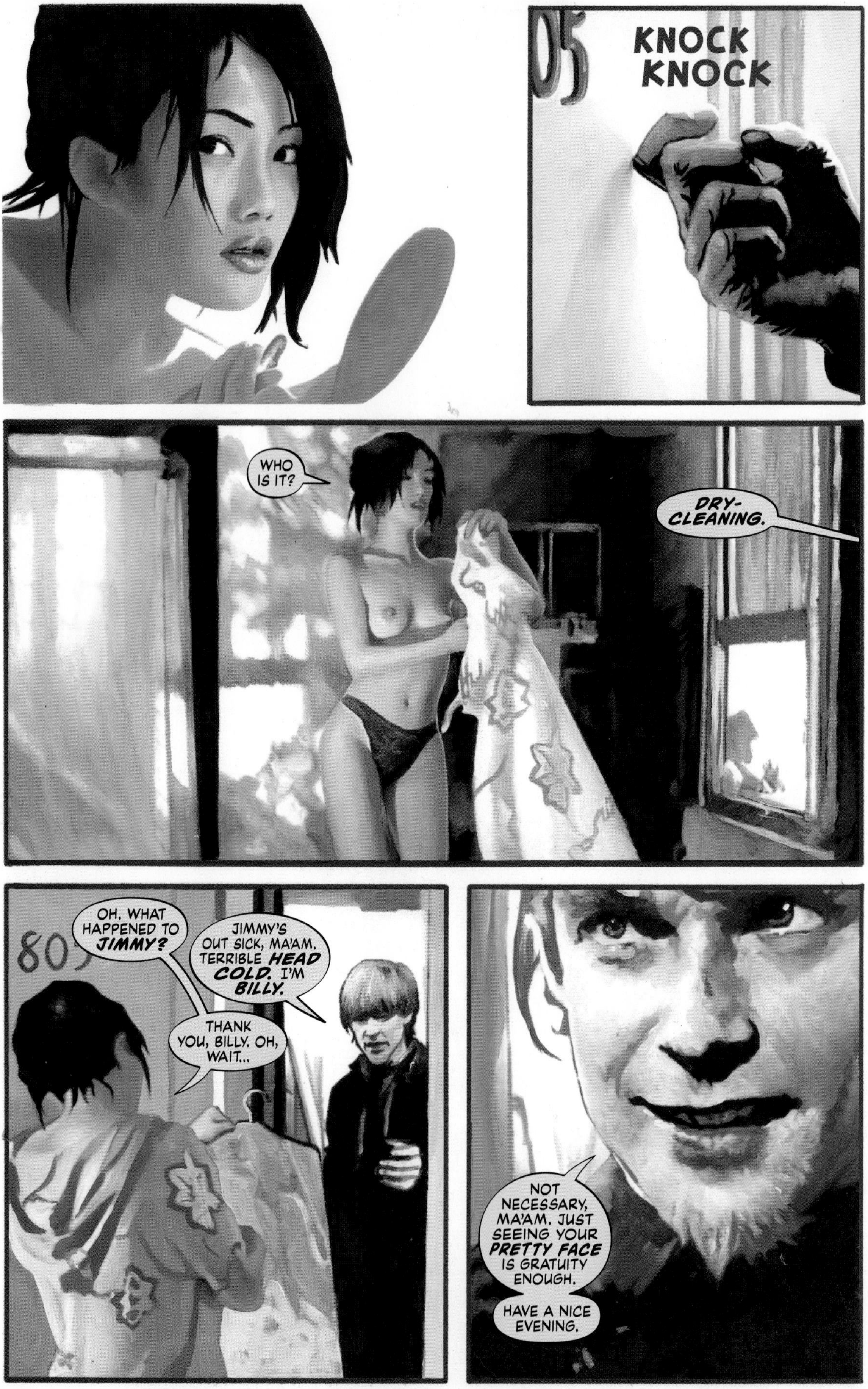
KNOCK KNOCK
WHO IS IT?
DRY-CLEANING.
OH. WHAT HAPPENED TO JIMMY?
JIMMY'S OUT SICK, MA'AM. TERRIBLE HEAD COLD. I'M BILLY.
THANK YOU, BILLY. OH, WAIT...
NOT NECESSARY, MA'AM. JUST SEEING YOUR PRETTY FACE IS GRATUITY ENOUGH.
HAVE A NICE EVENING.

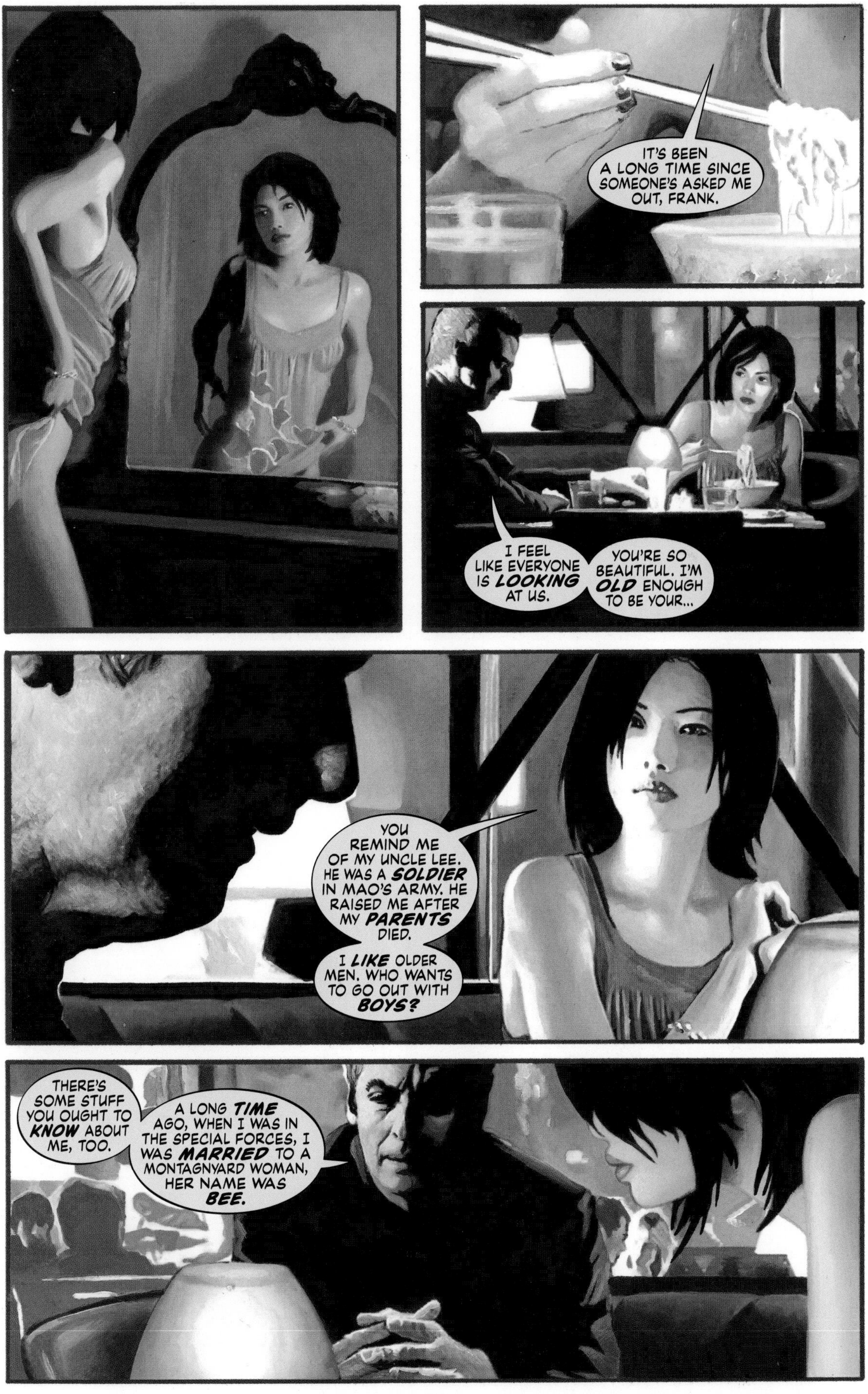
IT'S BEEN A LONG TIME SINCE SOMEONE'S ASKED ME OUT, FRANK.
I FEEL LIKE EVERYONE IS LOOKING AT US.
YOU'RE SO BEAUTIFUL. I'M OLD ENOUGH TO BE YOUR...
YOU REMIND ME OF MY UNCLE LEE. HE WAS A SOLDIER IN MAO'S ARMY. HE RAISED ME AFTER MY PARENTS DIED.
I LIKE OLDER MEN. WHO WANTS TO GO OUT WITH BOYS?
THERE'S SOME STUFF YOU OUGHT TO KNOW ABOUT ME, TOO.
A LONG TIME AGO, WHEN I WAS IN THE SPECIAL FORCES, I WAS MARRIED TO A MONTAGNYARD WOMAN, HER NAME WAS BEE.

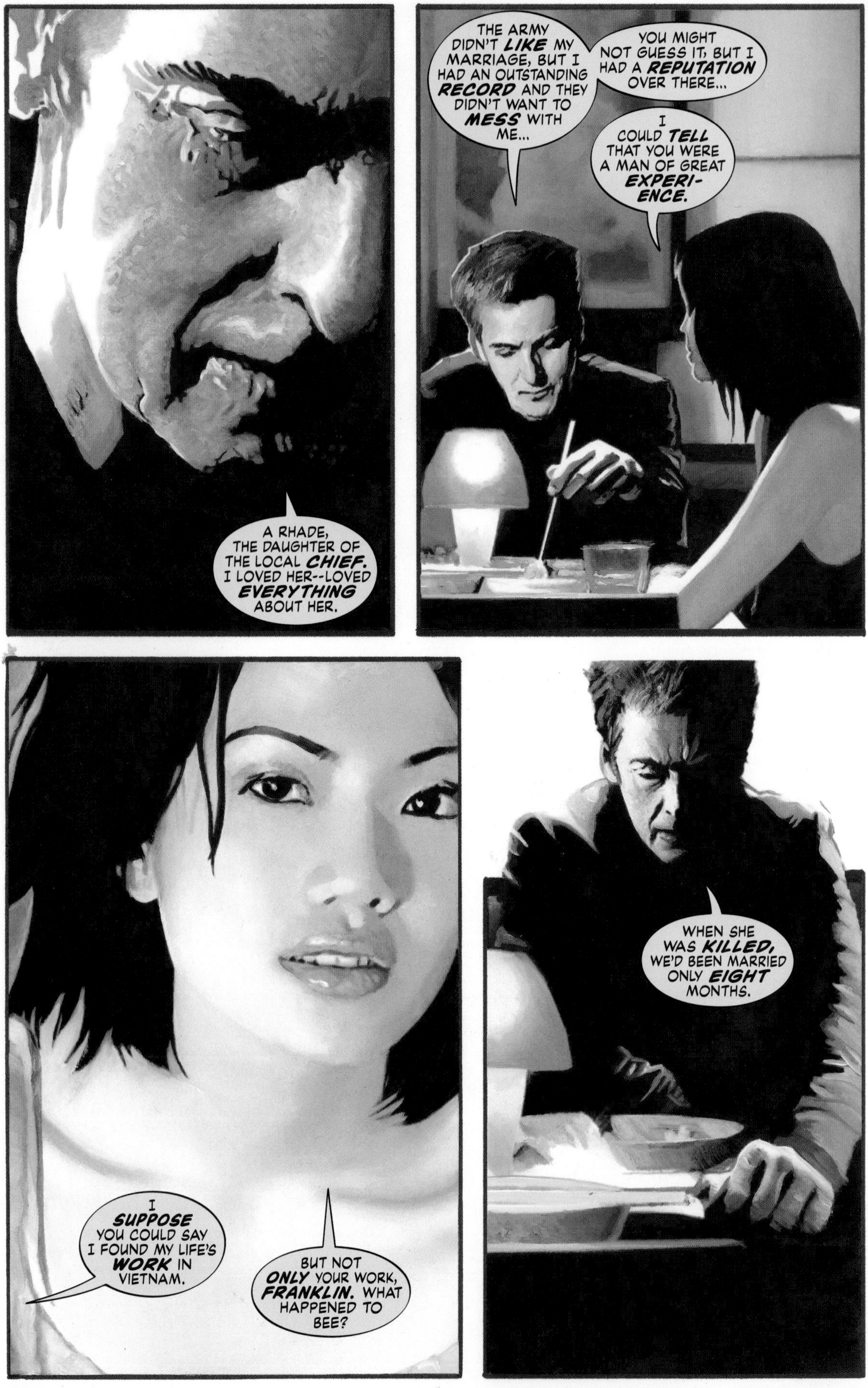
A RHADE, THE DAUGHTER OF THE LOCAL CHIEF. I LOVED HER--LOVED EVERYTHING ABOUT HER.
THE ARMY DIDN'T LIKE MY MARRIAGE, BUT I HAD AN OUTSTANDING RECORD AND THEY DIDN'T WANT TO MESS WITH ME...
YOU MIGHT NOT GUESS IT, BUT I HAD A REPUTATION OVER THERE...
I COULD TELL THAT YOU WERE A MAN OF GREAT EXPERI- ENCE.
I SUPPOSE YOU COULD SAY I FOUND MY LIFE'S WORK IN VIETNAM.
BUT NOT ONLY YOUR WORK, FRANKLIN. WHAT HAPPENED TO BEE?
WHEN SHE WAS KILLED, WE'D BEEN MARRIED ONLY EIGHT MONTHS.

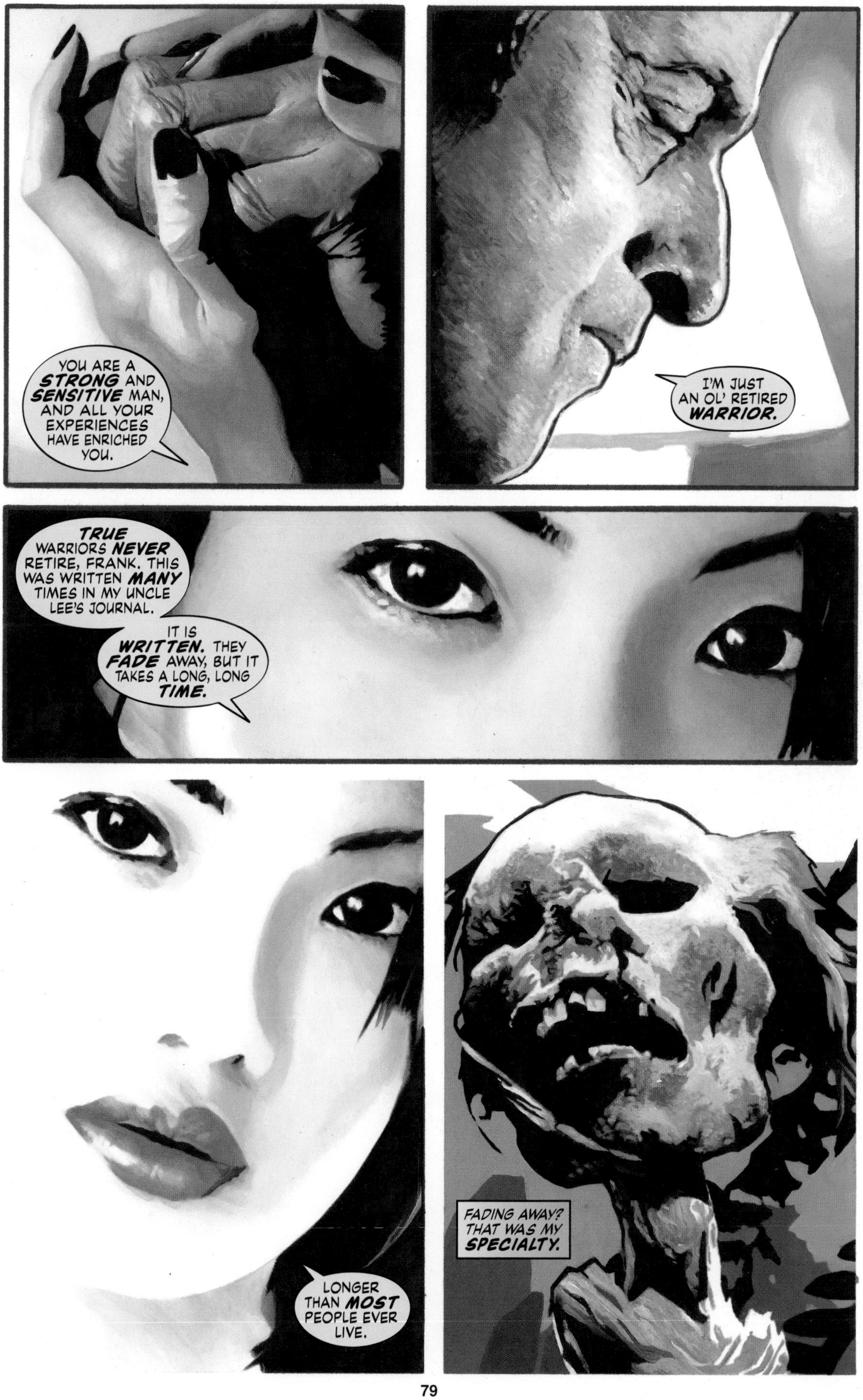
YOU ARE A STRONG AND SENSITIVE MAN, AND ALL YOUR EXPERIENCES HAVE ENRICHED YOU.
I'M JUST AN OL' RETIRED WARRIOR.
TRUE WARRIORS NEVER RETIRE, FRANK. THIS WAS WRITTEN MANY TIMES IN MY UNCLE LEE'S JOURNAL.
IT IS WRITTEN. THEY FADE AWAY, BUT IT TAKES A LONG, LONG TIME.
LONGER THAN MOST PEOPLE EVER LIVE.
FADING AWAY? THAT WAS MY SPECIALTY.

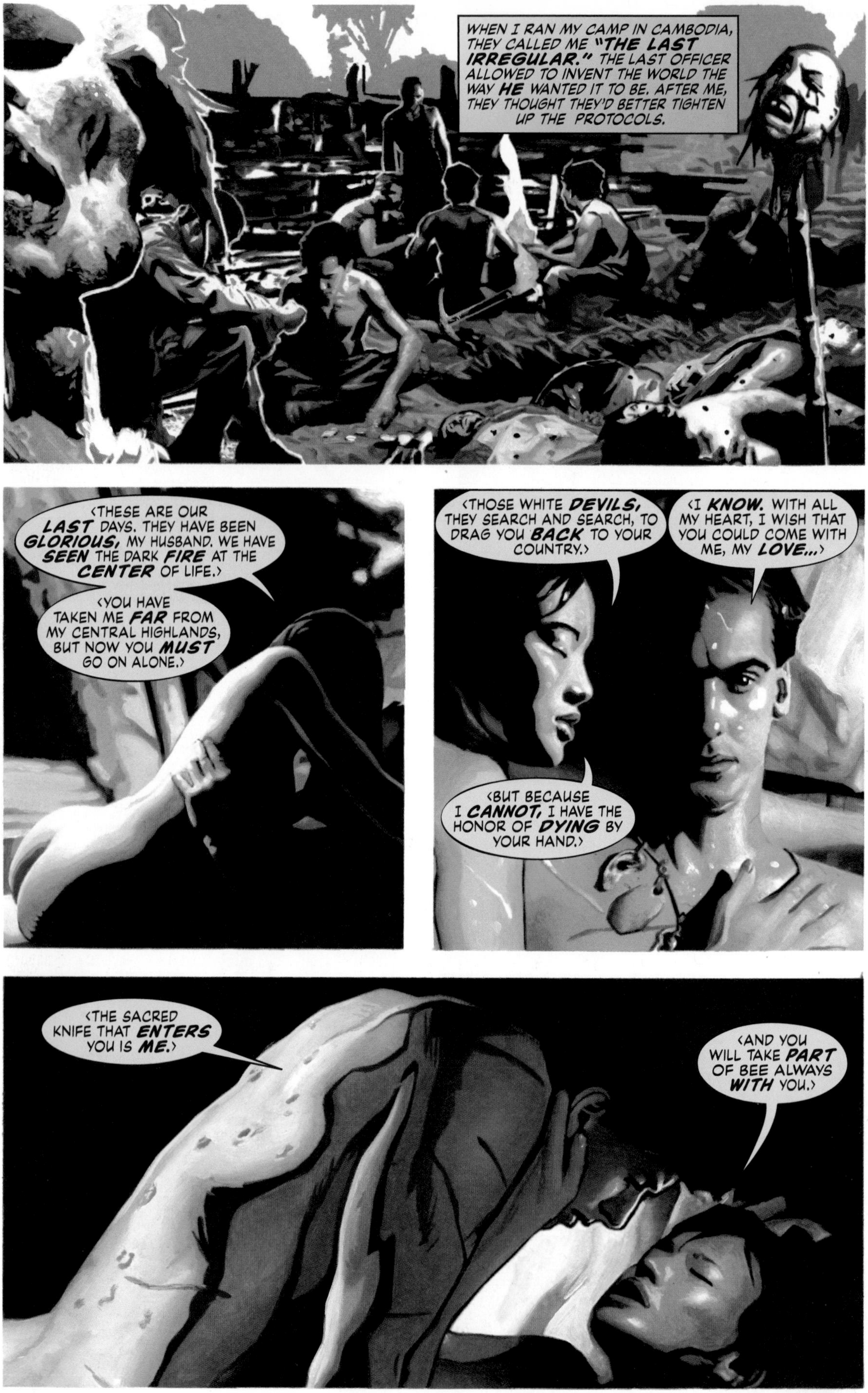
WHEN I RAN MY CAMP IN CAMBODIA, THEY CALLED ME "THE LAST IRREGULAR." THE LAST OFFICER ALLOWED TO INVENT THE WORLD THE WAY HE WANTED IT TO BE. AFTER ME, THEY THOUGHT THEY'D BETTER TIGHTEN UP THE PROTOCOLS.
<THESE ARE OUR LAST DAYS. THEY HAVE BEEN GLORIOUS, MY HUSBAND. WE HAVE SEEN THE DARK FIRE AT THE CENTER OF LIFE.>
<YOU HAVE TAKEN ME FAR FROM MY CENTRAL HIGHLANDS, BUT NOW YOU MUST GO ON ALONE.>
<THOSE WHITE DEVILS, THEY SEARCH AND SEARCH, TO DRAG YOU BACK TO YOUR COUNTRY.>
<I KNOW. WITH ALL MY HEART, I WISH THAT YOU COULD COME WITH ME, MY LOVE...>
<BUT BECAUSE I CANNOT, I HAVE THE HONOR OF DYING BY YOUR HAND.>
<THE SACRED KNIFE THAT ENTERS YOU IS ME.>
<AND YOU WILL TAKE PART OF BEE ALWAYS WITH YOU.>

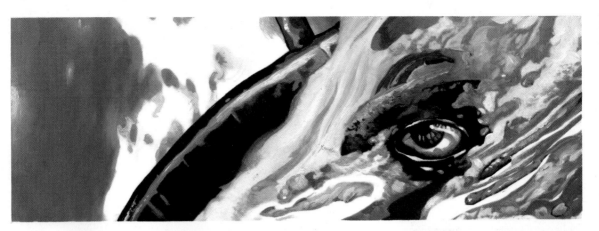

ALWAYS.

THE SACRED PATTERN HAD BEEN SET.

"UNCLE LEE KNEW MUCH *VIOLENCE* IN HIS LIFE..."

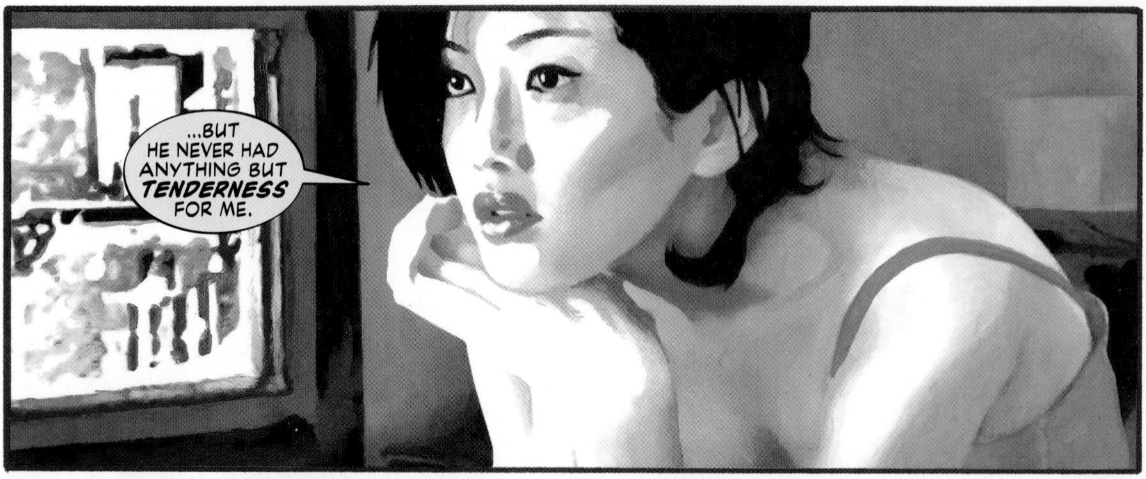
...BUT HE NEVER HAD ANYTHING BUT TENDERNESS FOR ME.

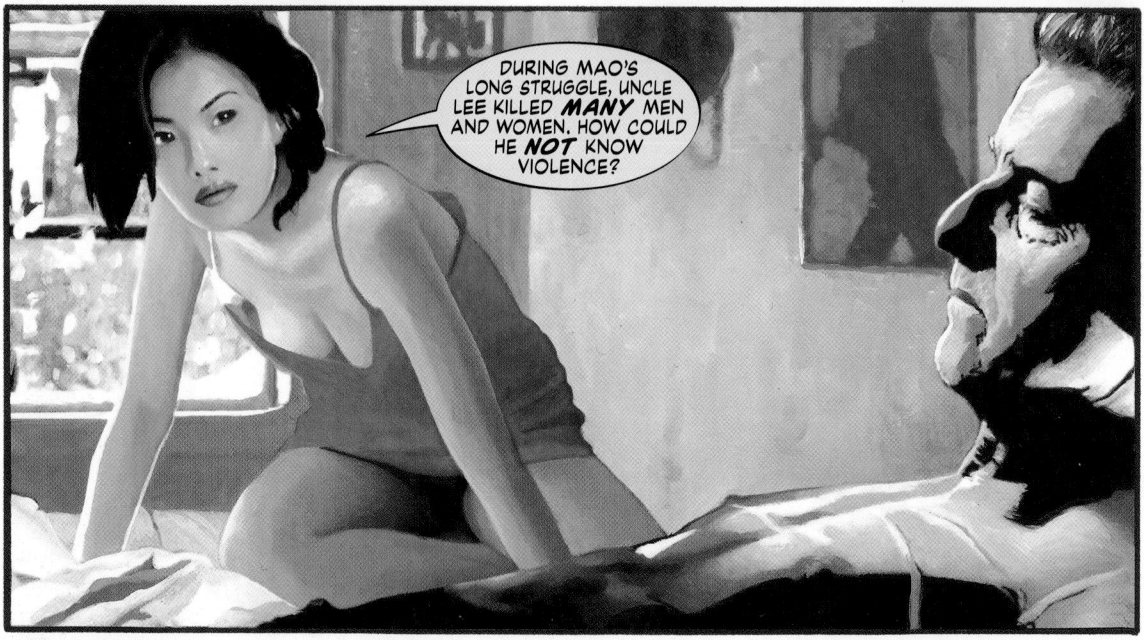
DURING MAO'S LONG STRUGGLE, UNCLE LEE KILLED MANY MEN AND WOMEN. HOW COULD HE NOT KNOW VIOLENCE?

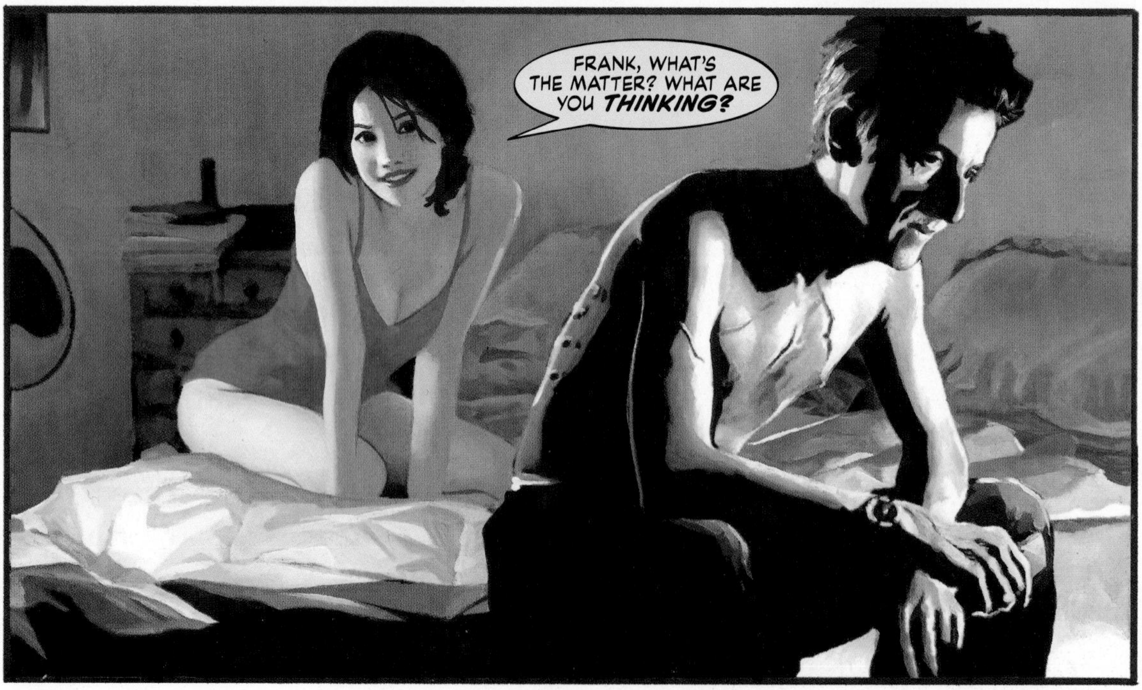
FRANK, WHAT'S THE MATTER? WHAT ARE YOU THINKING?

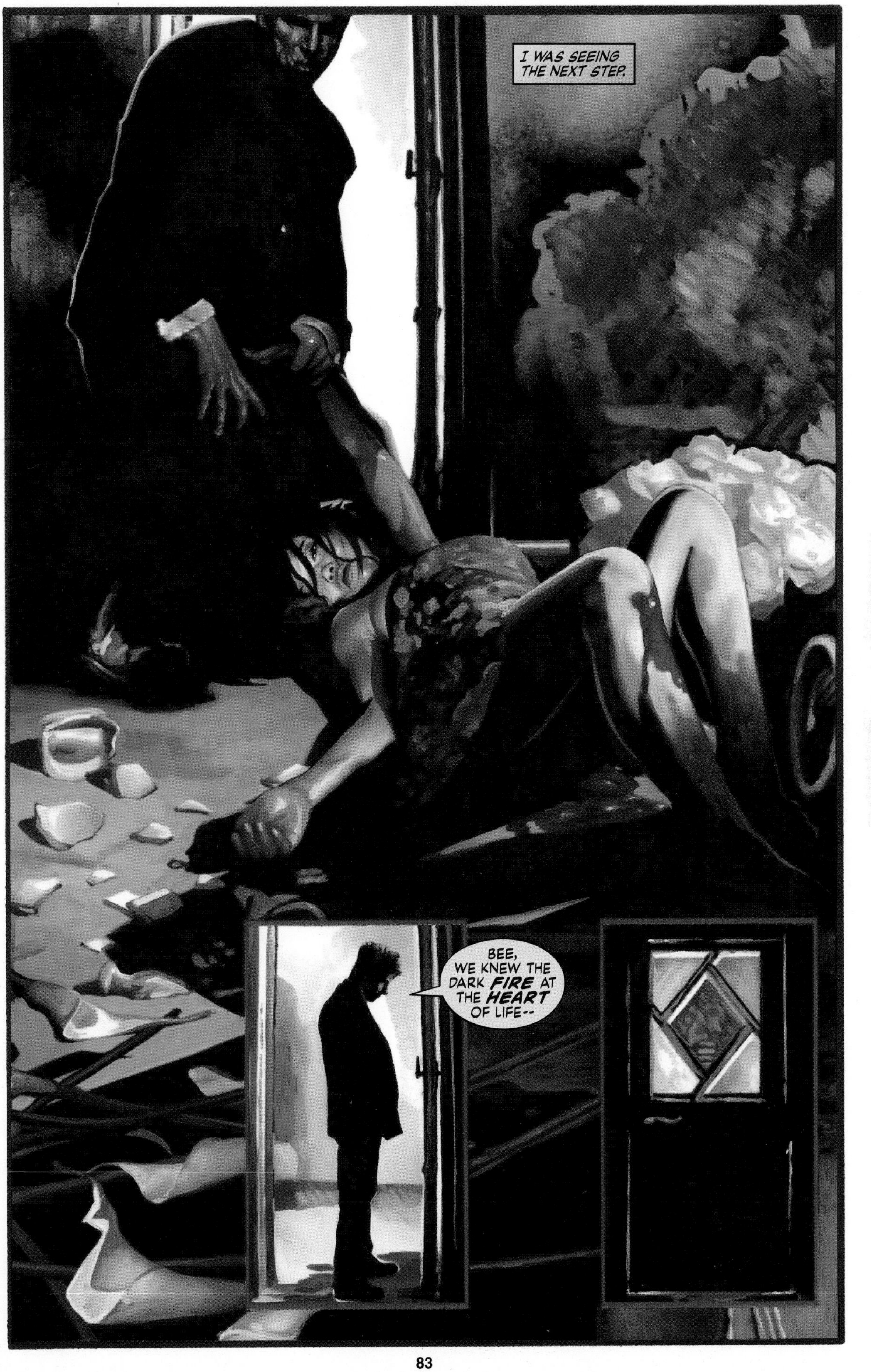
I WAS SEEING THE NEXT STEP.
BEE, WE KNEW THE DARK FIRE AT THE HEART OF LIFE--

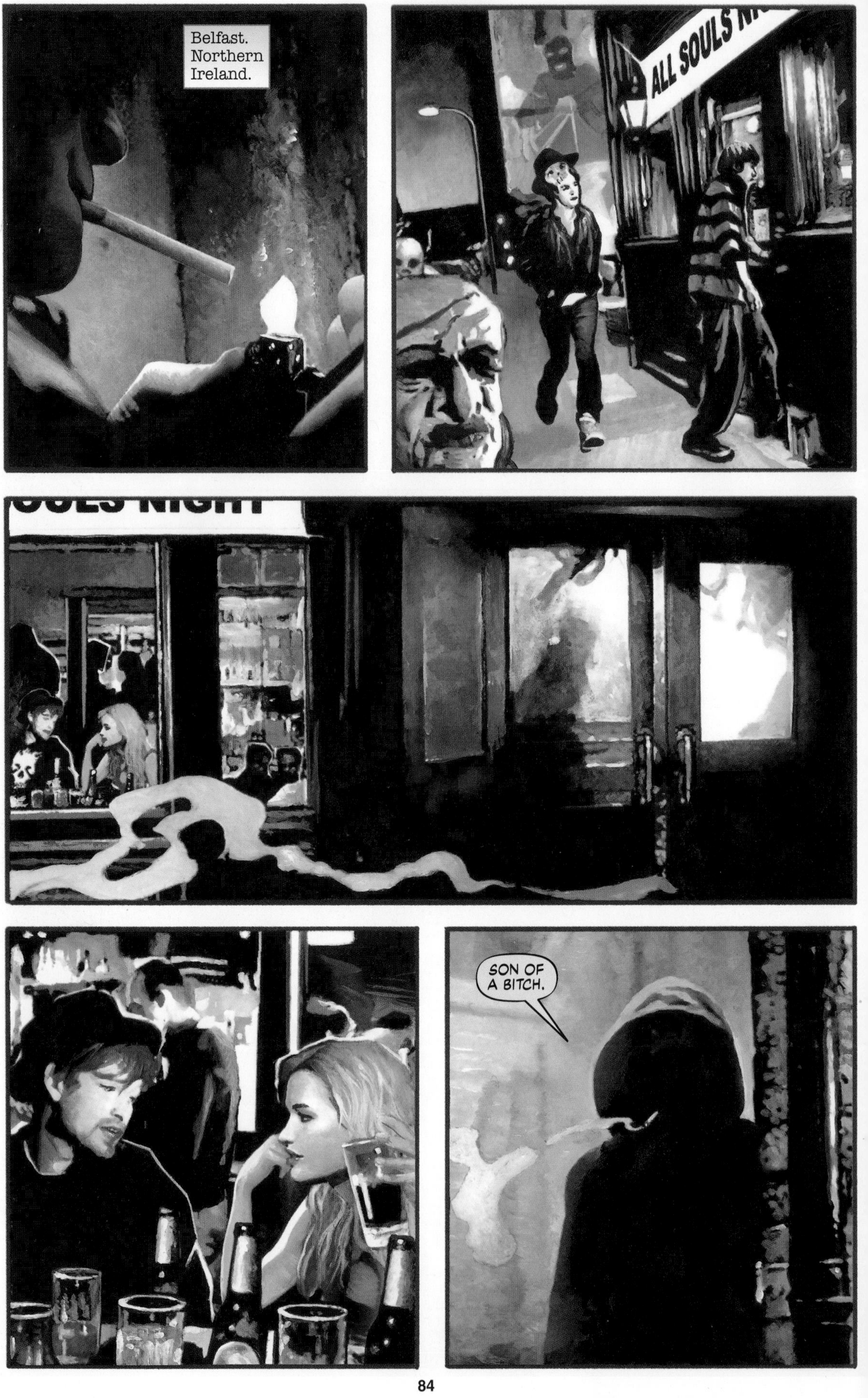
Belfast. Northern Ireland.
ALL SOULS
SON OF A BITCH.

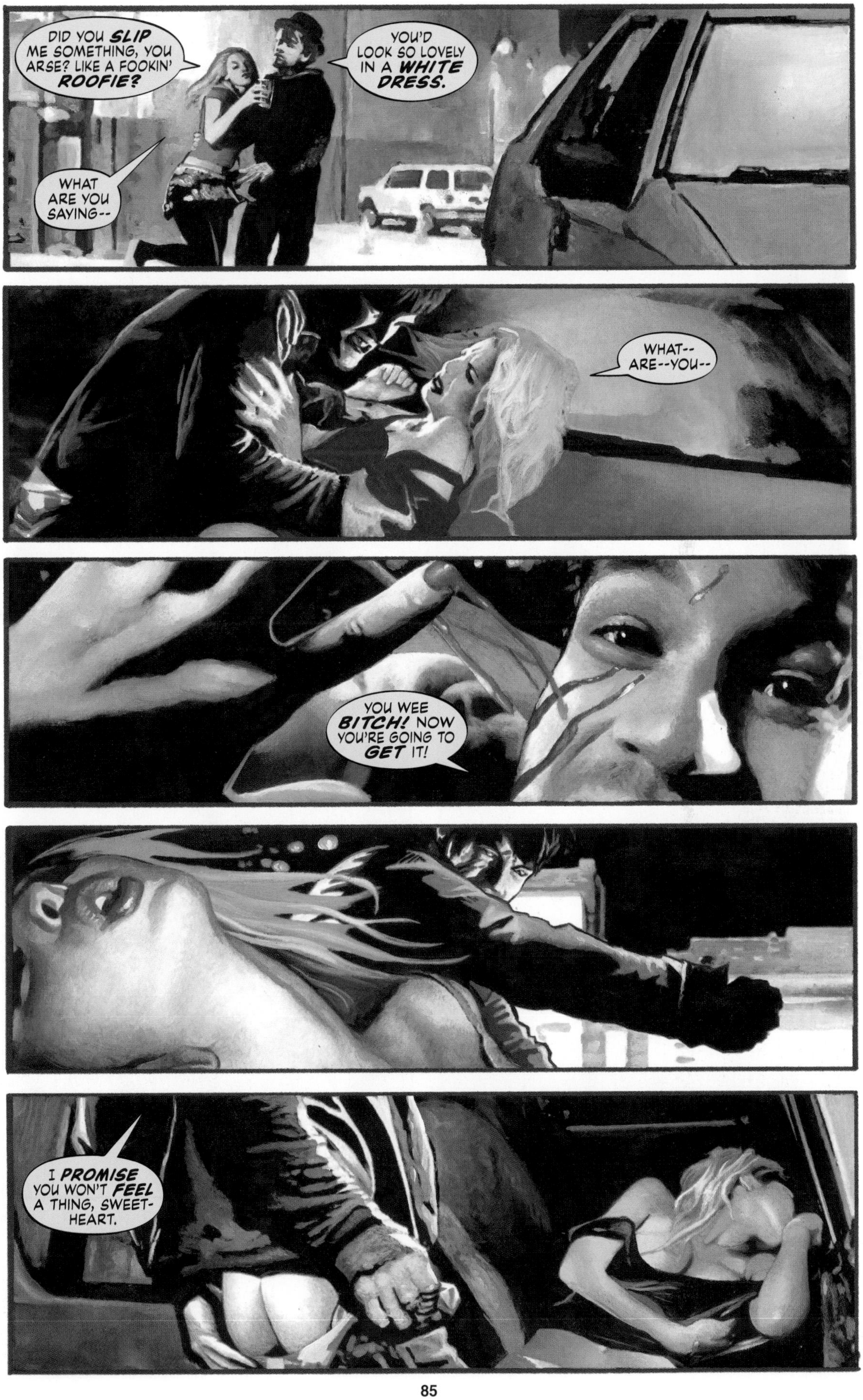
DID YOU SLIP ME SOMETHING, YOU ARSE? LIKE A FOOKIN' ROOFIE?
WHAT ARE YOU SAYING--
YOU'D LOOK SO LOVELY IN A WHITE DRESS.
WHAT--ARE--YOU--
YOU WEE BITCH! NOW YOU'RE GOING TO GET IT!
I PROMISE YOU WON'T FEEL A THING, SWEET-HEART.

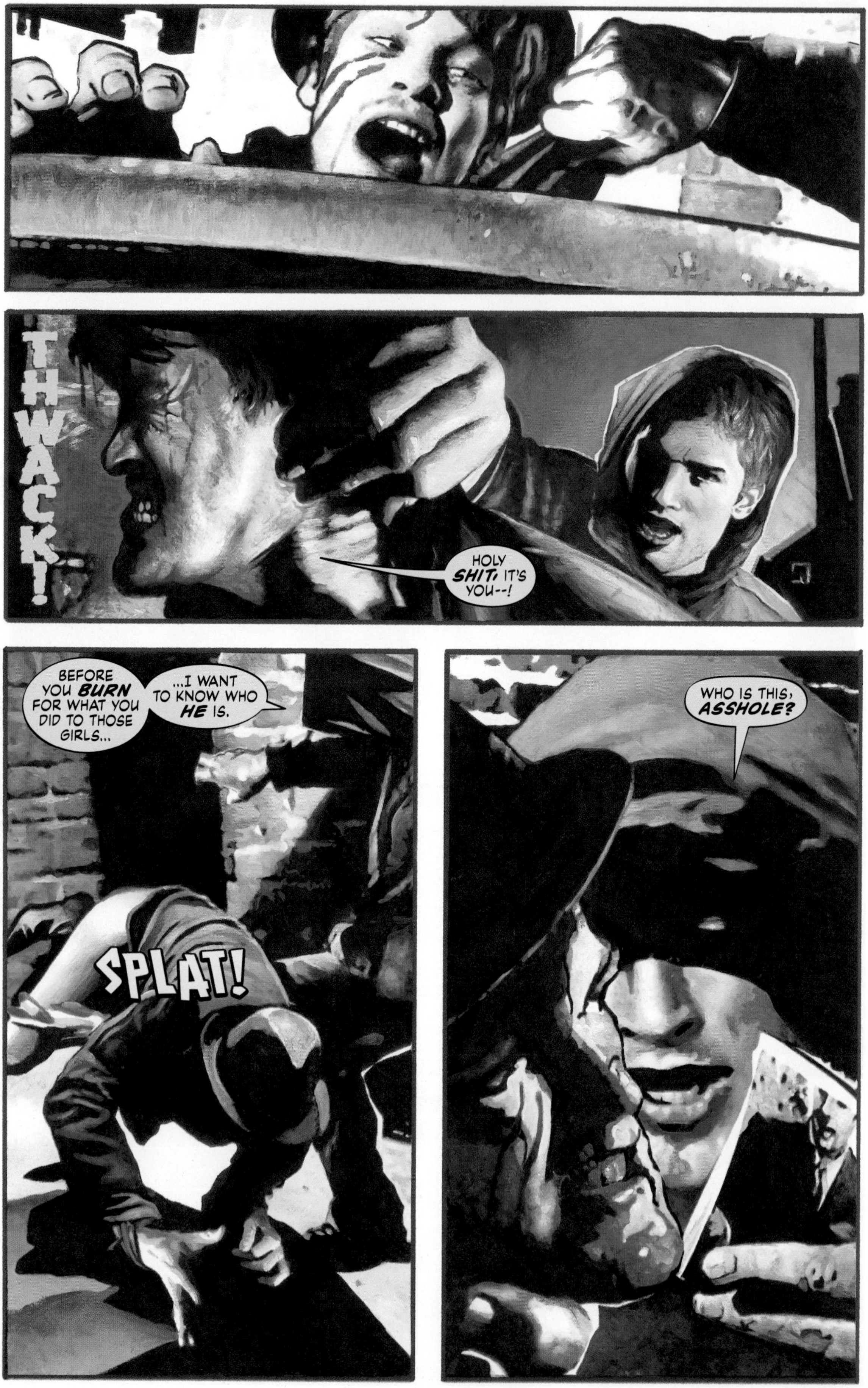
THWACK!
HOLY SHIT, IT'S YOU--!
BEFORE YOU BURN FOR WHAT YOU DID TO THOSE GIRLS...
...I WANT TO KNOW WHO HE IS.
SPLAT!
WHO IS THIS, ASSHOLE?

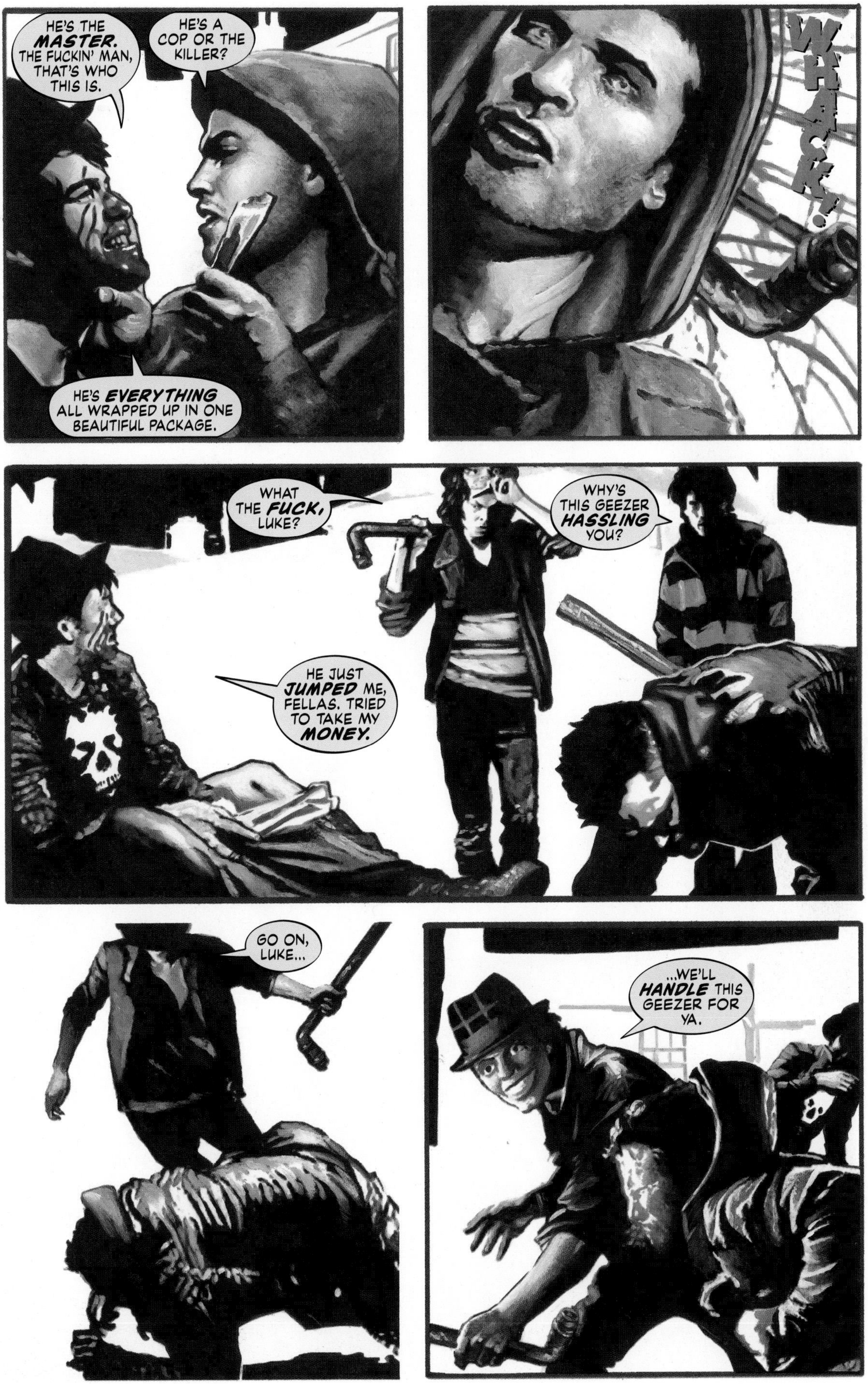
HE'S THE **MASTER.** THE FUCKIN' MAN, THAT'S WHO THIS IS.
HE'S A COP OR THE KILLER?
HE'S **EVERYTHING** ALL WRAPPED UP IN ONE BEAUTIFUL PACKAGE.
WHACK!
WHAT THE **FUCK,** LUKE?
WHY'S THIS GEEZER **HASSLING** YOU?
HE JUST **JUMPED** ME, FELLAS. TRIED TO TAKE MY **MONEY.**
GO ON, LUKE...
...WE'LL **HANDLE** THIS GEEZER FOR YA.

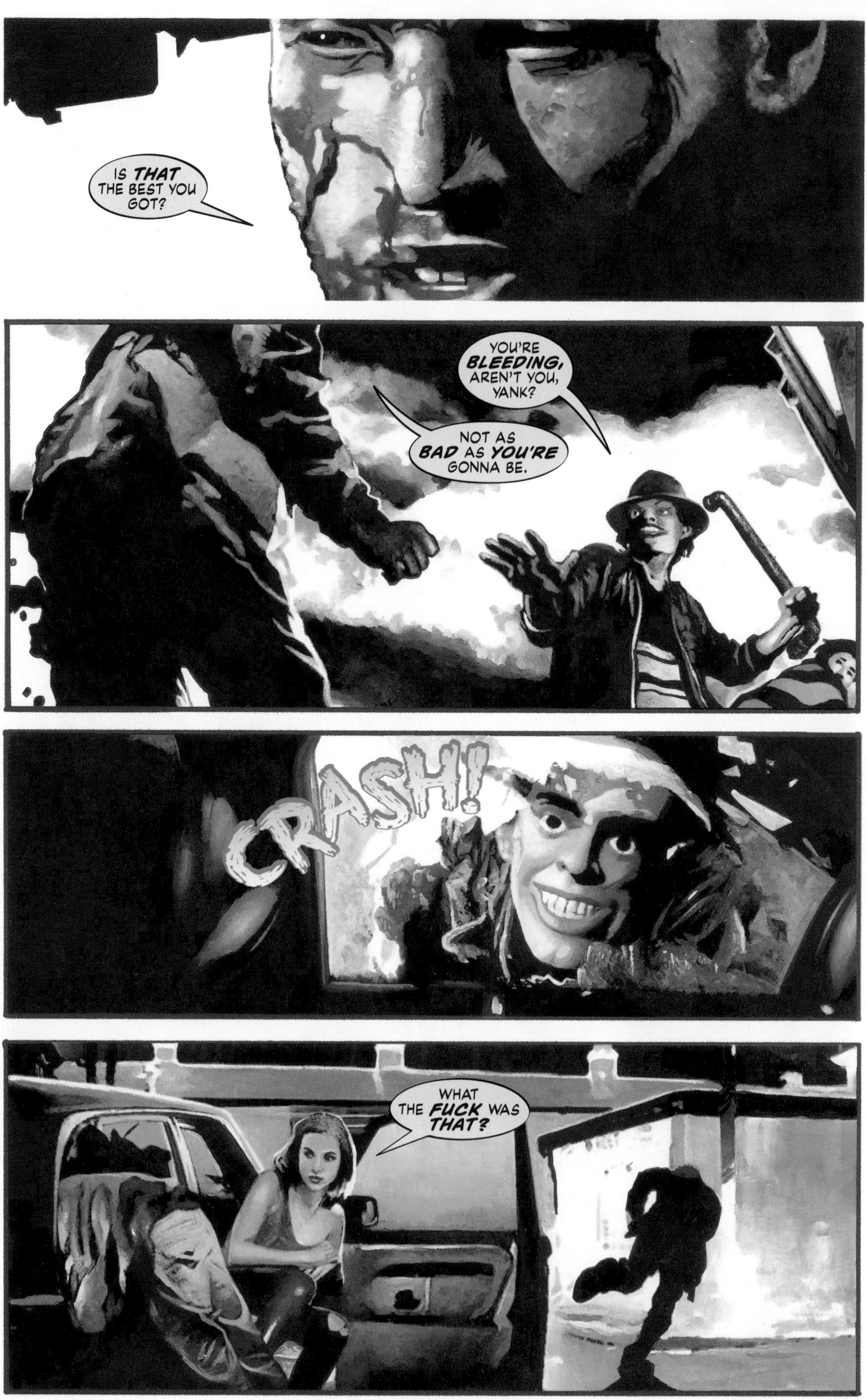
IS THAT THE BEST YOU GOT?
YOU'RE BLEEDING, AREN'T YOU, YANK?
NOT AS BAD AS YOU'RE GONNA BE.
CRASH!
WHAT THE FUCK WAS THAT?

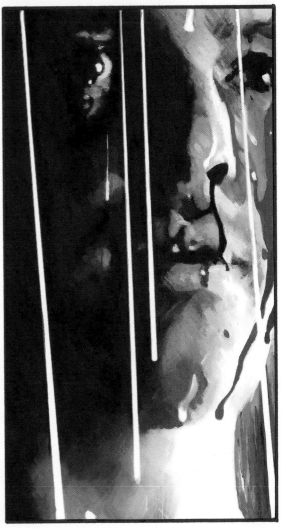

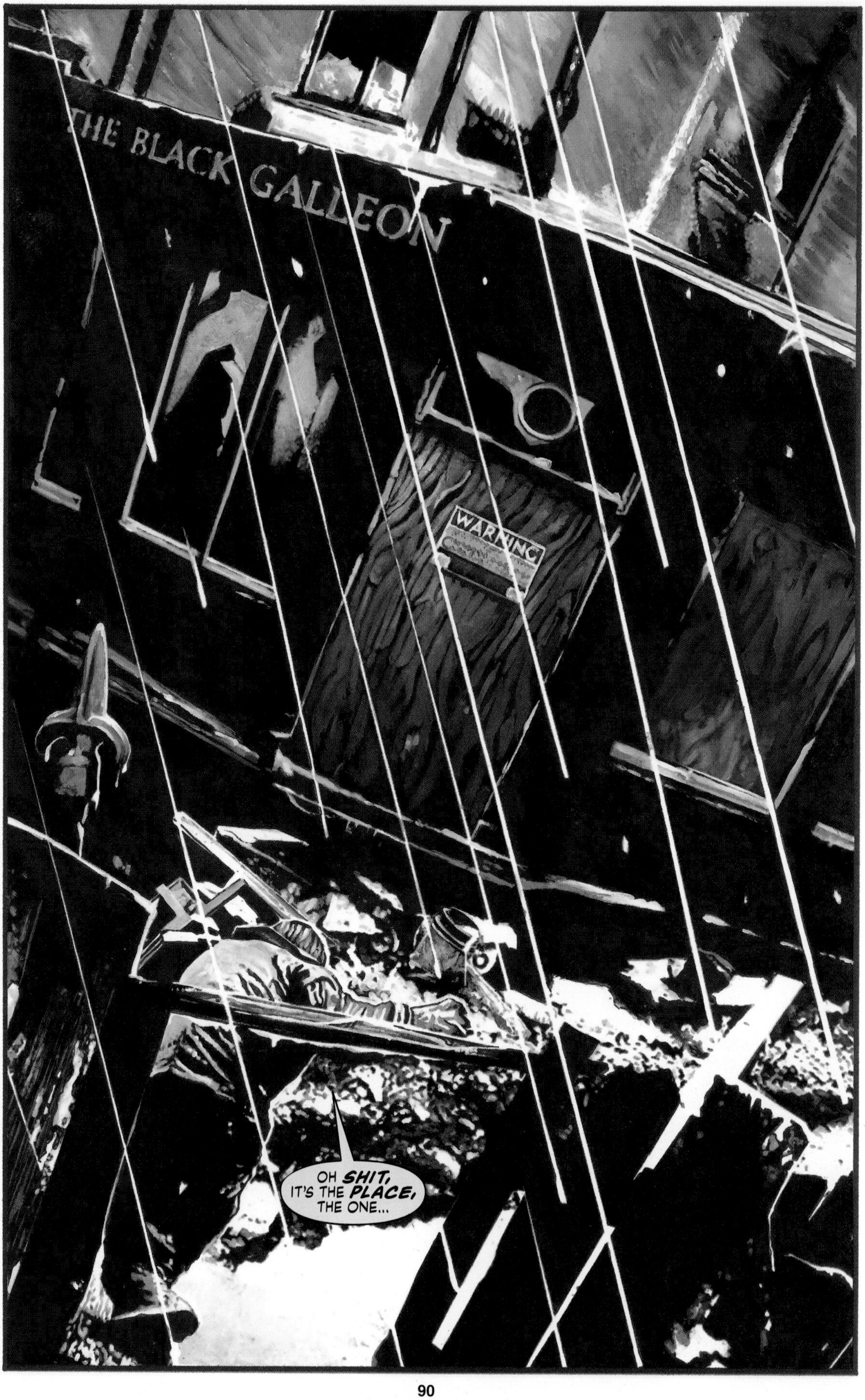
THE BLACK GALLEON
WARNING
OH SHIT, IT'S THE PLACE, THE ONE...

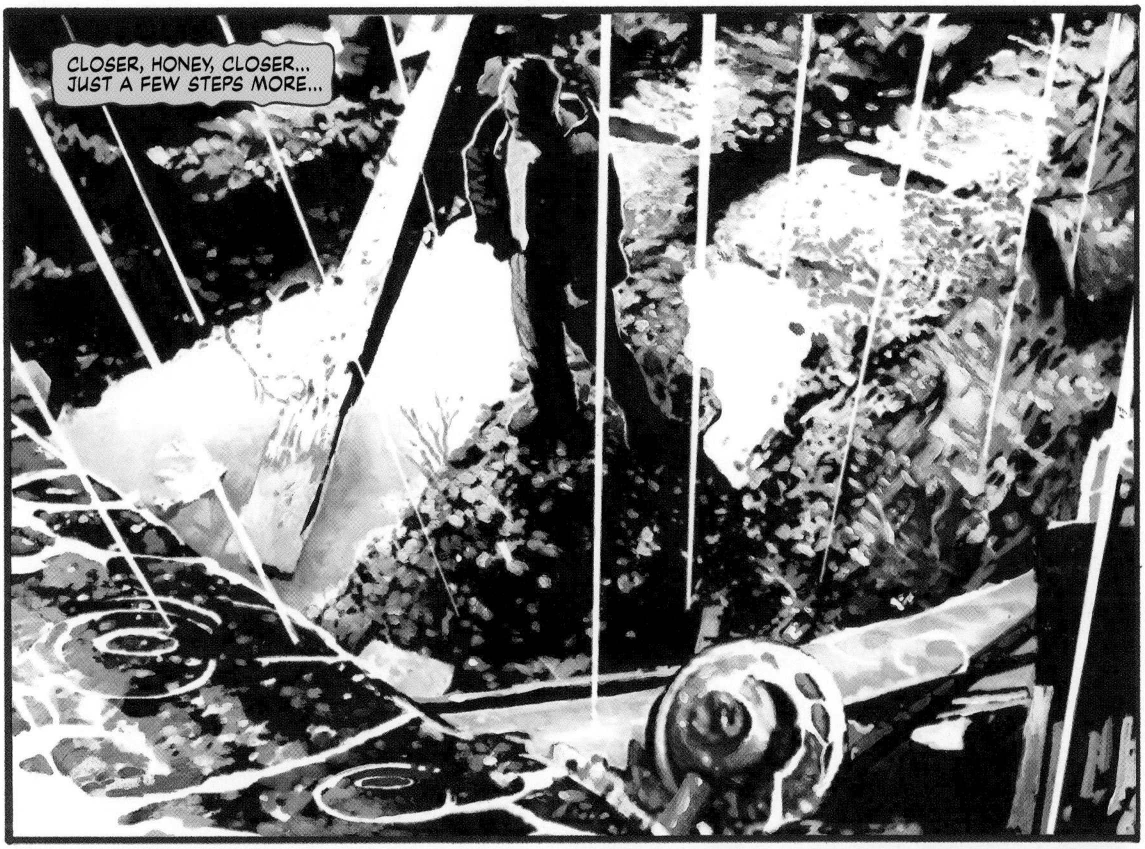
CLOSER, HONEY, CLOSER... JUST A FEW STEPS MORE...

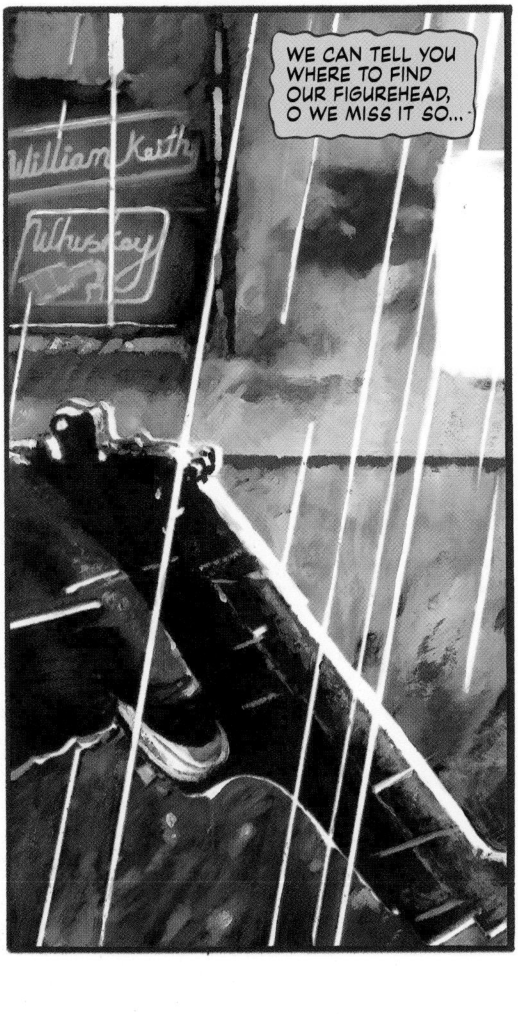
WE CAN TELL YOU WHERE TO FIND OUR FIGUREHEAD, O WE MISS IT SO...

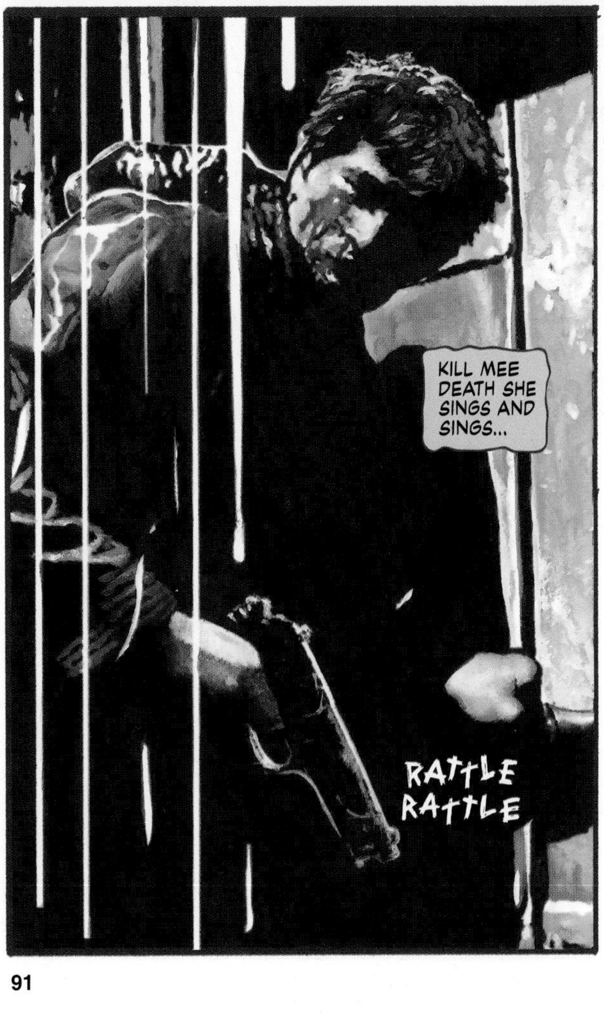
KILL MEE DEATH SHE SINGS AND SINGS...
RATTLE RATTLE

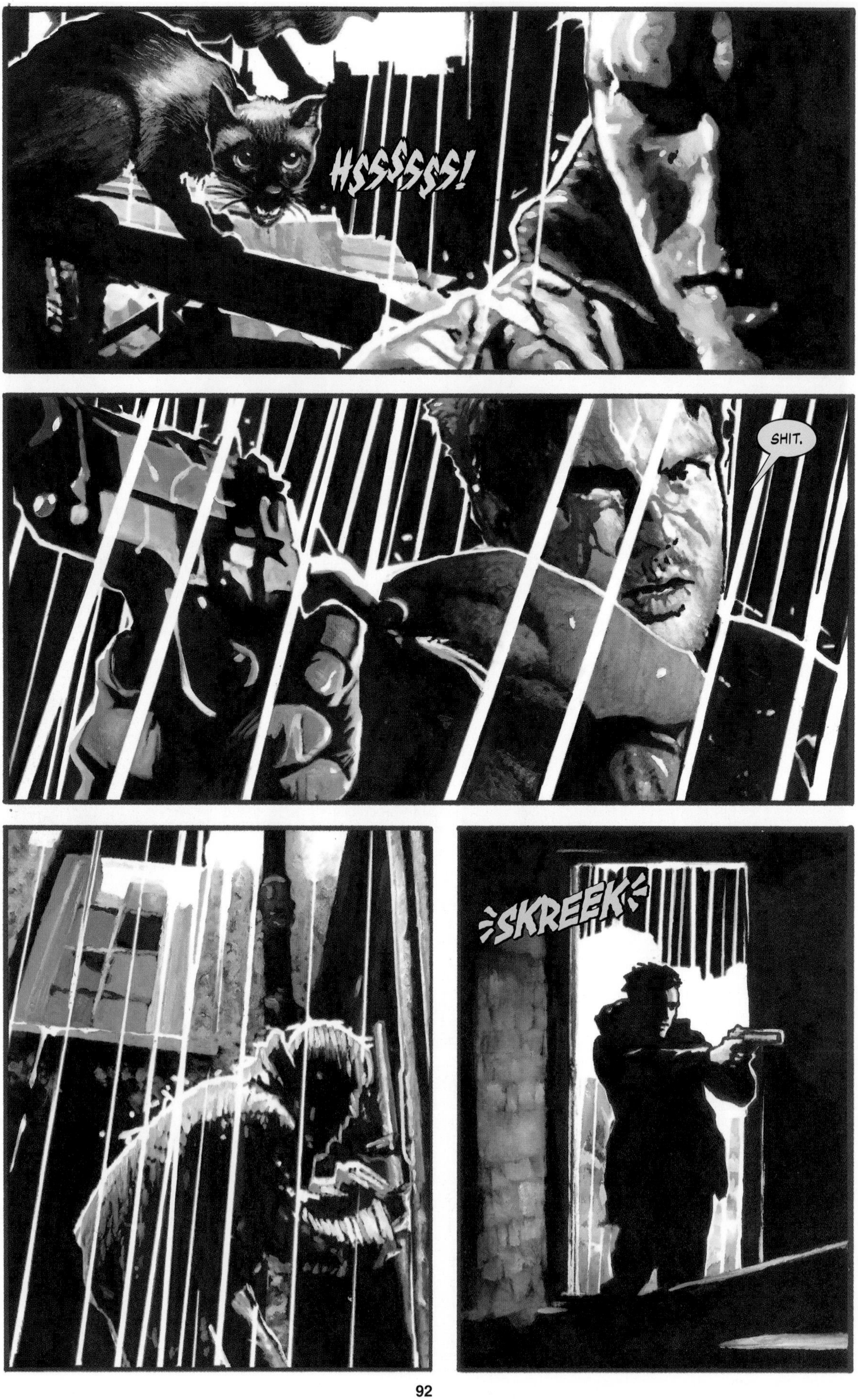
HSSSSSS!
SHIT.
SKREEK

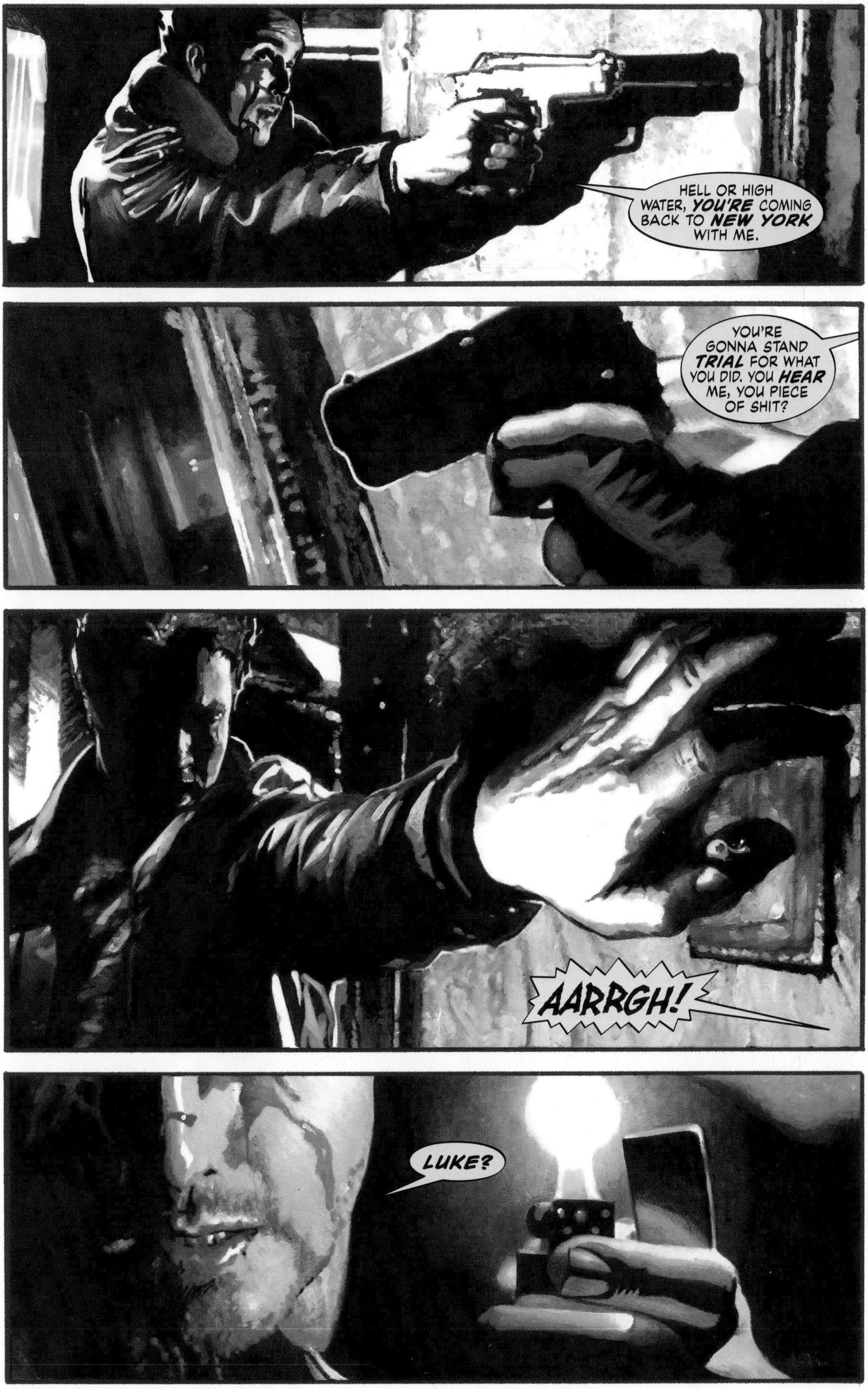
HELL OR HIGH WATER, YOU'RE COMING BACK TO NEW YORK WITH ME.
YOU'RE GONNA STAND TRIAL FOR WHAT YOU DID. YOU HEAR ME, YOU PIECE OF SHIT?
AARRGH!
LUKE?

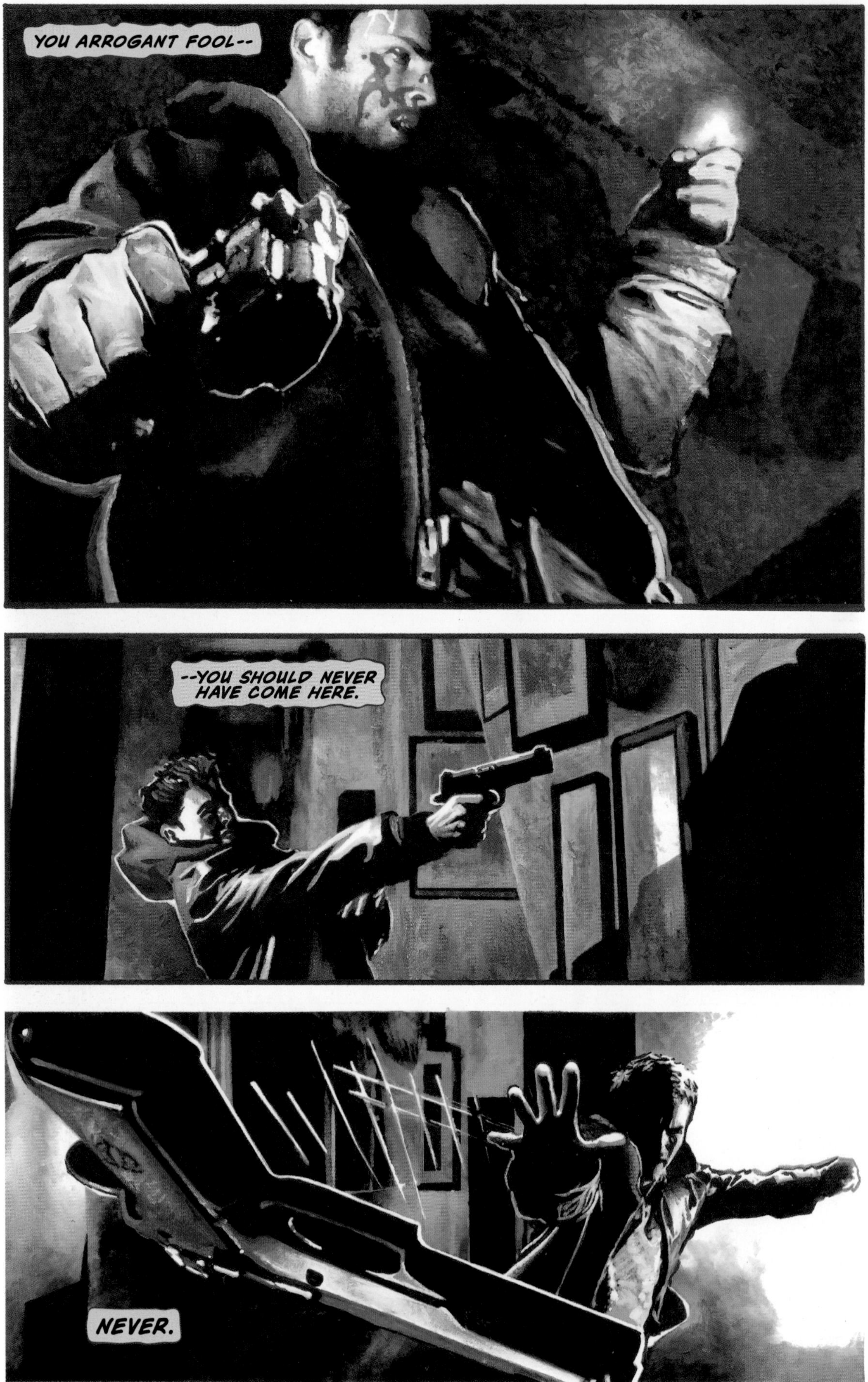
YOU ARROGANT FOOL--
--YOU SHOULD NEVER HAVE COME HERE.
NEVER.

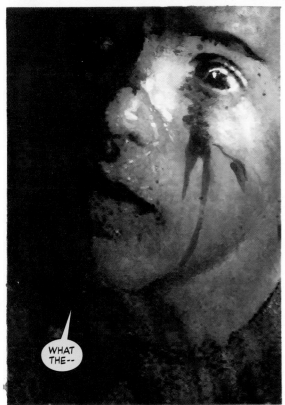

WHAT
THE--

--FUCK!

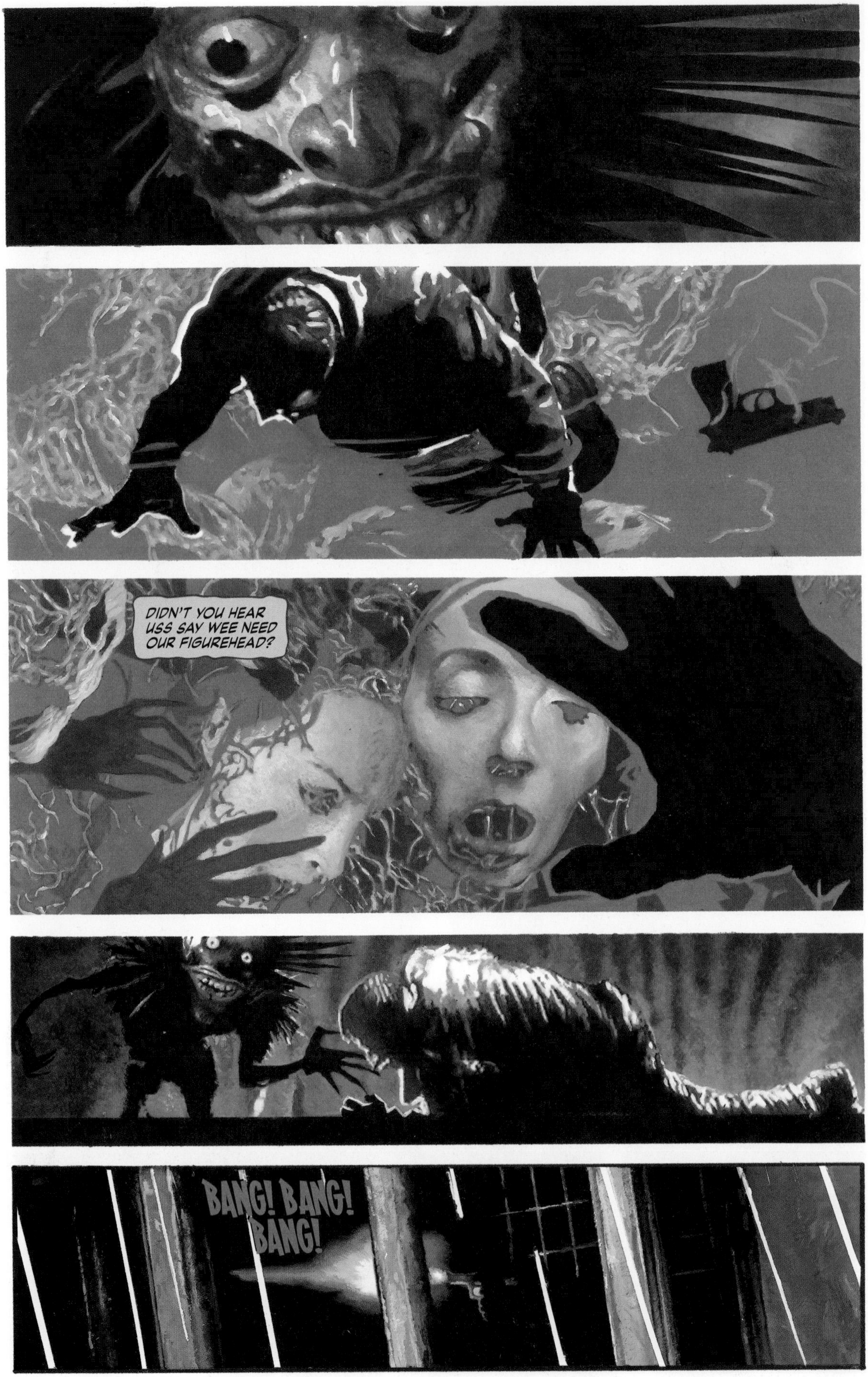
DIDN'T YOU HEAR USS SAY WEE NEED OUR FIGUREHEAD?
BANG! BANG! BANG!

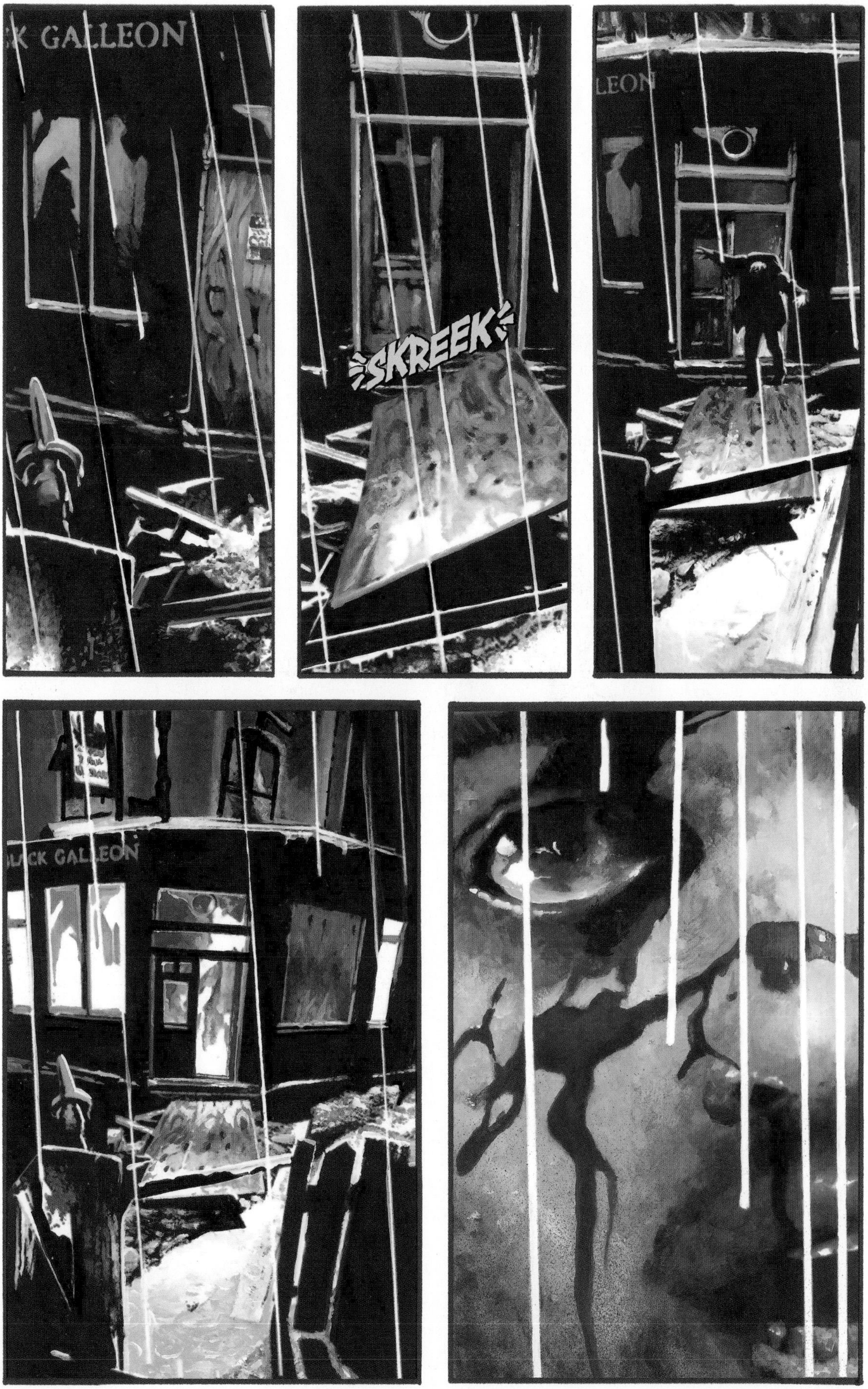
GALLEON
SKREEK
BLACK GALLEON

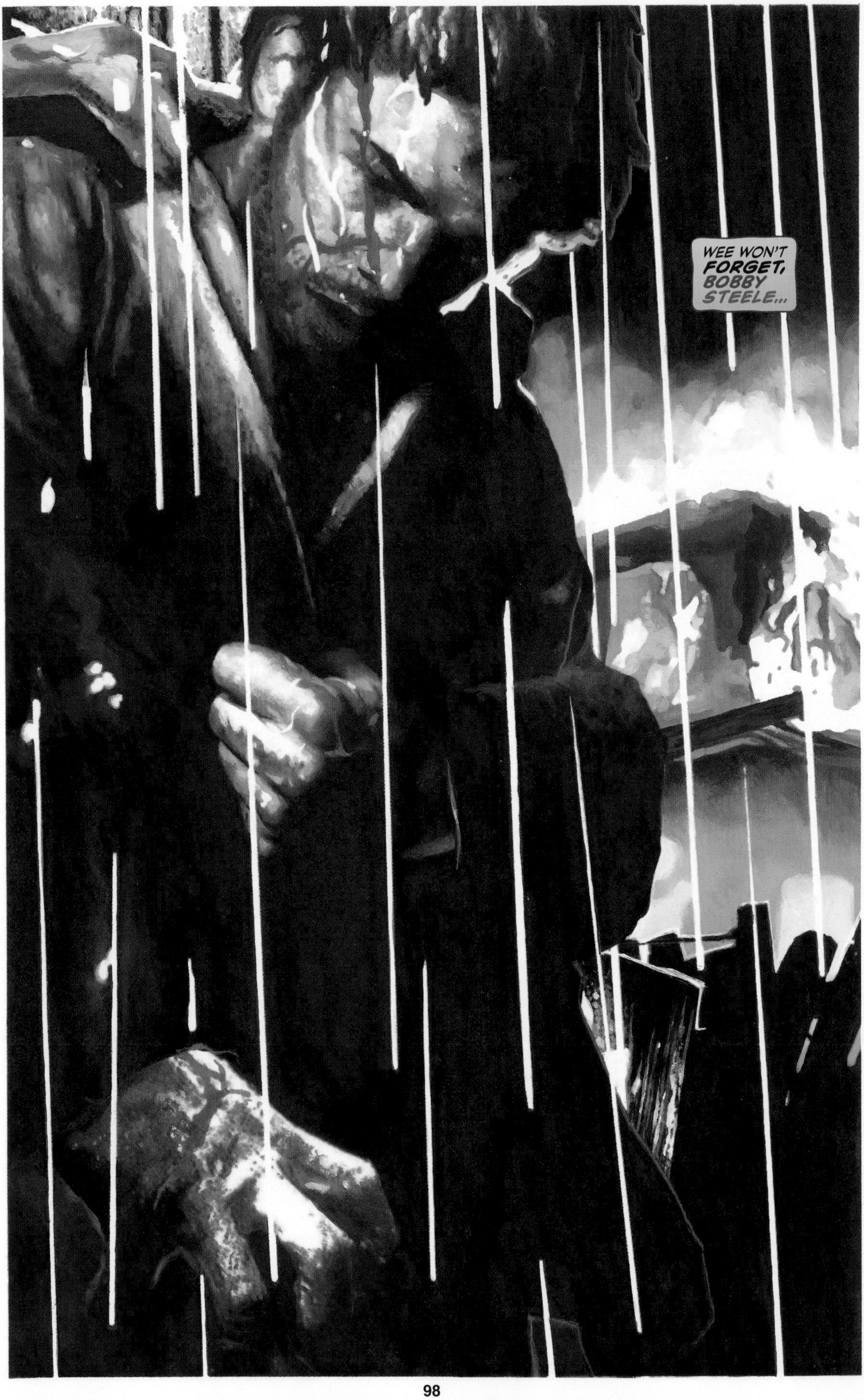
WEE WON'T FORGET, BOBBY STEELE...

O MY BACKWARD ILL-TRAINED HEART...

Allentown, Pennsylvania 1973.

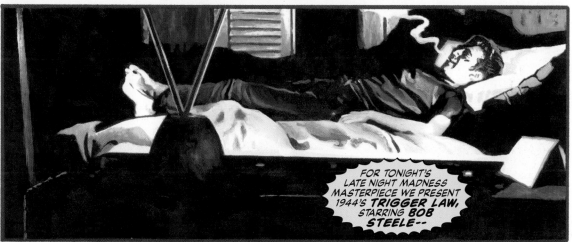

FOR TONIGHT'S LATE NIGHT MADNESS MASTERPIECE WE PRESENT 1944'S *TRIGGER LAW,* STARRING *BOB STEELE*--

--GREATEST OF ALL UNKNOWN COWBOY HEROES BACK IN THE DAY...

AND *HE'S GOING* TO COME FOR YOU, *FEE.*

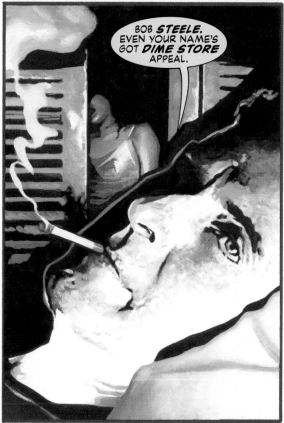

BOB *STEELE.* EVEN YOUR NAME'S GOT *DIME STORE* APPEAL.

99

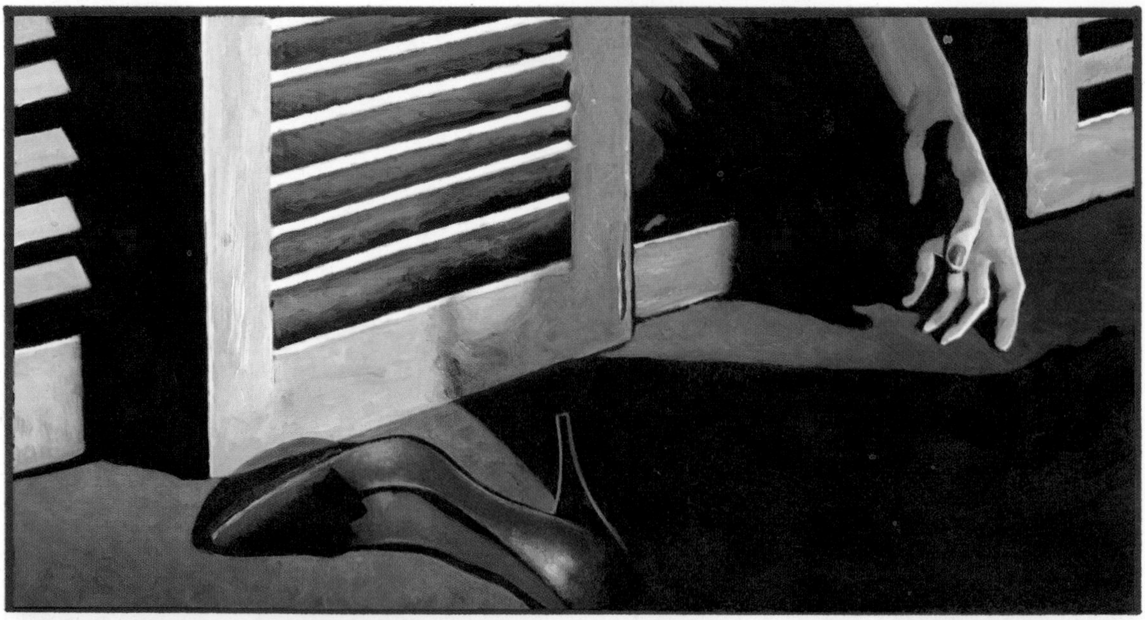

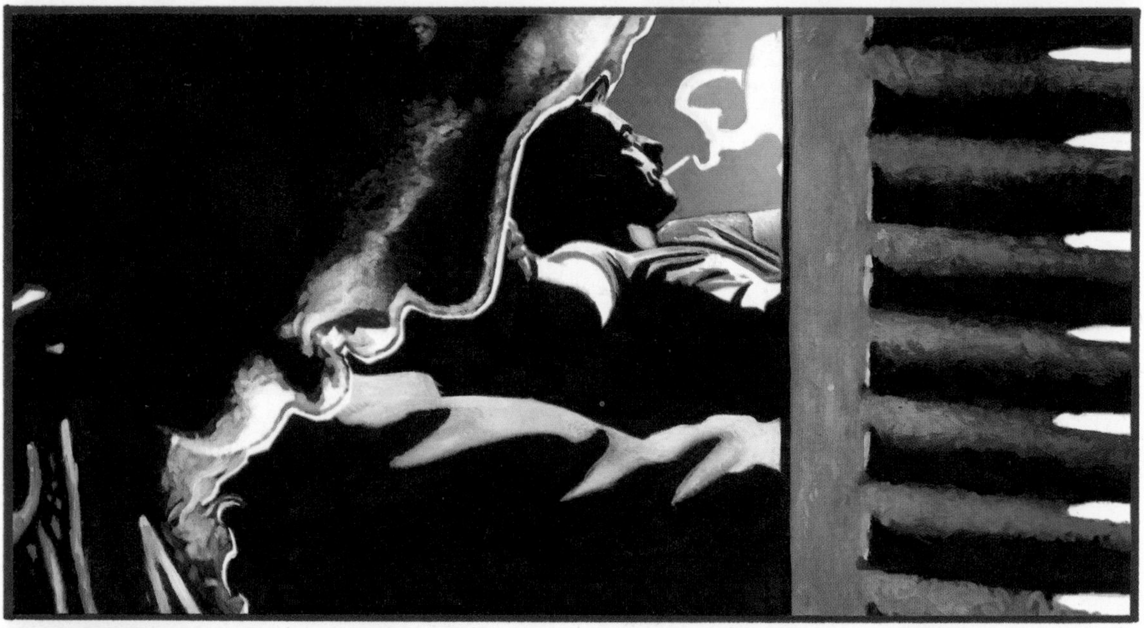

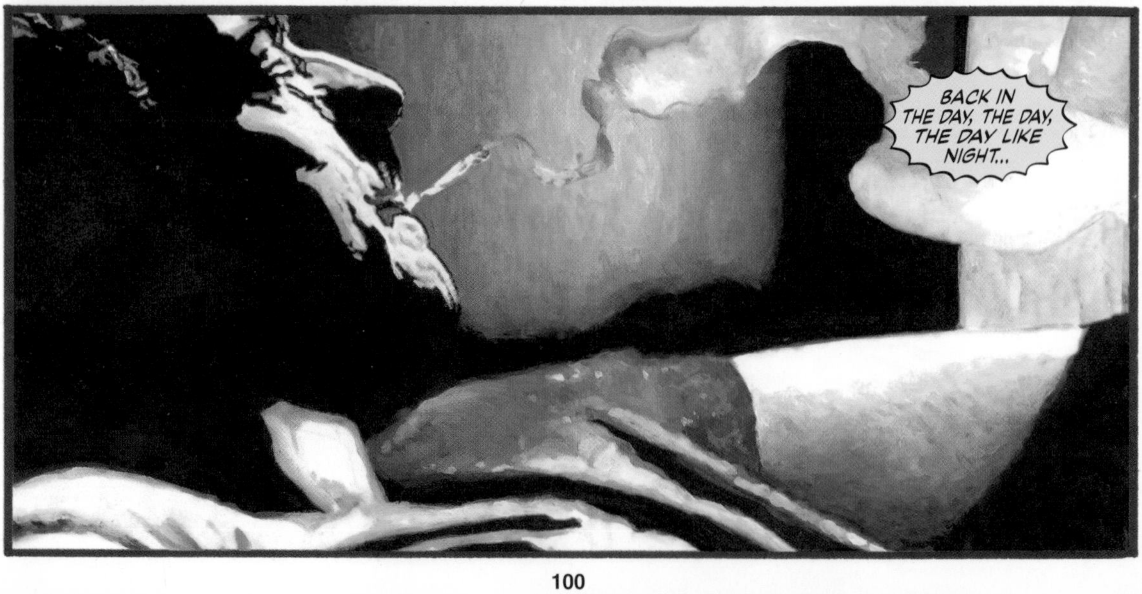
BACK IN THE DAY, THE DAY, THE DAY LIKE NIGHT...

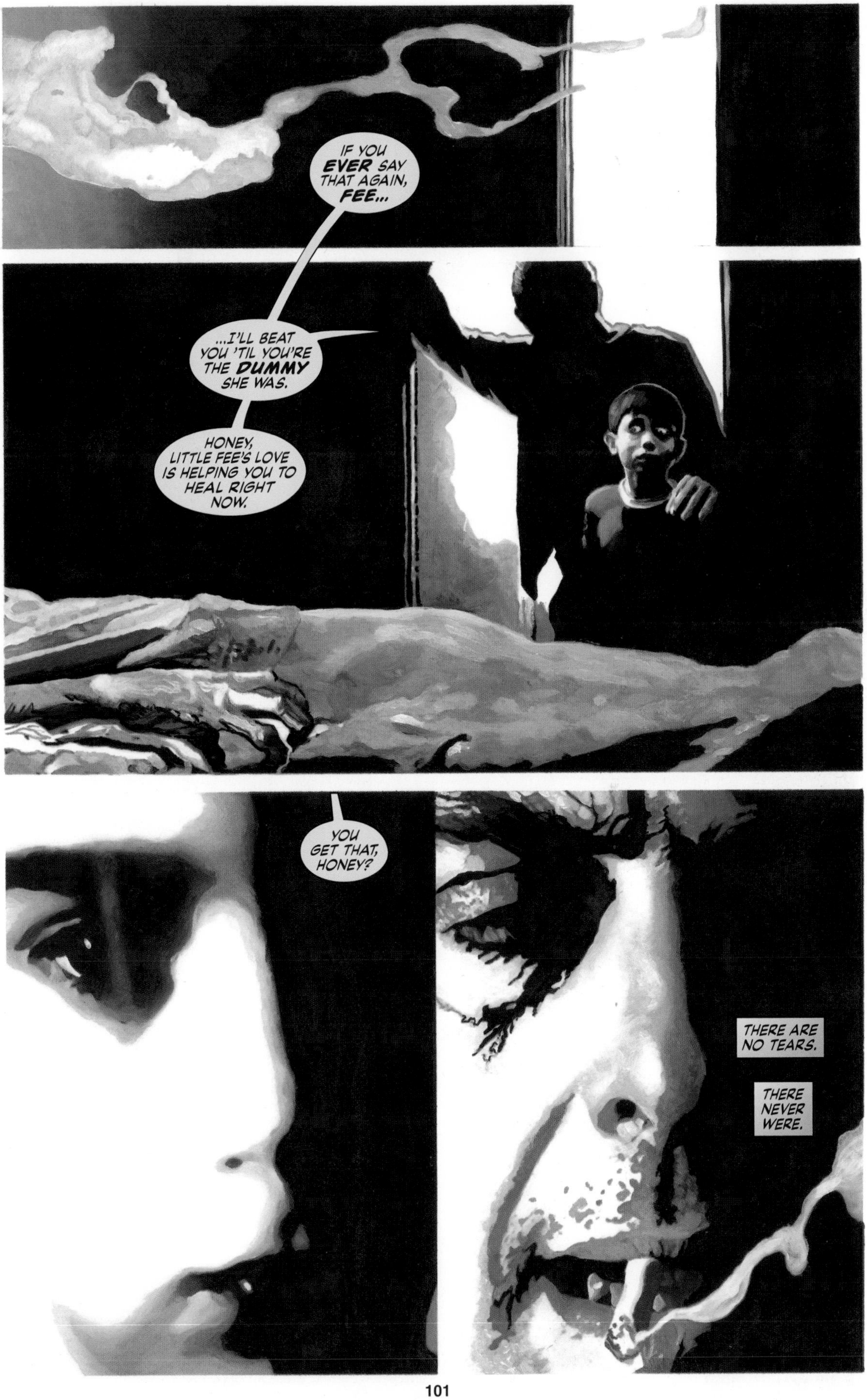
IF YOU EVER SAY THAT AGAIN, FEE...
...I'LL BEAT YOU 'TIL YOU'RE THE DUMMY SHE WAS.
HONEY, LITTLE FEE'S LOVE IS HELPING YOU TO HEAL RIGHT NOW.
YOU GET THAT, HONEY?
THERE ARE NO TEARS.
THERE NEVER WERE.

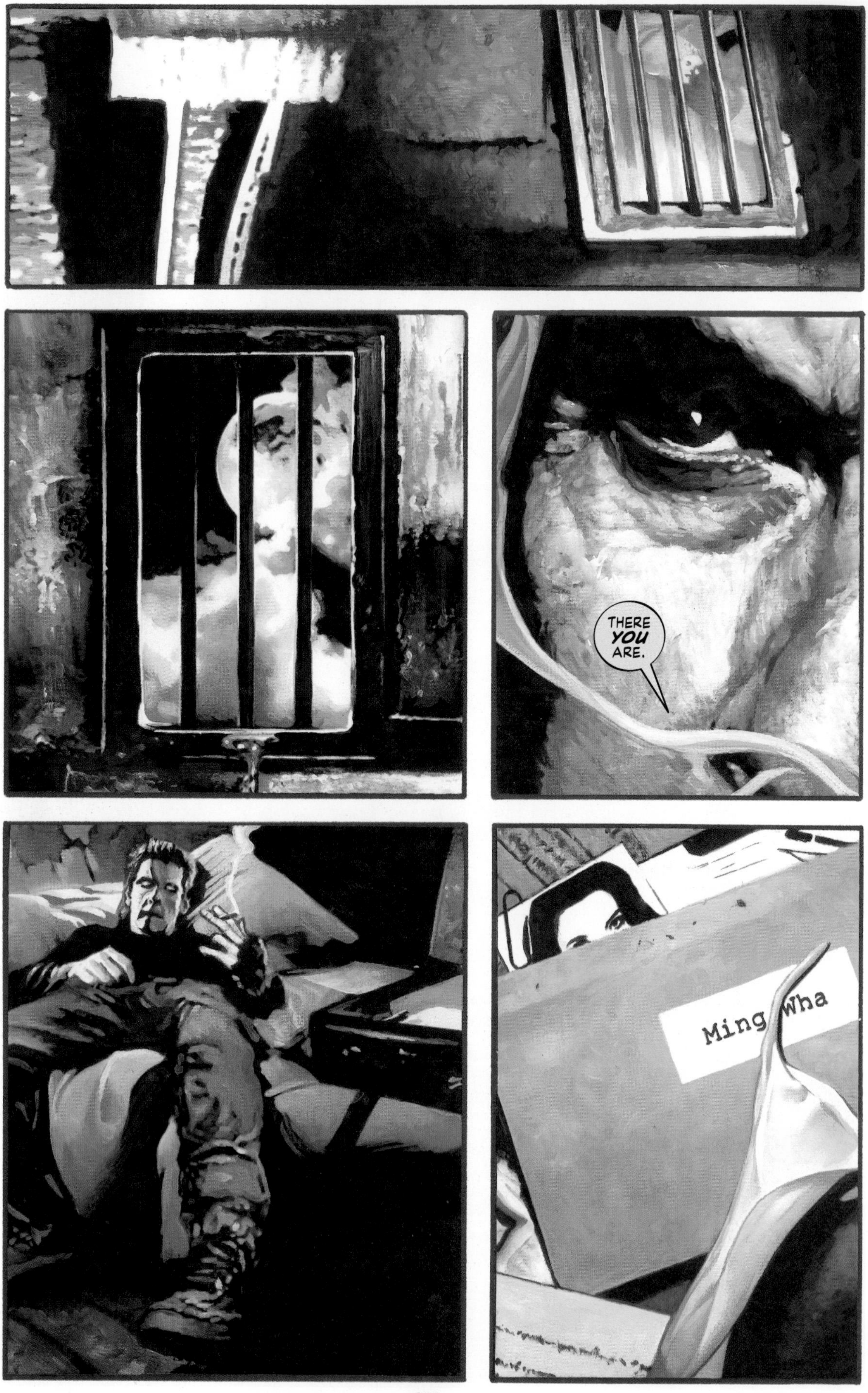
THERE YOU ARE.
Ming Wha

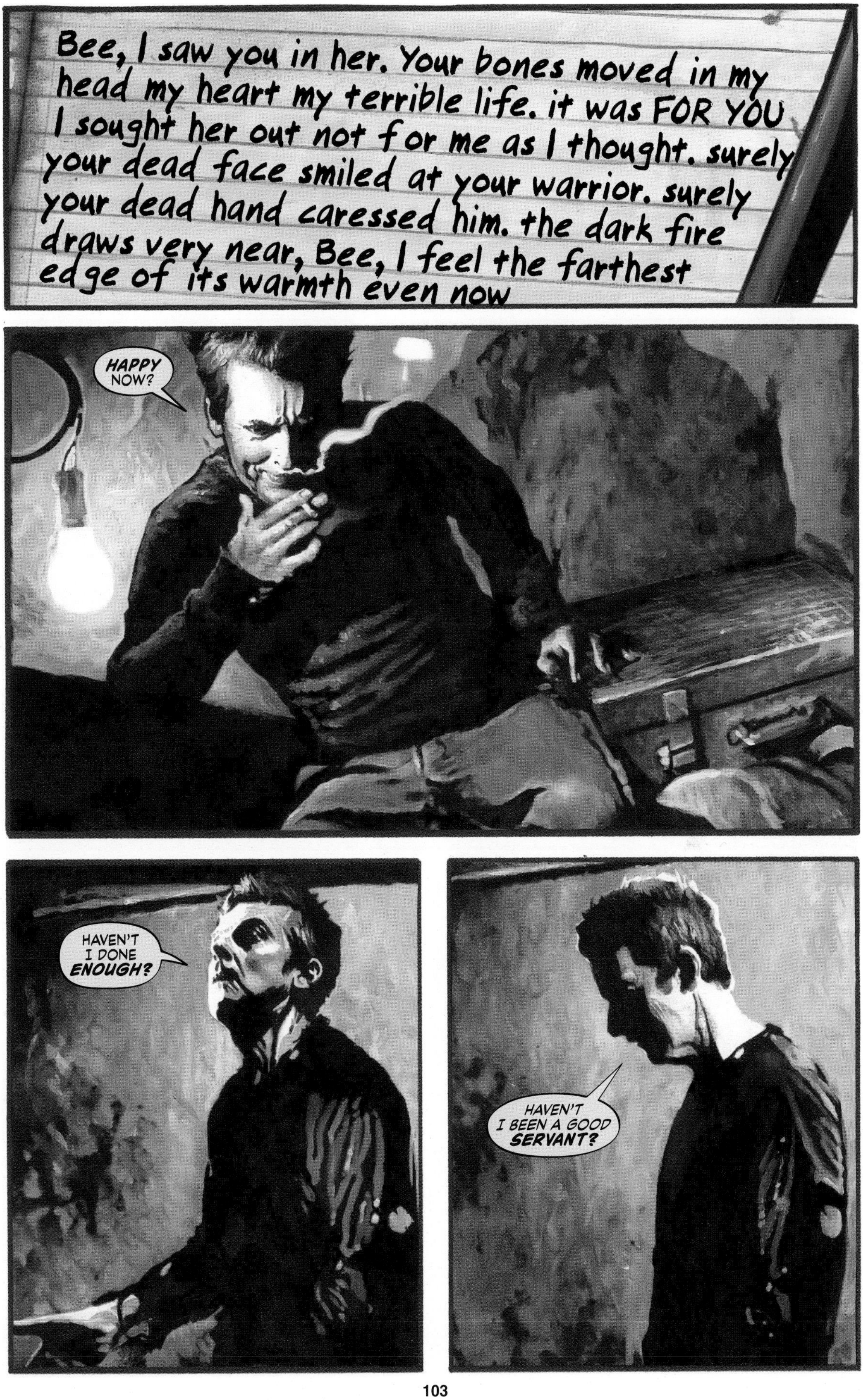
Bee, I saw you in her. Your bones moved in my head my heart my terrible life. it was FOR YOU I sought her out not for me as I thought. surely your dead face smiled at your warrior. surely your dead hand caressed him. the dark fire draws very near, Bee, I feel the farthest edge of its warmth even now
HAPPY NOW?
HAVEN'T I DONE ENOUGH?
HAVEN'T I BEEN A GOOD SERVANT?

Ulster County.
Upstate New York.

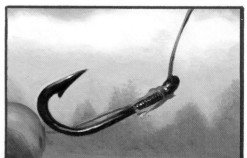

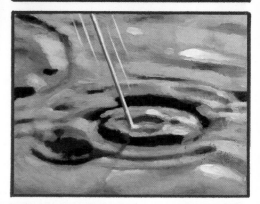

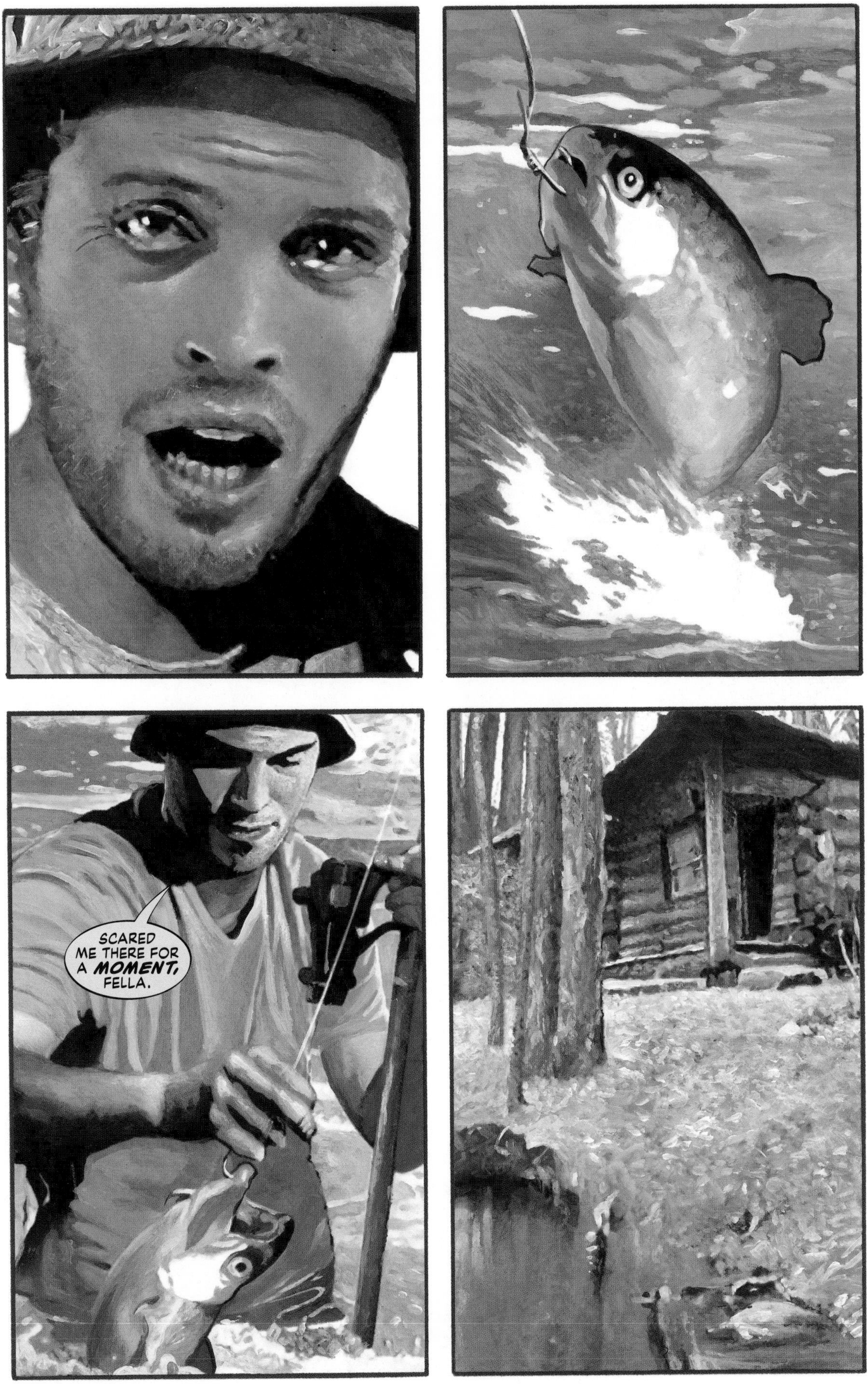
SCARED ME THERE FOR A **MOMENT,** FELLA.

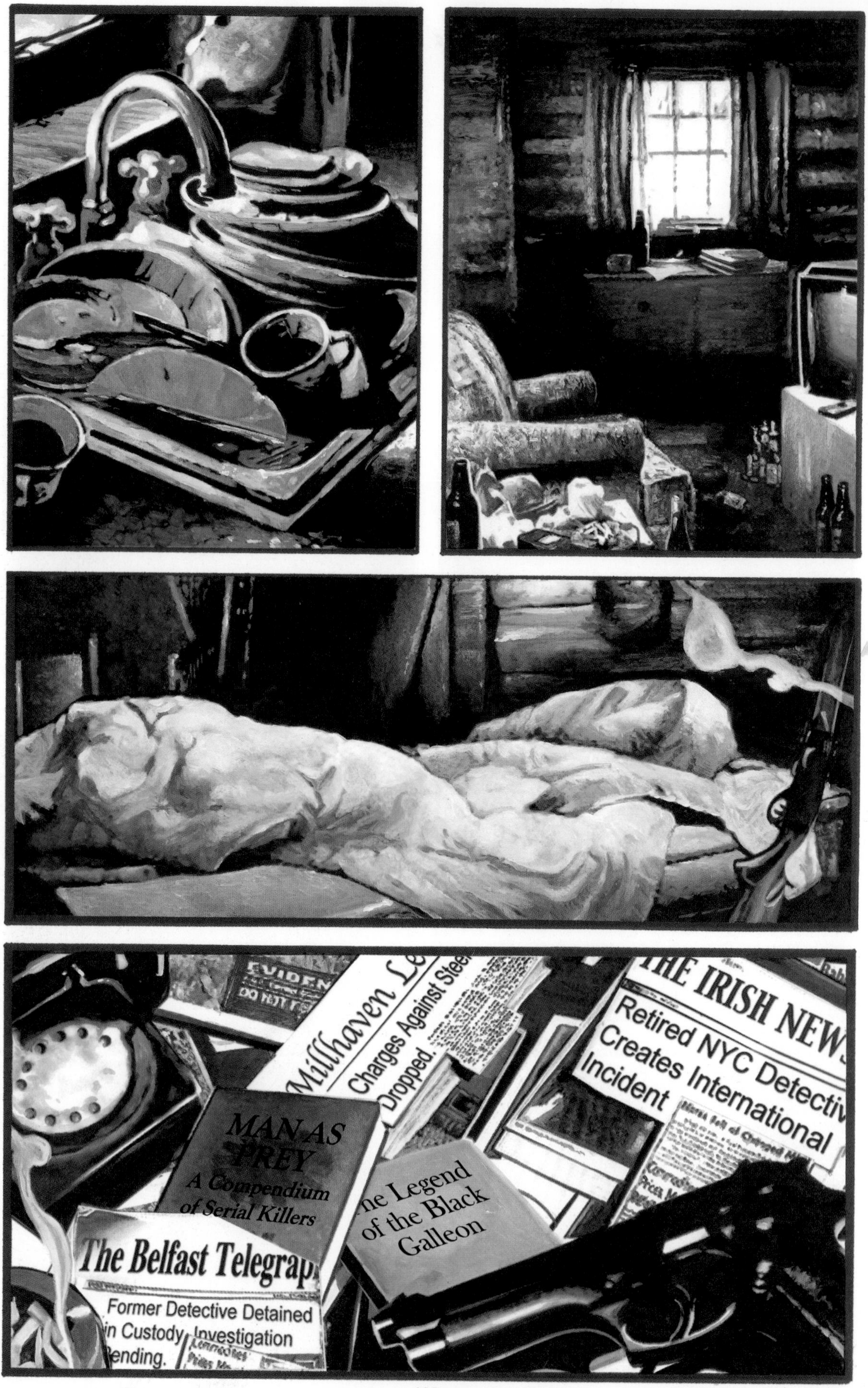
HE IRISH NEWS
Retired NYC Detectiv
Creates International
Incident
Millhaven Le
Charges Against Stee
Dropped.
MAN AS PREY
A Compendium of Serial Killers
he Legend of the Black Galleon
The Belfast Telegrap
Former Detective Detained in Custody. Investigation Pending.

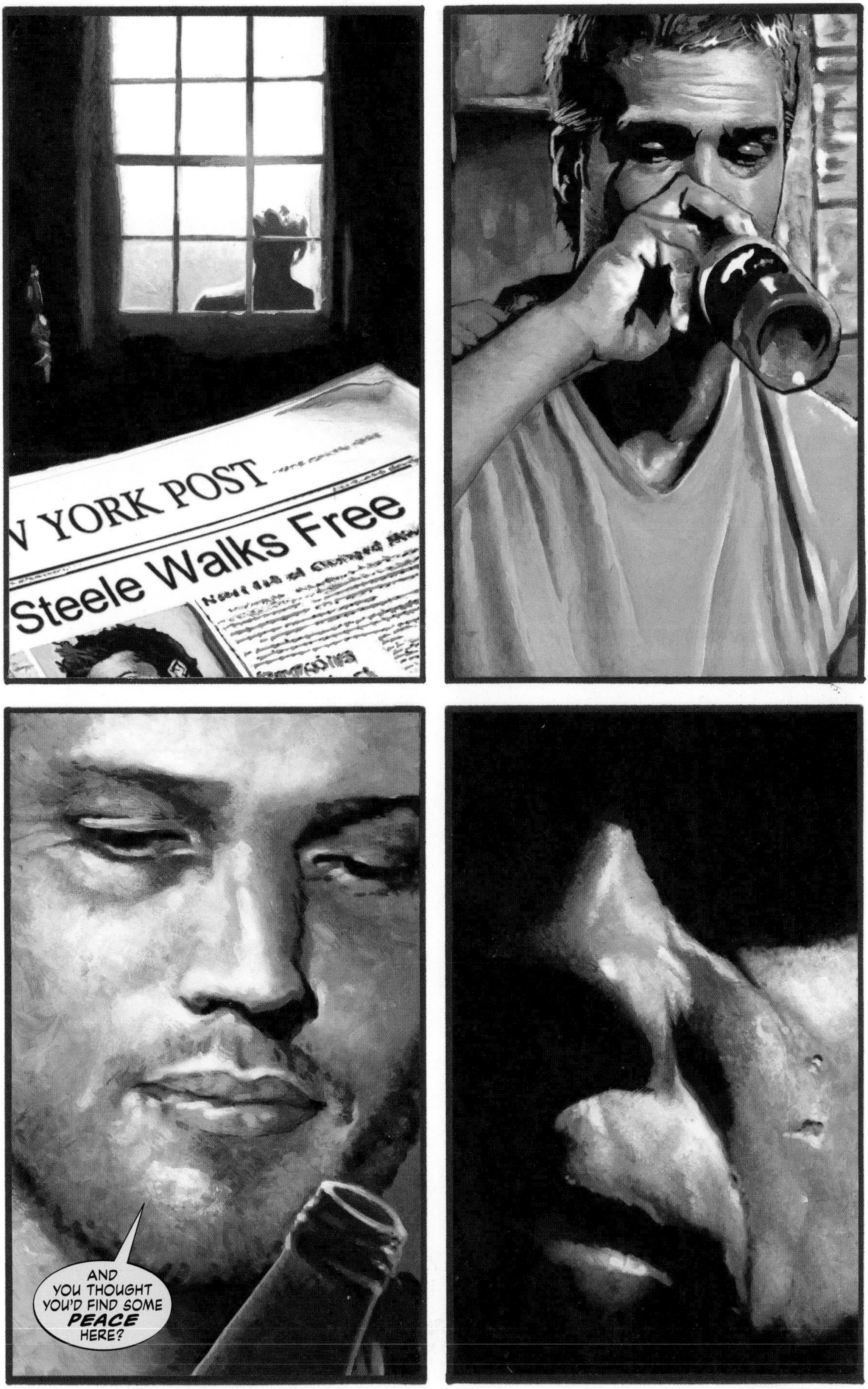
YORK POST
Steele Walks Free
AND YOU THOUGHT YOU'D FIND SOME *PEACE* HERE?

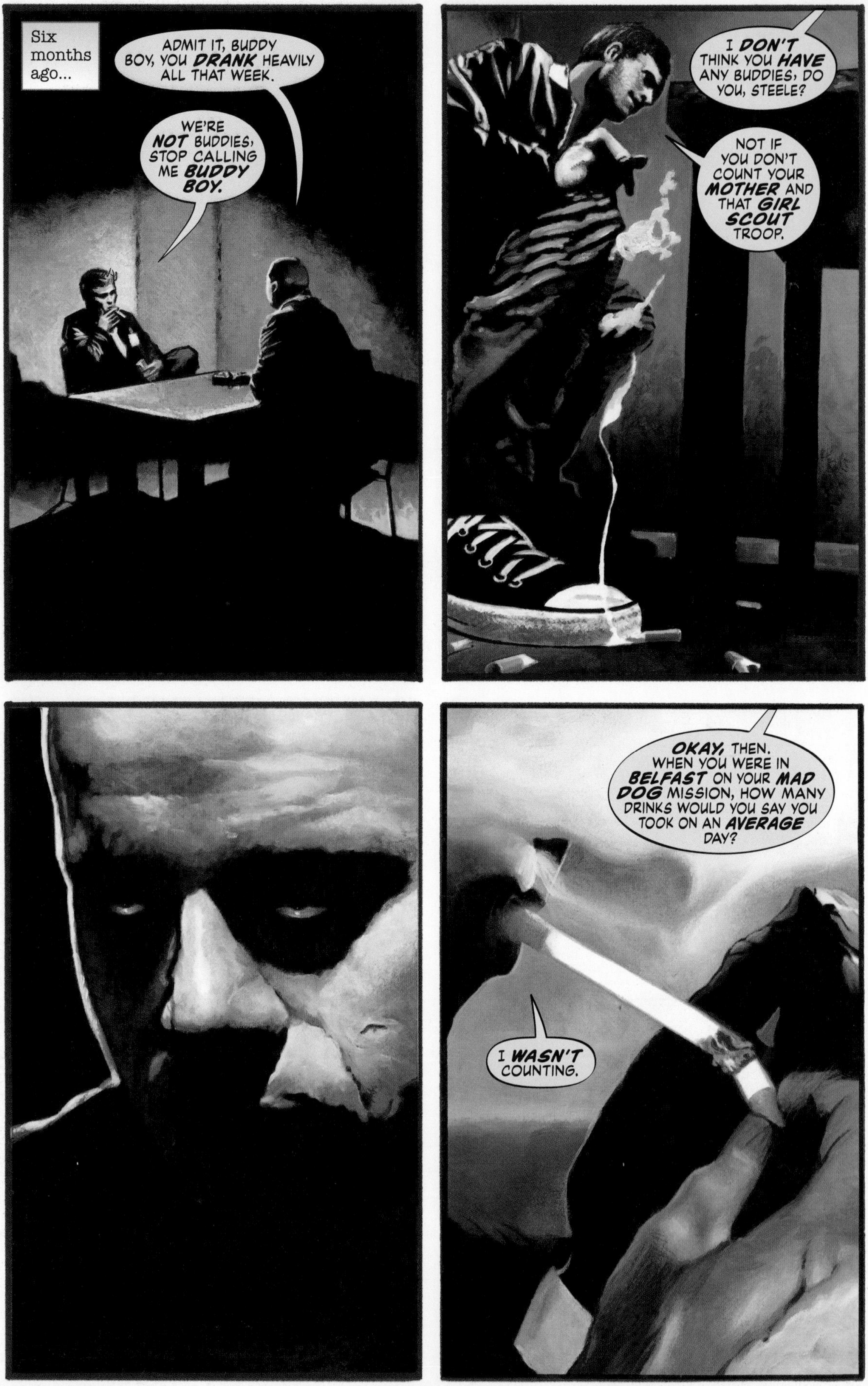

Six months ago...
ADMIT IT, BUDDY BOY, YOU **DRANK** HEAVILY ALL THAT WEEK.
WE'RE **NOT** BUDDIES, STOP CALLING ME **BUDDY BOY.**
I **DON'T** THINK YOU **HAVE** ANY BUDDIES, DO YOU, STEELE?
NOT IF YOU DON'T COUNT YOUR **MOTHER** AND THAT **GIRL SCOUT** TROOP.
OKAY, THEN. WHEN YOU WERE IN **BELFAST** ON YOUR **MAD DOG** MISSION, HOW MANY DRINKS WOULD YOU SAY YOU TOOK ON AN **AVERAGE** DAY?
I **WASN'T** COUNTING.

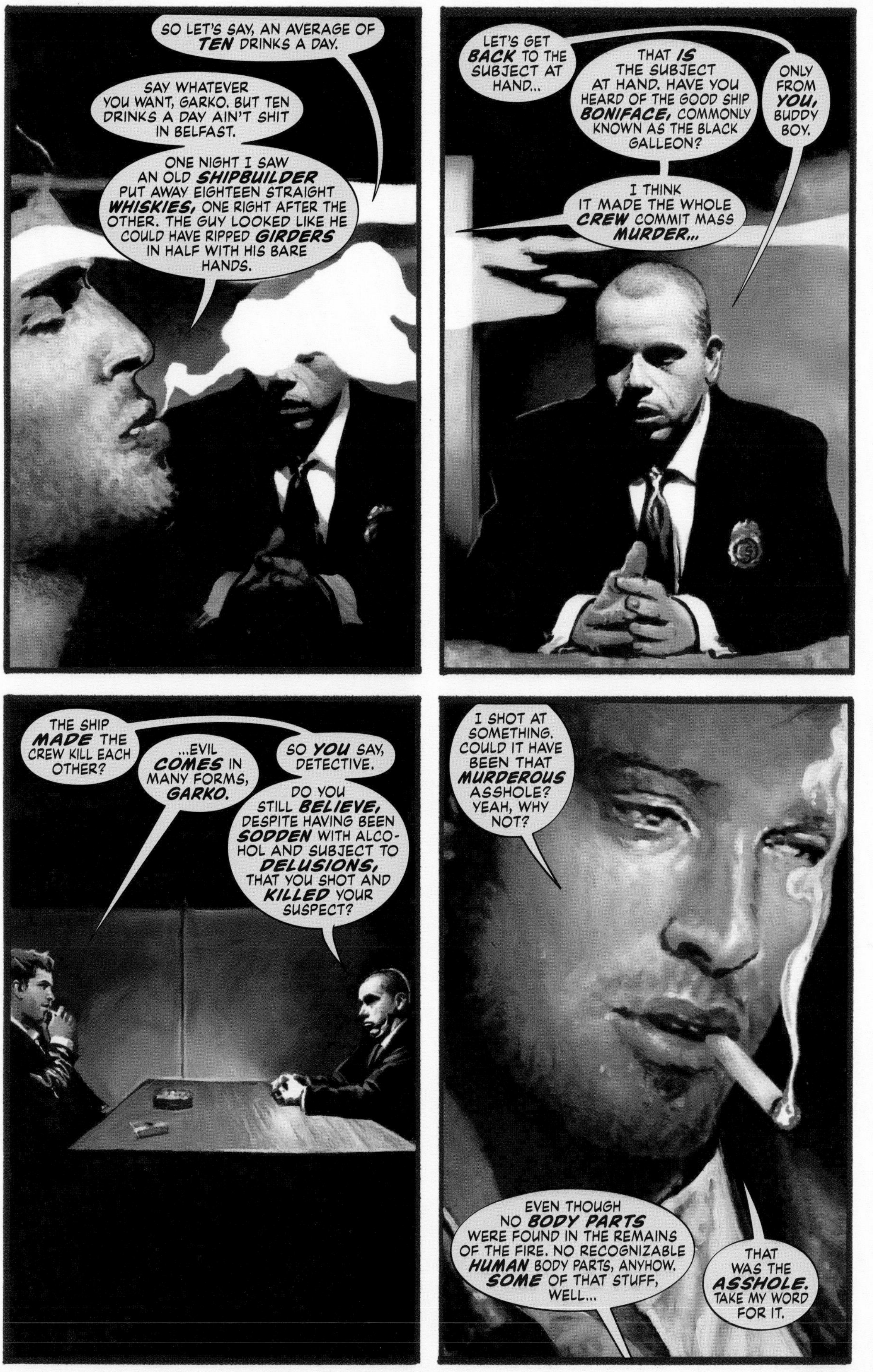
SO LET'S SAY, AN AVERAGE OF TEN DRINKS A DAY.
SAY WHATEVER YOU WANT, GARKO. BUT TEN DRINKS A DAY AIN'T SHIT IN BELFAST.
ONE NIGHT I SAW AN OLD SHIPBUILDER PUT AWAY EIGHTEEN STRAIGHT WHISKIES, ONE RIGHT AFTER THE OTHER. THE GUY LOOKED LIKE HE COULD HAVE RIPPED GIRDERS IN HALF WITH HIS BARE HANDS.
LET'S GET BACK TO THE SUBJECT AT HAND...
THAT IS THE SUBJECT AT HAND. HAVE YOU HEARD OF THE GOOD SHIP BONIFACE, COMMONLY KNOWN AS THE BLACK GALLEON?
ONLY FROM YOU, BUDDY BOY.
I THINK IT MADE THE WHOLE CREW COMMIT MASS MURDER...
THE SHIP MADE THE CREW KILL EACH OTHER?
...EVIL COMES IN MANY FORMS, GARKO.
SO YOU SAY, DETECTIVE.
DO YOU STILL BELIEVE, DESPITE HAVING BEEN SODDEN WITH ALCOHOL AND SUBJECT TO DELUSIONS, THAT YOU SHOT AND KILLED YOUR SUSPECT?
I SHOT AT SOMETHING. COULD IT HAVE BEEN THAT MURDEROUS ASSHOLE? YEAH, WHY NOT?
EVEN THOUGH NO BODY PARTS WERE FOUND IN THE REMAINS OF THE FIRE. NO RECOGNIZABLE HUMAN BODY PARTS, ANYHOW. SOME OF THAT STUFF, WELL...
THAT WAS THE ASSHOLE. TAKE MY WORD FOR IT.

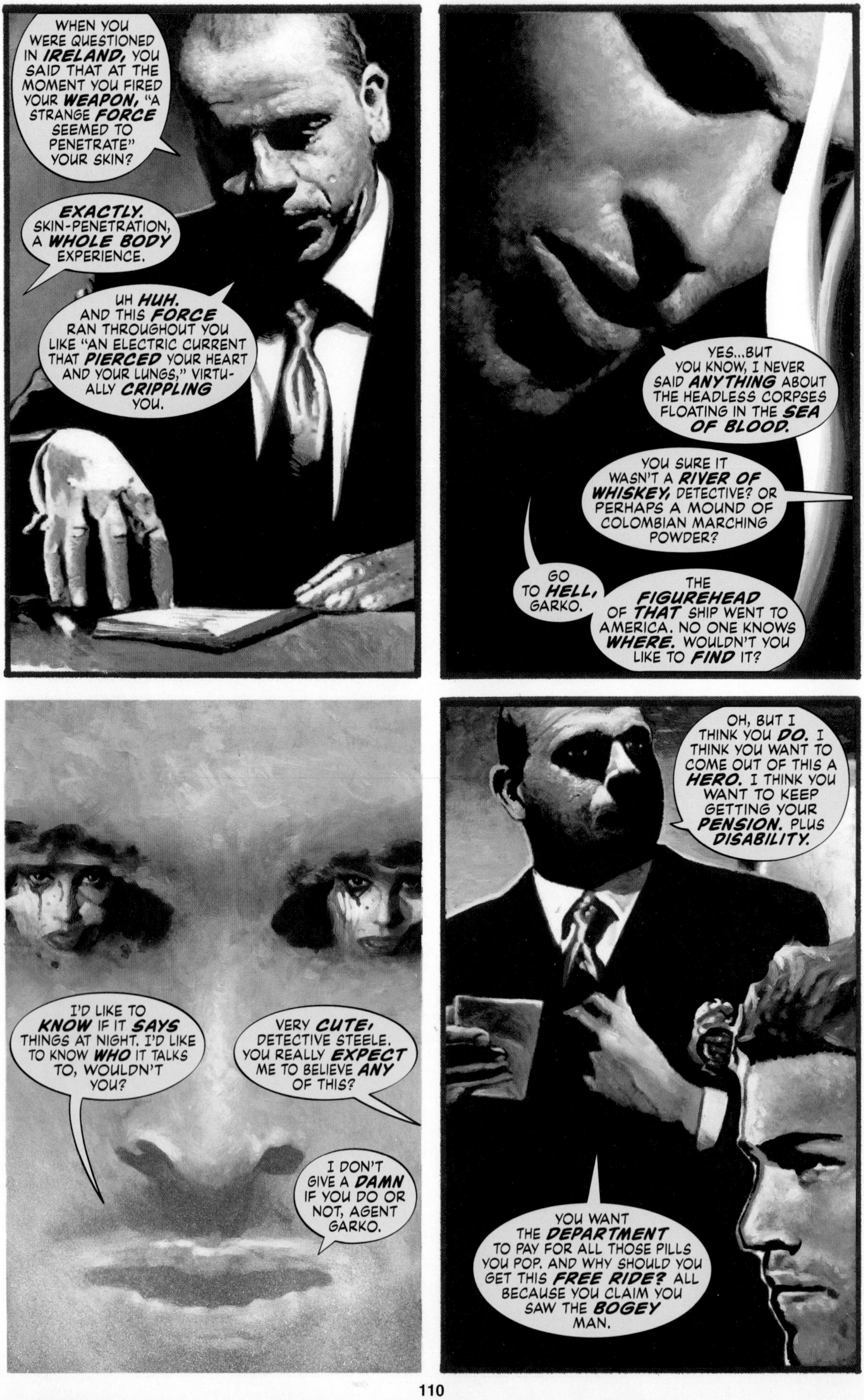
WHEN YOU WERE QUESTIONED IN IRELAND, YOU SAID THAT AT THE MOMENT YOU FIRED YOUR WEAPON, "A STRANGE FORCE SEEMED TO PENETRATE" YOUR SKIN?
EXACTLY. SKIN-PENETRATION, A WHOLE BODY EXPERIENCE.
UH HUH. AND THIS FORCE RAN THROUGHOUT YOU LIKE "AN ELECTRIC CURRENT THAT PIERCED YOUR HEART AND YOUR LUNGS," VIRTU-ALLY CRIPPLING YOU.
YES...BUT YOU KNOW, I NEVER SAID ANYTHING ABOUT THE HEADLESS CORPSES FLOATING IN THE SEA OF BLOOD.
YOU SURE IT WASN'T A RIVER OF WHISKEY, DETECTIVE? OR PERHAPS A MOUND OF COLOMBIAN MARCHING POWDER?
GO TO HELL, GARKO.
THE FIGUREHEAD OF THAT SHIP WENT TO AMERICA. NO ONE KNOWS WHERE. WOULDN'T YOU LIKE TO FIND IT?
I'D LIKE TO KNOW IF IT SAYS THINGS AT NIGHT. I'D LIKE TO KNOW WHO IT TALKS TO, WOULDN'T YOU?
VERY CUTE, DETECTIVE STEELE. YOU REALLY EXPECT ME TO BELIEVE ANY OF THIS?
I DON'T GIVE A DAMN IF YOU DO OR NOT, AGENT GARKO.
OH, BUT I THINK YOU DO. I THINK YOU WANT TO COME OUT OF THIS A HERO. I THINK YOU WANT TO KEEP GETTING YOUR PENSION. PLUS DISABILITY.
YOU WANT THE DEPARTMENT TO PAY FOR ALL THOSE PILLS YOU POP. AND WHY SHOULD YOU GET THIS FREE RIDE? ALL BECAUSE YOU CLAIM YOU SAW THE BOGEY MAN.

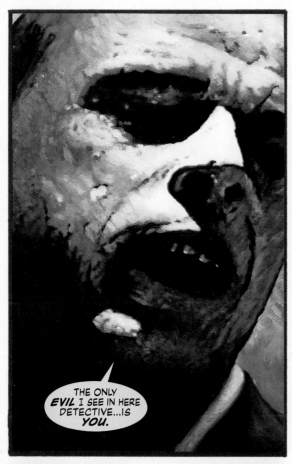

THE ONLY *EVIL* I SEE IN HERE DETECTIVE...IS *YOU.*

FIND A *LAWYER,* STEELE. YOU'RE GOING TO *NEED* ONE.

BRIING! BRIING!

Present day.
BRIING!
BRIING!
BRIING!
BRIING!
BRIING!
BRIING!
HELLO?

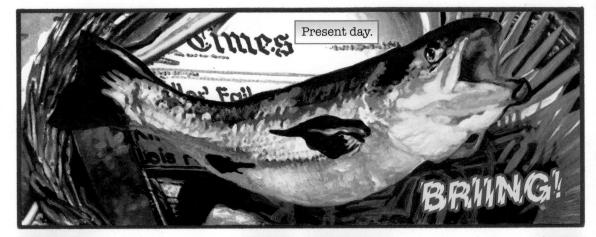

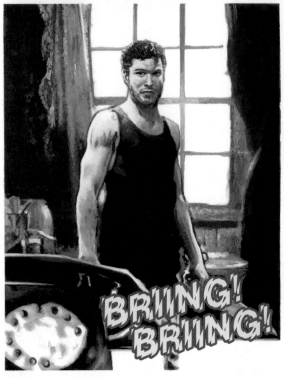

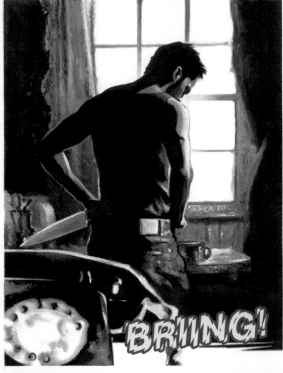

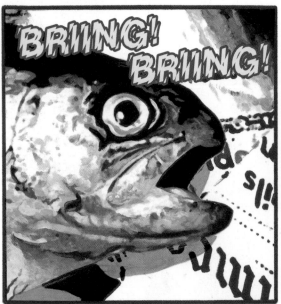

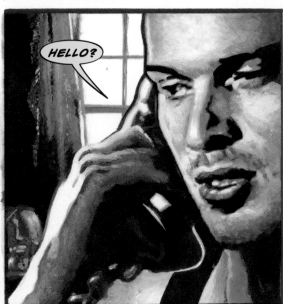

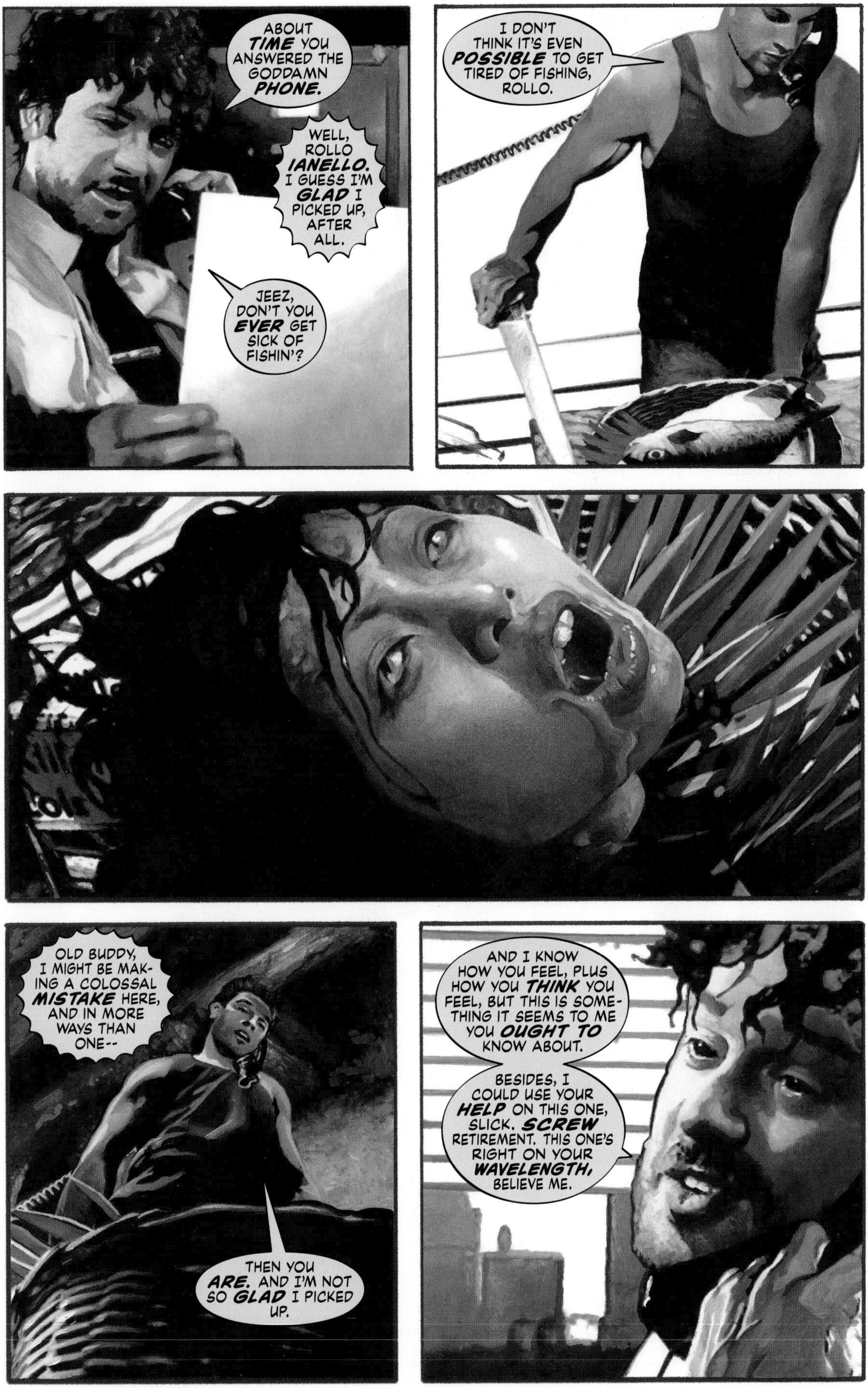
ABOUT TIME YOU ANSWERED THE GODDAMN PHONE.
WELL, ROLLO IANELLO. I GUESS I'M GLAD I PICKED UP, AFTER ALL.
JEEZ, DON'T YOU EVER GET SICK OF FISHIN'?
I DON'T THINK IT'S EVEN POSSIBLE TO GET TIRED OF FISHING, ROLLO.
OLD BUDDY, I MIGHT BE MAKING A COLOSSAL MISTAKE HERE, AND IN MORE WAYS THAN ONE--
THEN YOU ARE. AND I'M NOT SO GLAD I PICKED UP.
AND I KNOW HOW YOU FEEL, PLUS HOW YOU THINK YOU FEEL, BUT THIS IS SOMETHING IT SEEMS TO ME YOU OUGHT TO KNOW ABOUT.
BESIDES, I COULD USE YOUR HELP ON THIS ONE, SLICK. SCREW RETIREMENT. THIS ONE'S RIGHT ON YOUR WAVELENGTH, BELIEVE ME.

WE'RE TALKING ABOUT A REAL OLD-SCHOOL *BUTCHER* HERE, BOBBY. KIND OF GUY THAT USED TO SHINE YOUR *DAY* RIGHT UP.

AND BY THAT I MEAN YOUR OLD SCHOOL, OLD PARDNER. SOME OF THIS SHIT SEEMS *AWFULLY* FAMILIAR.

THIS ISN'T ABOUT WHITE *DRESSES*, NOW. IT'S ABOUT THE *OTHER* STUFF. THE GUY YOU WERE *REALLY* LOOKING FOR.

MAN AS PREY
A Compendium of Serial Killers

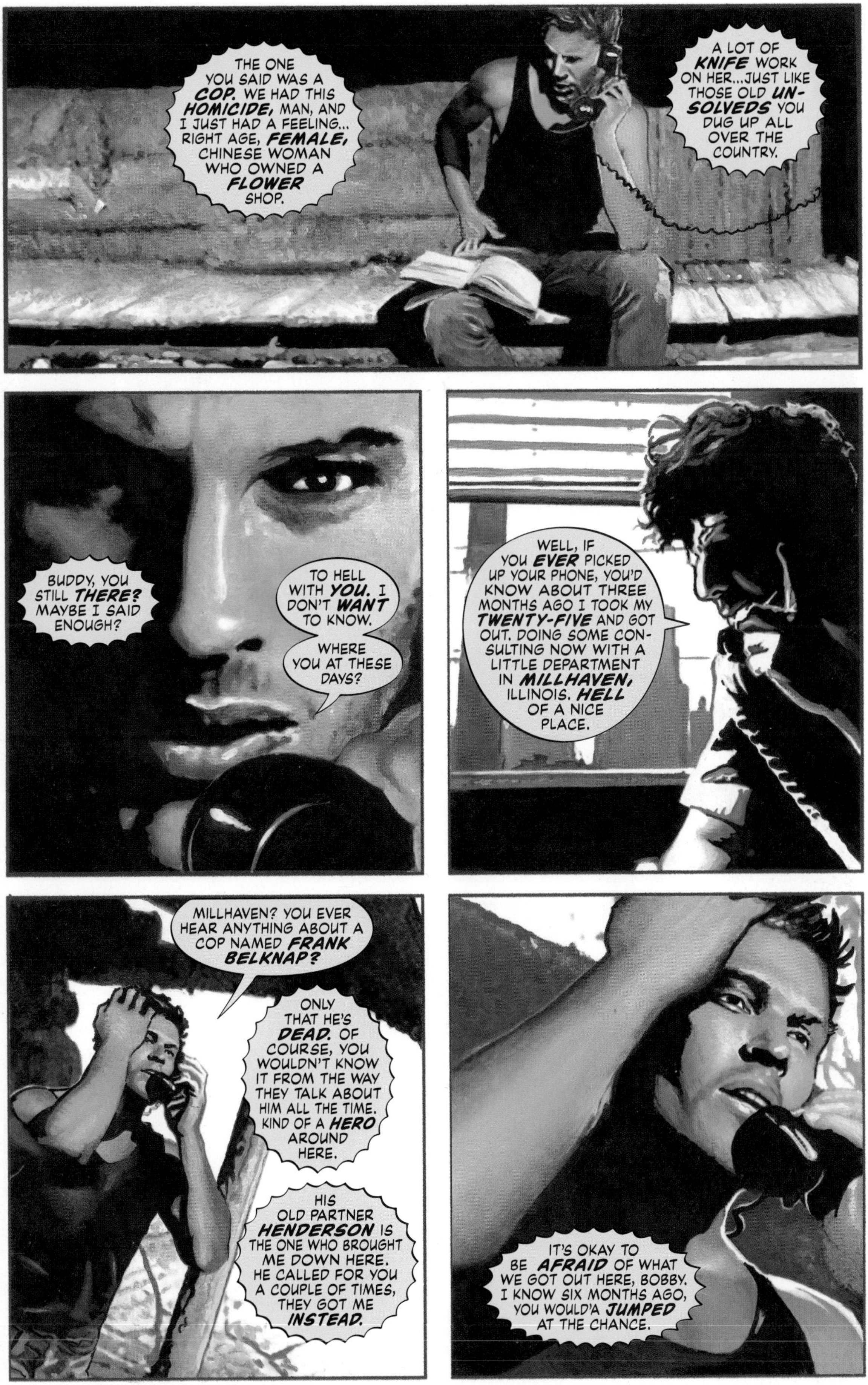
THE ONE YOU SAID WAS A COP. WE HAD THIS HOMICIDE, MAN, AND I JUST HAD A FEELING... RIGHT AGE, FEMALE, CHINESE WOMAN WHO OWNED A FLOWER SHOP.
A LOT OF KNIFE WORK ON HER...JUST LIKE THOSE OLD UN-SOLVEDS YOU DUG UP ALL OVER THE COUNTRY.
BUDDY, YOU STILL THERE? MAYBE I SAID ENOUGH?
TO HELL WITH YOU. I DON'T WANT TO KNOW.
WHERE YOU AT THESE DAYS?
WELL, IF YOU EVER PICKED UP YOUR PHONE, YOU'D KNOW ABOUT THREE MONTHS AGO I TOOK MY TWENTY-FIVE AND GOT OUT. DOING SOME CON-SULTING NOW WITH A LITTLE DEPARTMENT IN MILLHAVEN, ILLINOIS. HELL OF A NICE PLACE.
MILLHAVEN? YOU EVER HEAR ANYTHING ABOUT A COP NAMED FRANK BELKNAP?
ONLY THAT HE'S DEAD. OF COURSE, YOU WOULDN'T KNOW IT FROM THE WAY THEY TALK ABOUT HIM ALL THE TIME. KIND OF A HERO AROUND HERE.
HIS OLD PARTNER HENDERSON IS THE ONE WHO BROUGHT ME DOWN HERE. HE CALLED FOR YOU A COUPLE OF TIMES, THEY GOT ME INSTEAD.
IT'S OKAY TO BE AFRAID OF WHAT WE GOT OUT HERE, BOBBY. I KNOW SIX MONTHS AGO, YOU WOULD'A JUMPED AT THE CHANCE.

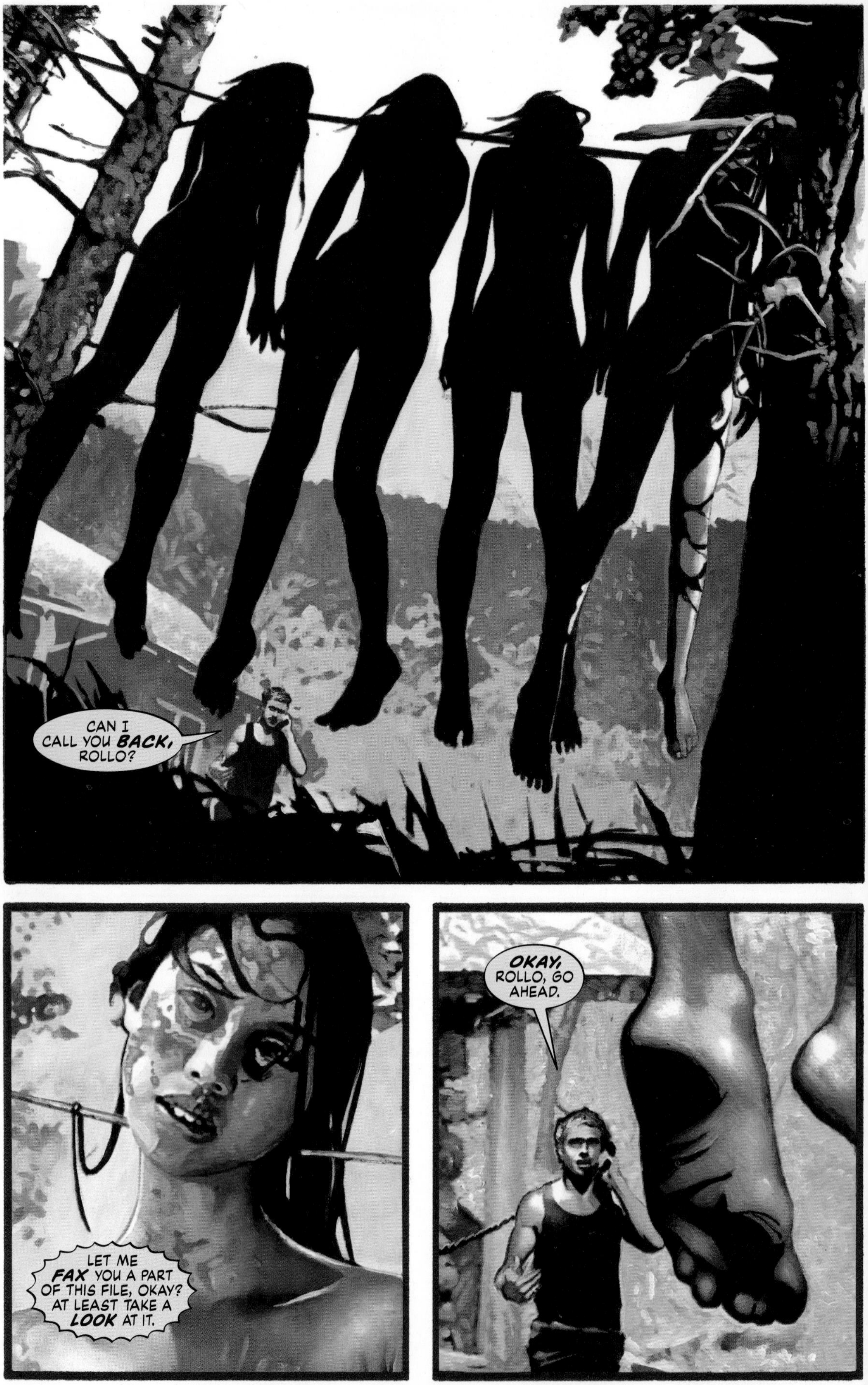
CAN I CALL YOU BACK, ROLLO?
LET ME FAX YOU A PART OF THIS FILE, OKAY? AT LEAST TAKE A LOOK AT IT.
OKAY, ROLLO, GO AHEAD.

HOLY FUCKIN' *MAIRZY* DOATES.

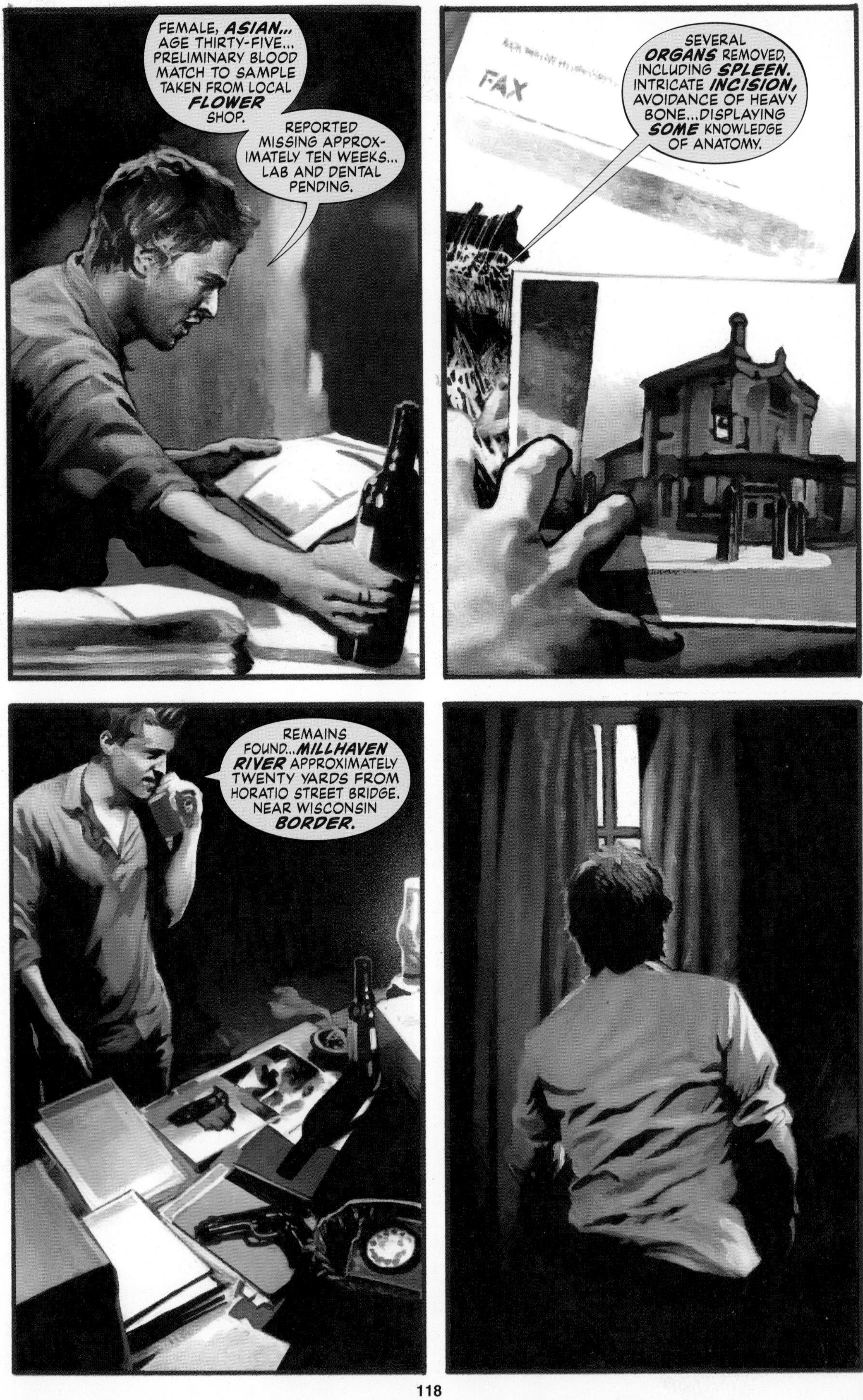
FEMALE, ASIAN... AGE THIRTY-FIVE... PRELIMINARY BLOOD MATCH TO SAMPLE TAKEN FROM LOCAL FLOWER SHOP.
REPORTED MISSING APPROX-IMATELY TEN WEEKS... LAB AND DENTAL PENDING.
FAX
SEVERAL ORGANS REMOVED, INCLUDING SPLEEN. INTRICATE INCISION, AVOIDANCE OF HEAVY BONE...DISPLAYING SOME KNOWLEDGE OF ANATOMY.
REMAINS FOUND...MILLHAVEN RIVER APPROXIMATELY TWENTY YARDS FROM HORATIO STREET BRIDGE. NEAR WISCONSIN BORDER.

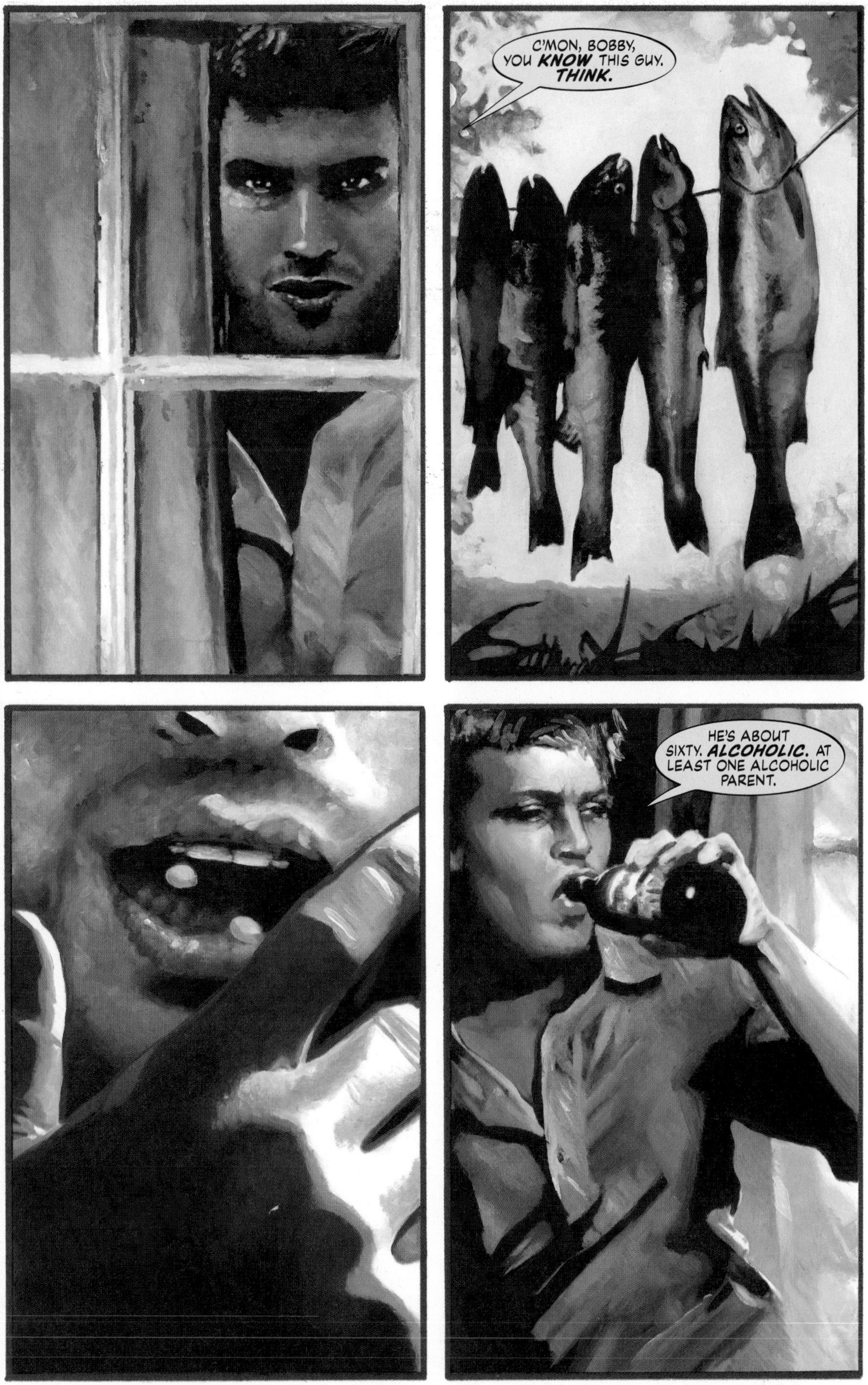
C'MON, BOBBY, YOU KNOW THIS GUY. THINK.
HE'S ABOUT SIXTY. ALCOHOLIC. AT LEAST ONE ALCOHOLIC PARENT.

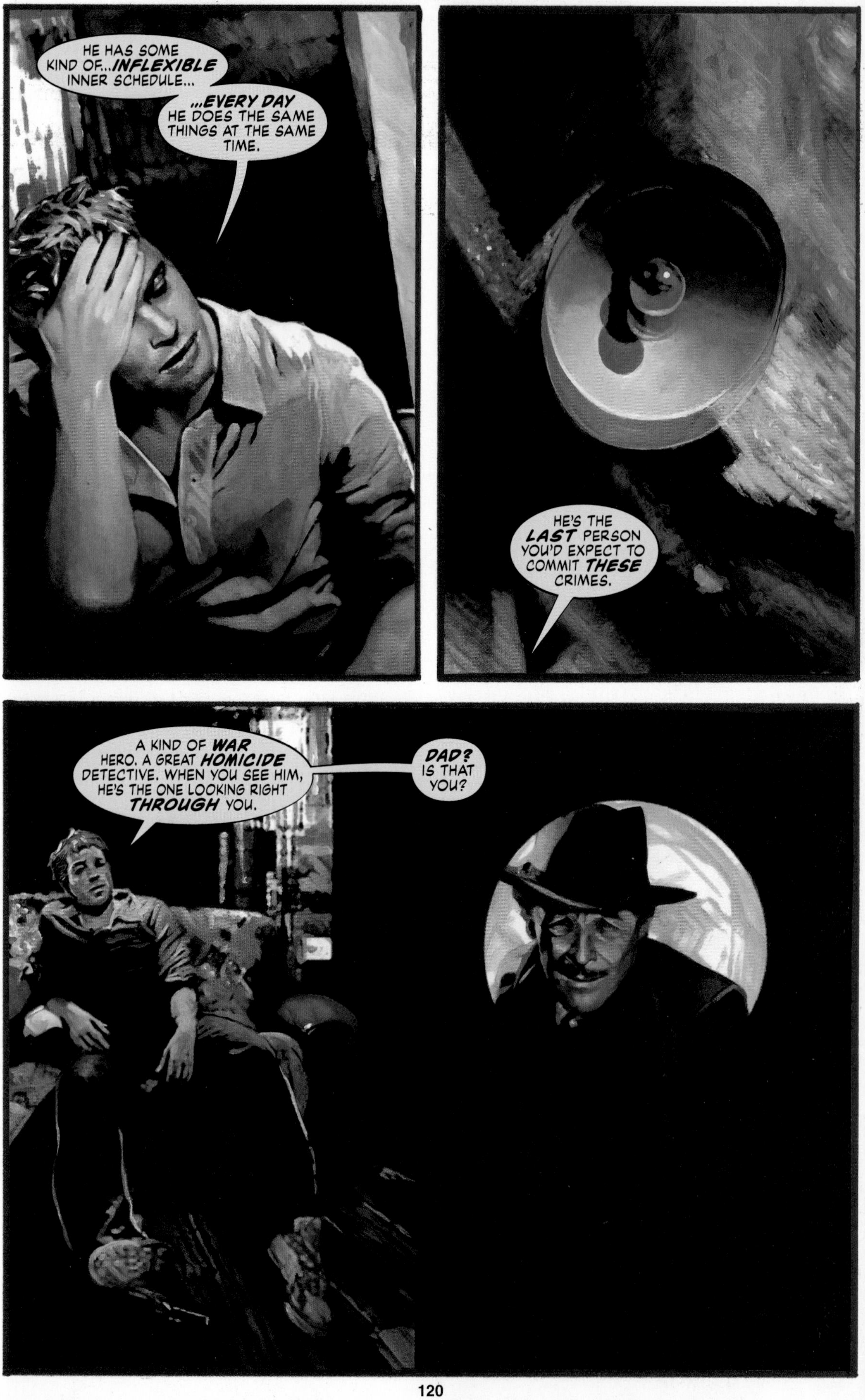
HE HAS SOME KIND OF...INFLEXIBLE INNER SCHEDULE...
...EVERY DAY HE DOES THE SAME THINGS AT THE SAME TIME.
HE'S THE LAST PERSON YOU'D EXPECT TO COMMIT THESE CRIMES.
A KIND OF WAR HERO. A GREAT HOMICIDE DETECTIVE. WHEN YOU SEE HIM, HE'S THE ONE LOOKING RIGHT THROUGH YOU.
DAD? IS THAT YOU?

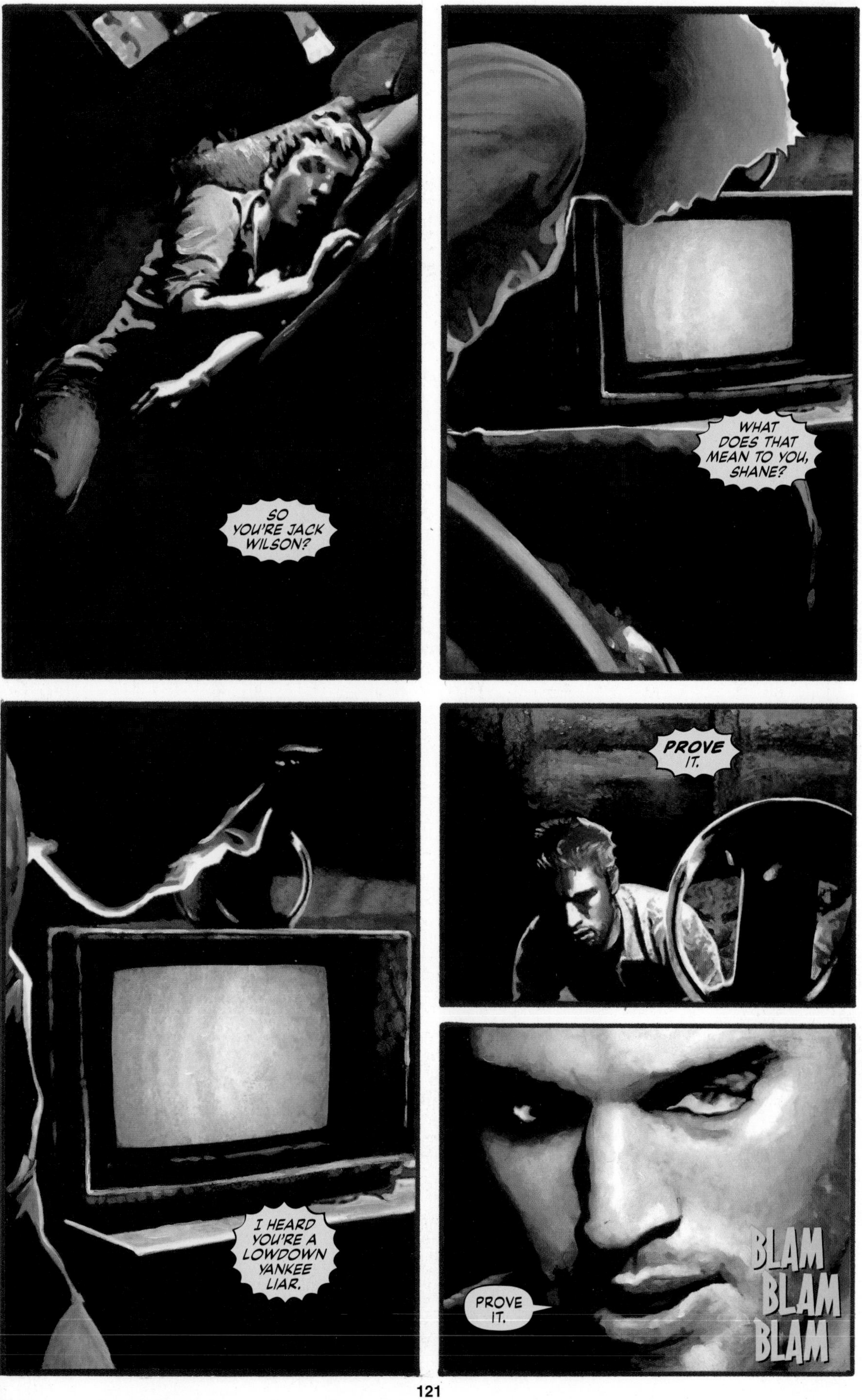
SO YOU'RE JACK WILSON?
WHAT DOES THAT MEAN TO YOU, SHANE?
I HEARD YOU'RE A LOWDOWN YANKEE LIAR.
PROVE IT.
PROVE IT.
BLAM BLAM BLAM

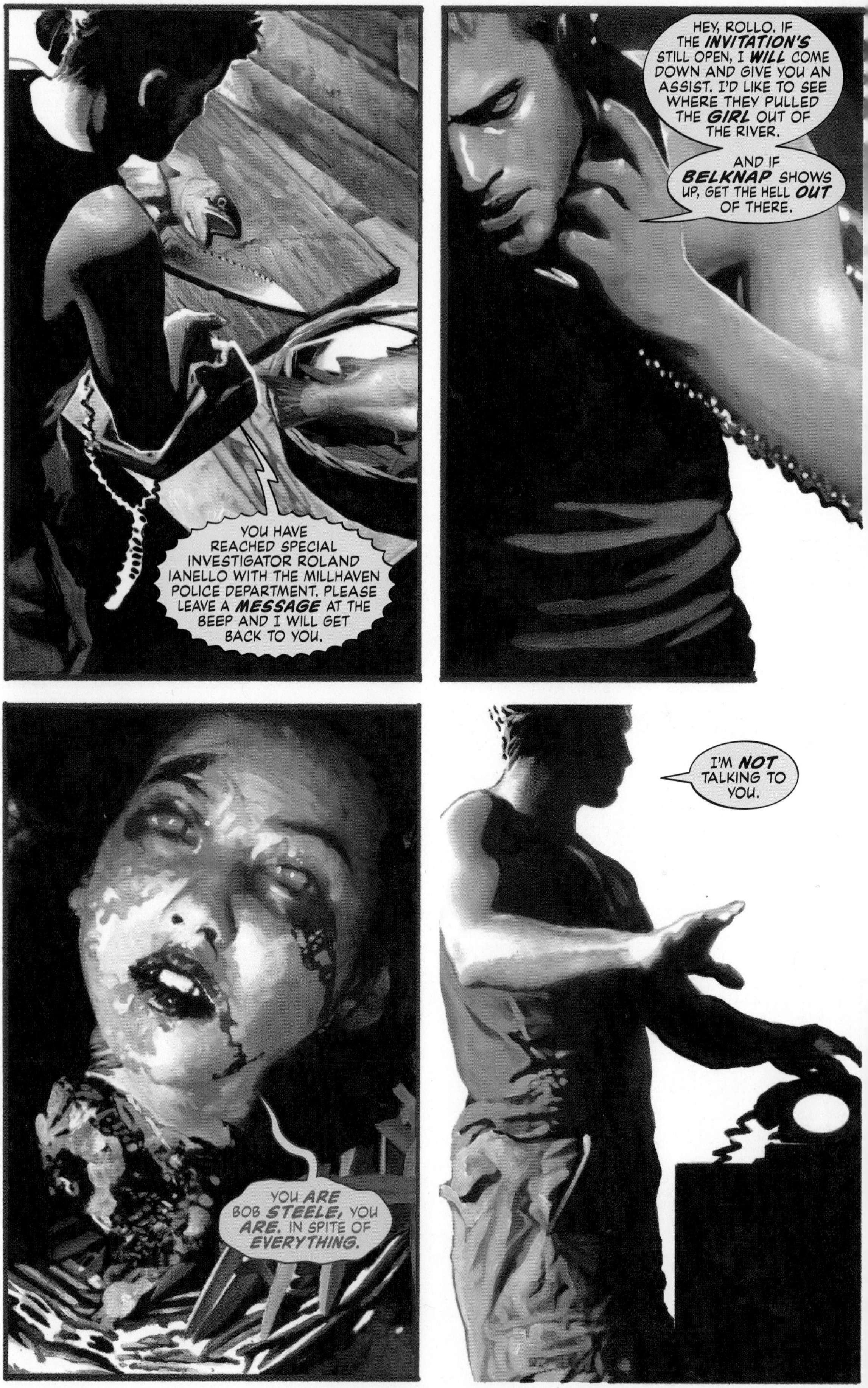
YOU HAVE REACHED SPECIAL INVESTIGATOR ROLAND IANELLO WITH THE MILLHAVEN POLICE DEPARTMENT. PLEASE LEAVE A MESSAGE AT THE BEEP AND I WILL GET BACK TO YOU.
HEY, ROLLO. IF THE INVITATION'S STILL OPEN, I WILL COME DOWN AND GIVE YOU AN ASSIST. I'D LIKE TO SEE WHERE THEY PULLED THE GIRL OUT OF THE RIVER.
AND IF BELKNAP SHOWS UP, GET THE HELL OUT OF THERE.
YOU ARE BOB STEELE, YOU ARE. IN SPITE OF EVERYTHING.
I'M NOT TALKING TO YOU.

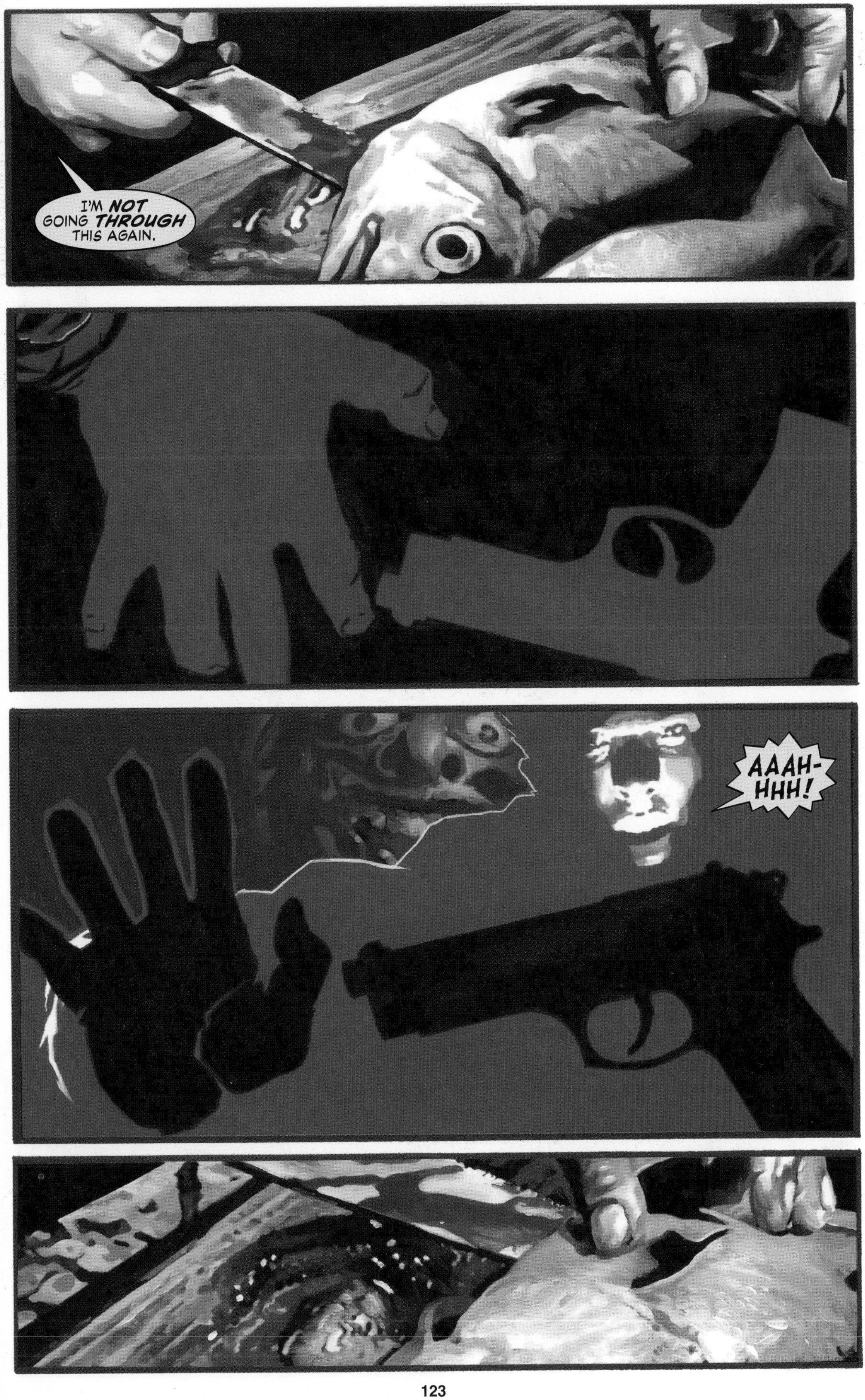
I'M **NOT** GOING **THROUGH** THIS AGAIN.
AAAH-HHH!

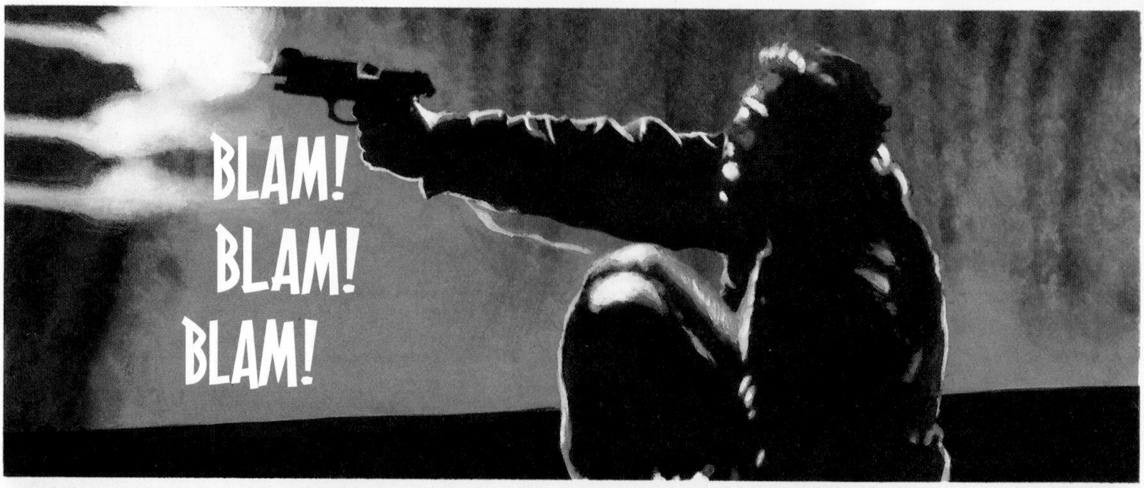
BLAM!
BLAM!
BLAM!

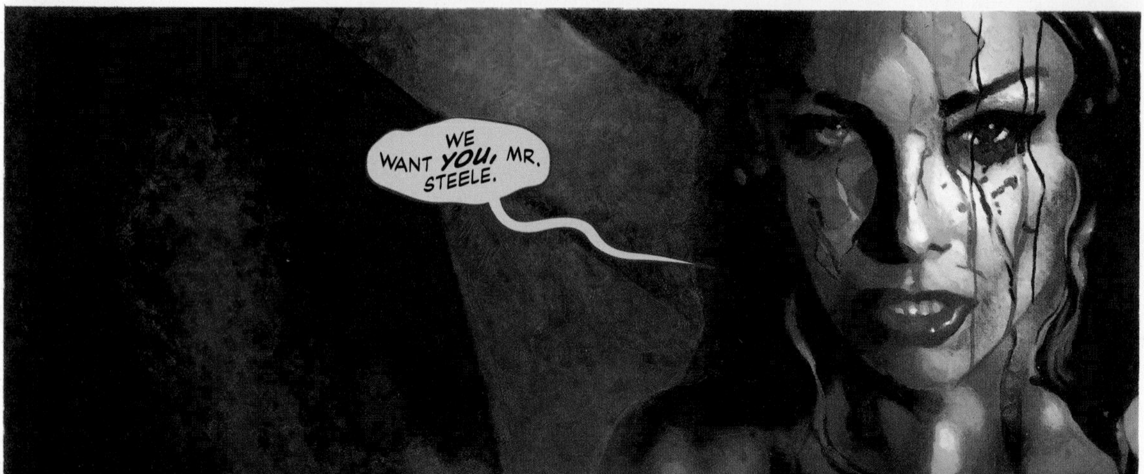
WE WANT YOU, MR. STEELE.

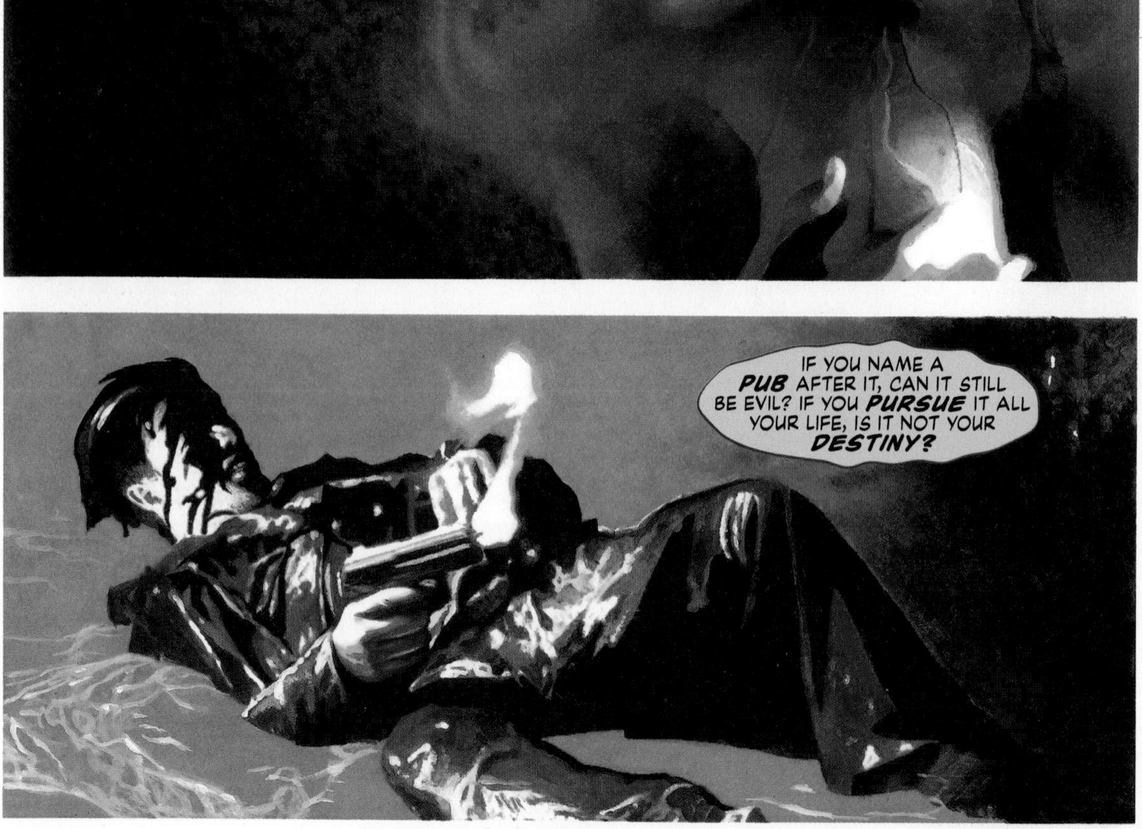
IF YOU NAME A PUB AFTER IT, CAN IT STILL BE EVIL? IF YOU PURSUE IT ALL YOUR LIFE, IS IT NOT YOUR DESTINY?

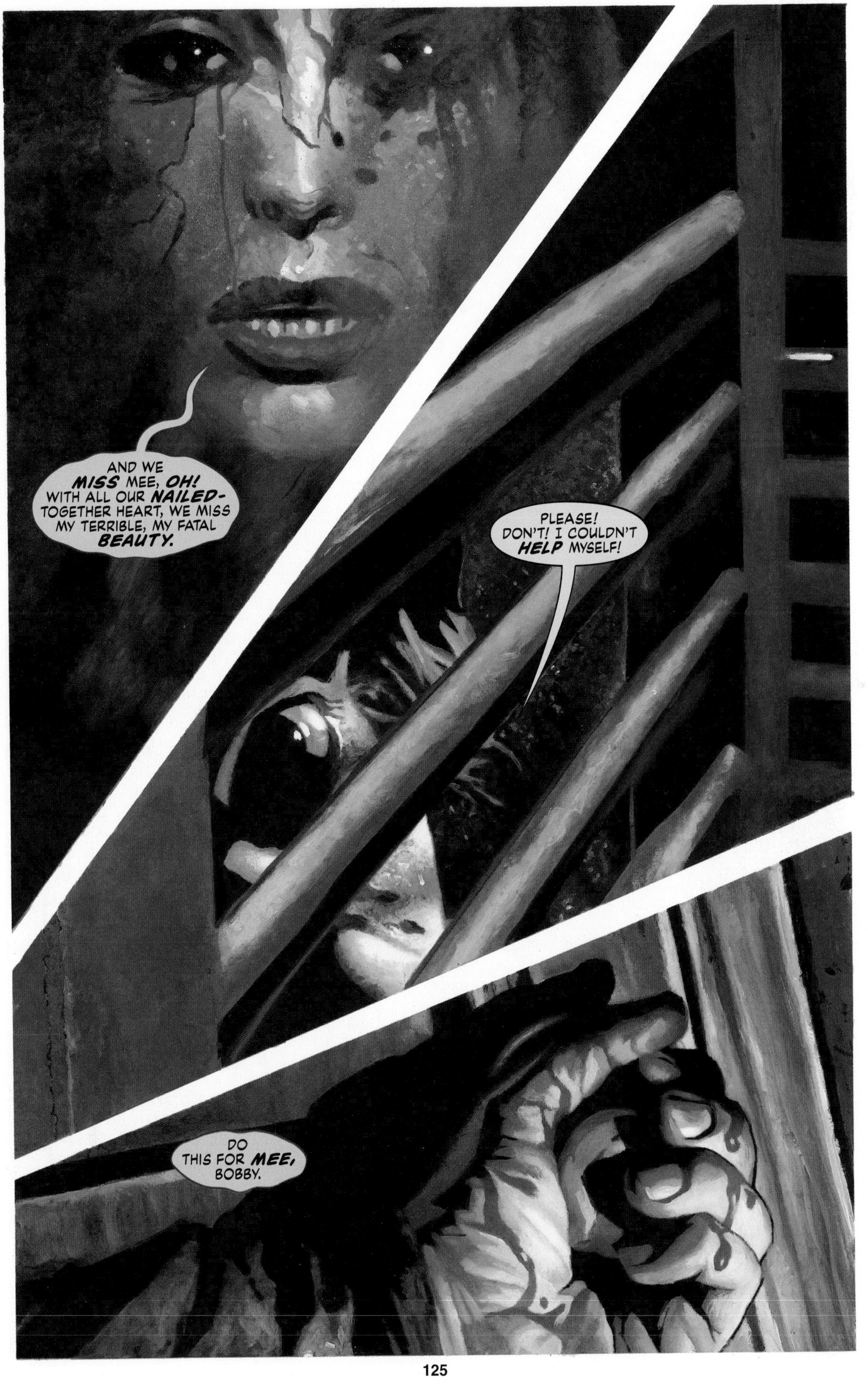
AND WE MISS MEE, OH! WITH ALL OUR NAILED-TOGETHER HEART, WE MISS MY TERRIBLE, MY FATAL BEAUTY.
PLEASE! DON'T! I COULDN'T HELP MYSELF!
DO THIS FOR MEE, BOBBY.

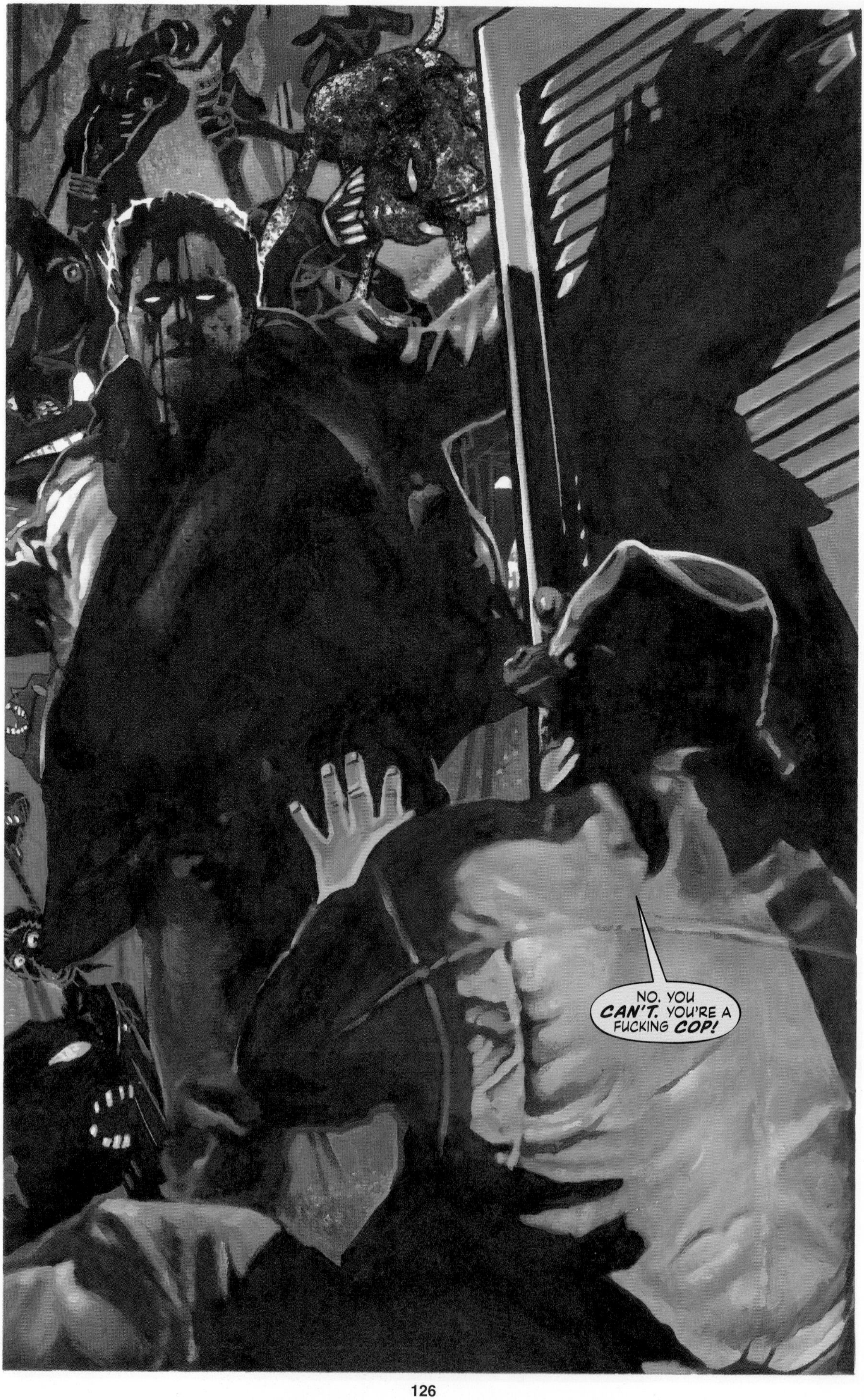
NO. YOU **CAN'T.** YOU'RE A FUCKING **COP!**

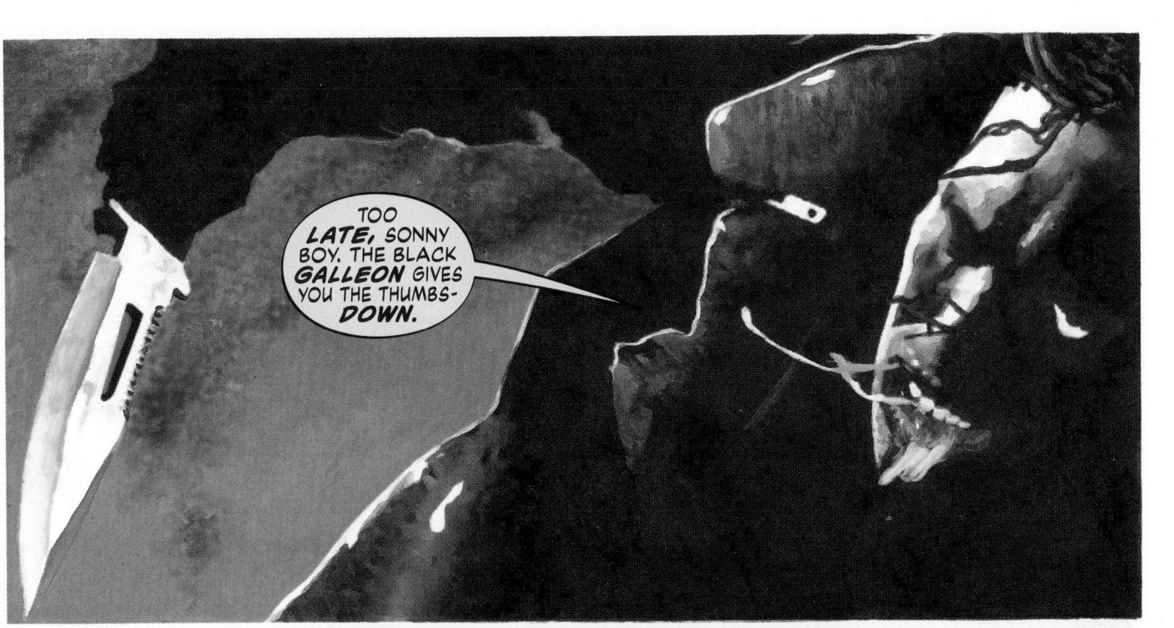
TOO LATE, SONNY BOY. THE BLACK GALLEON GIVES YOU THE THUMBS-DOWN.

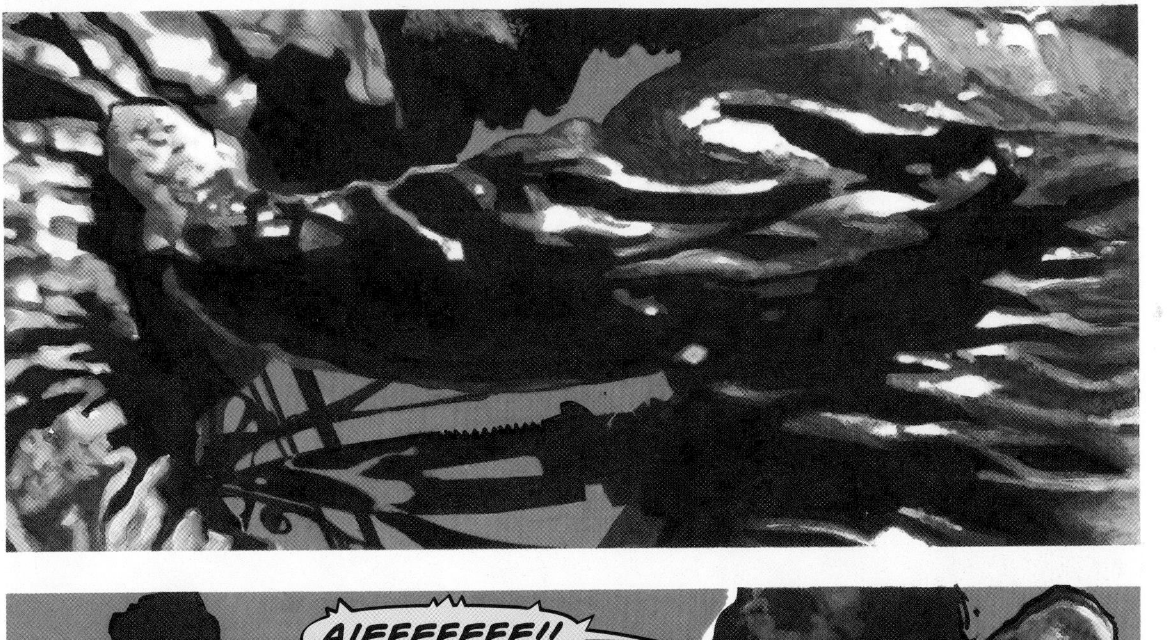

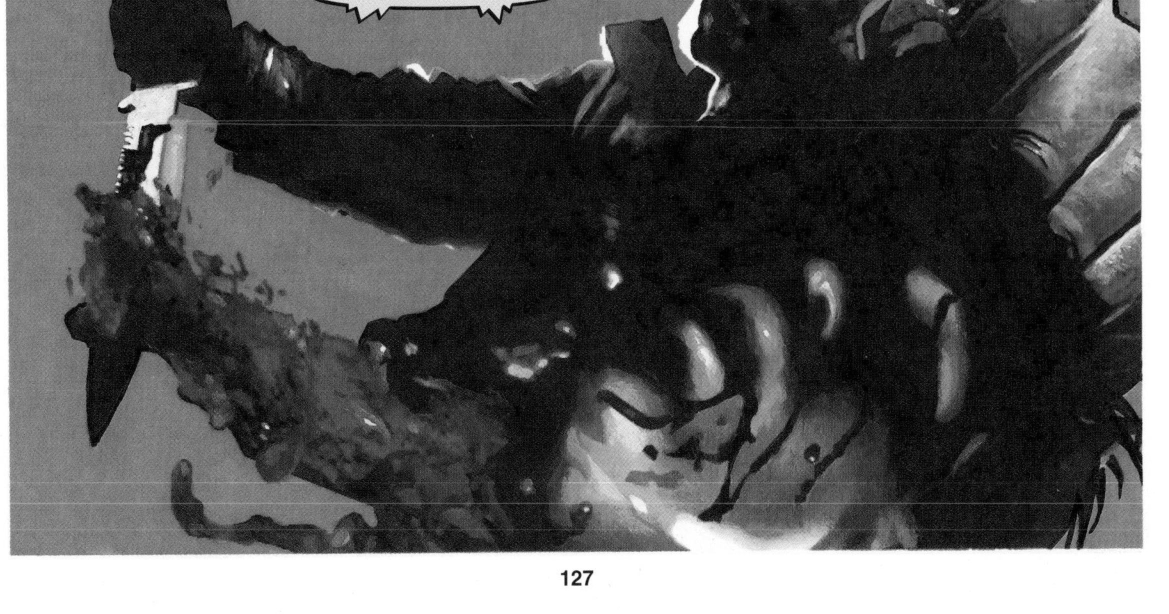
AIEEEEEEE!!

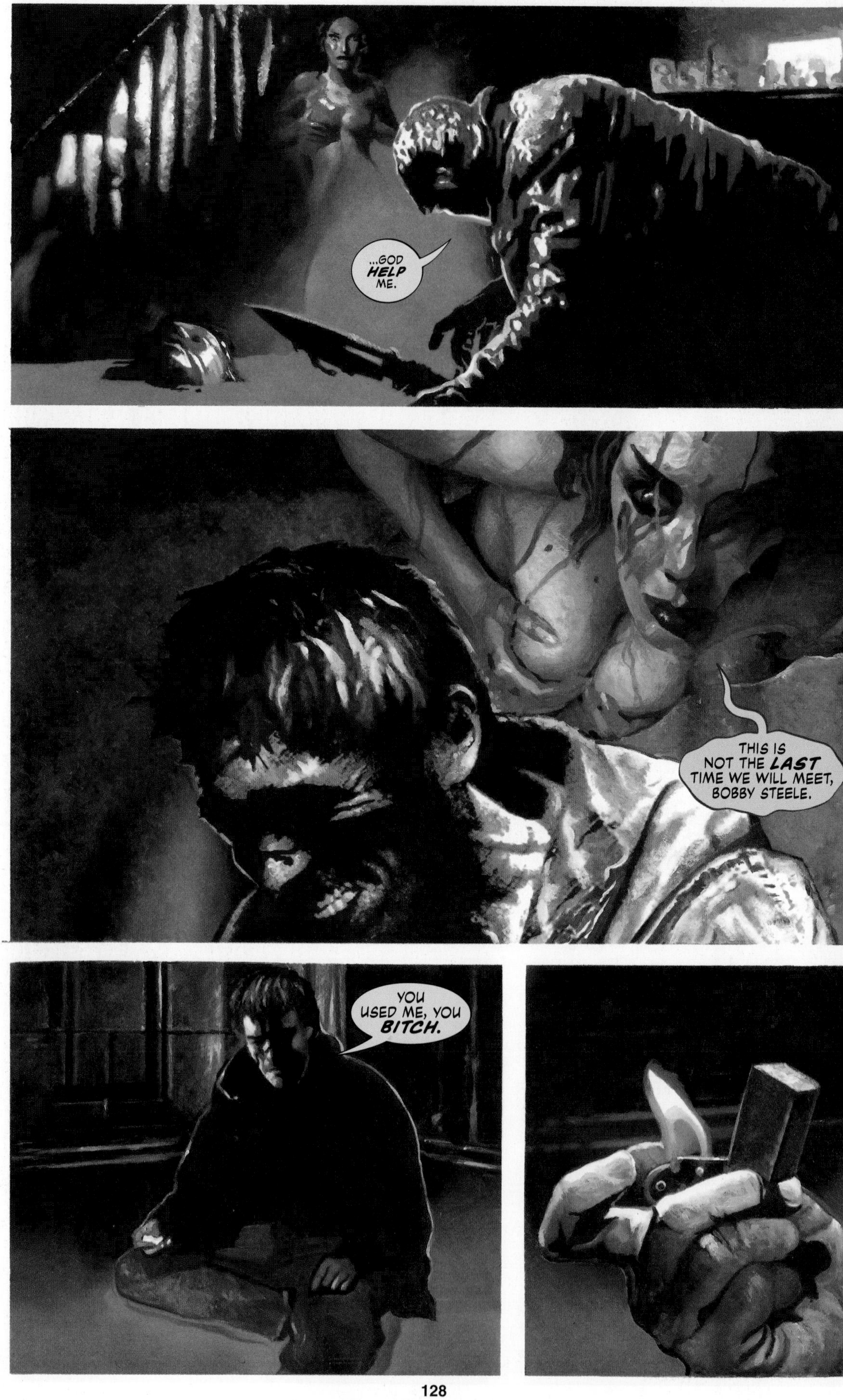
...GOD HELP ME.
THIS IS NOT THE LAST TIME WE WILL MEET, BOBBY STEELE.
YOU USED ME, YOU BITCH.

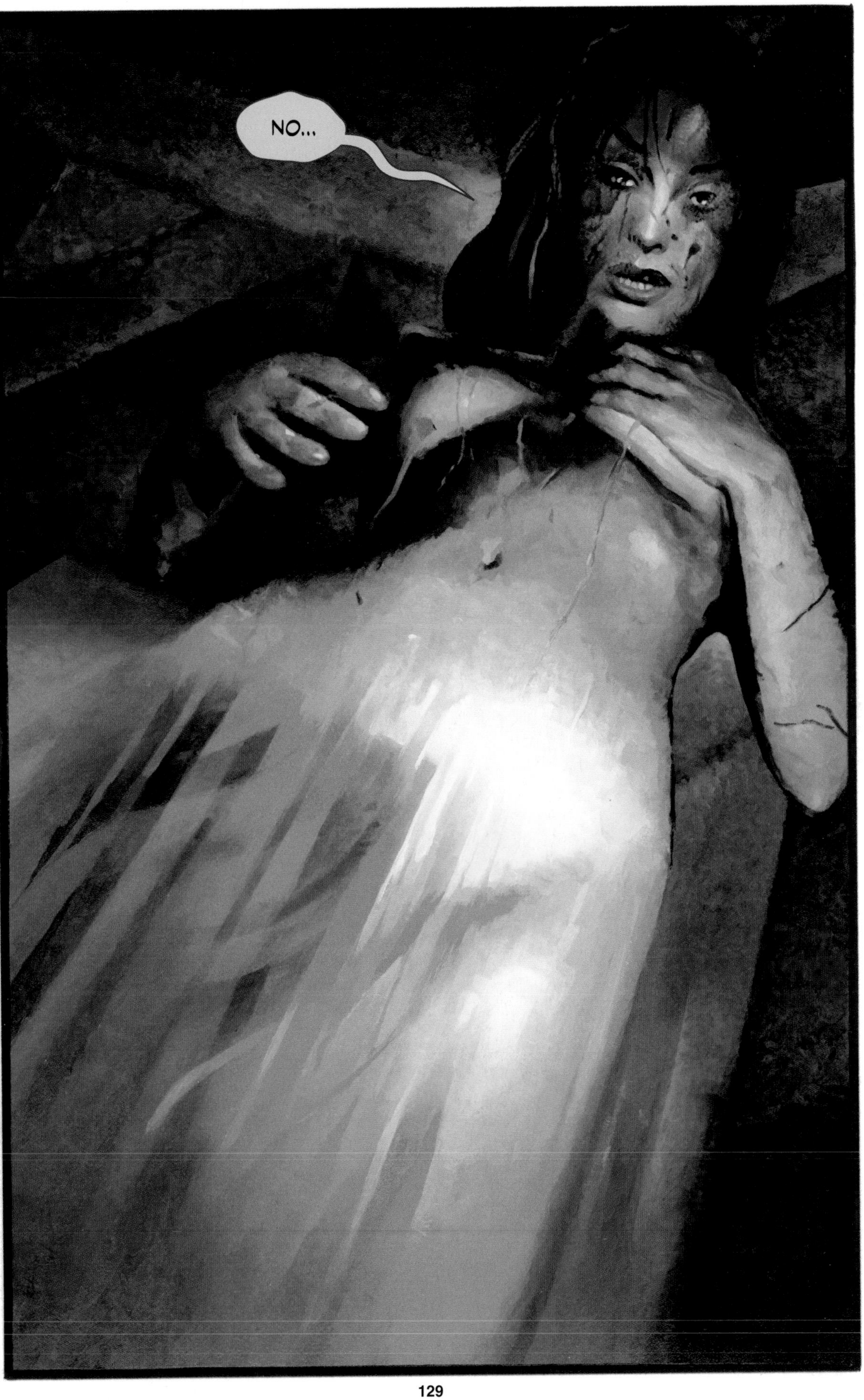
NO...

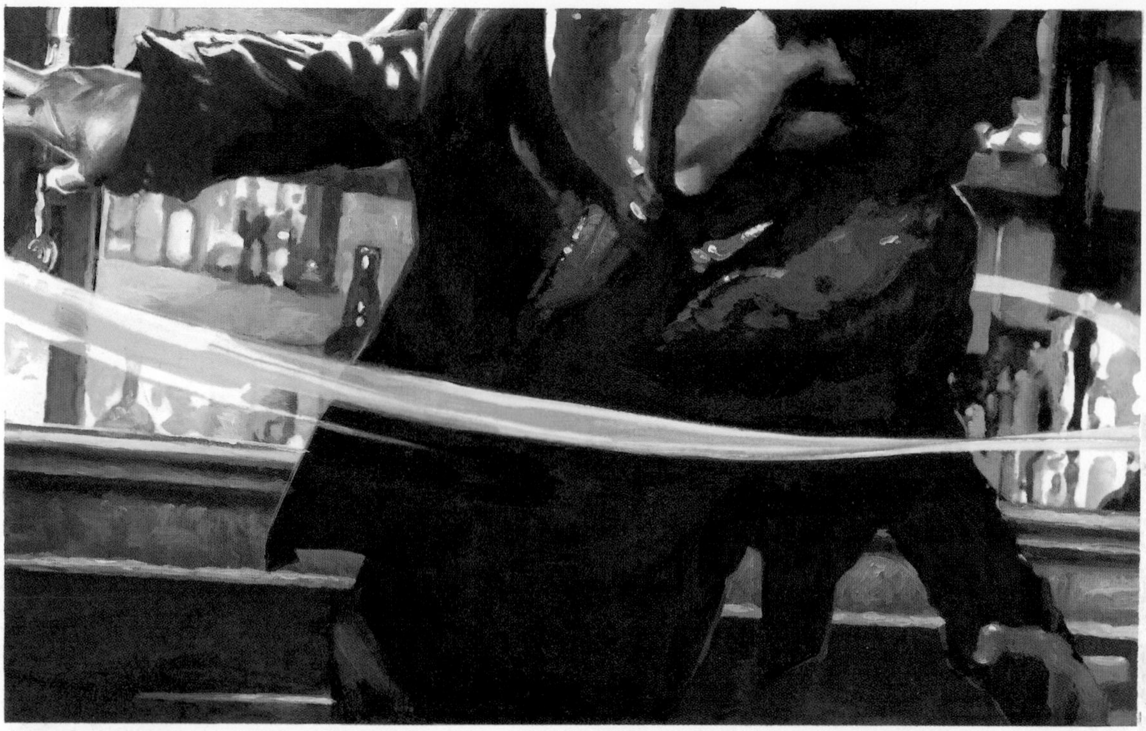

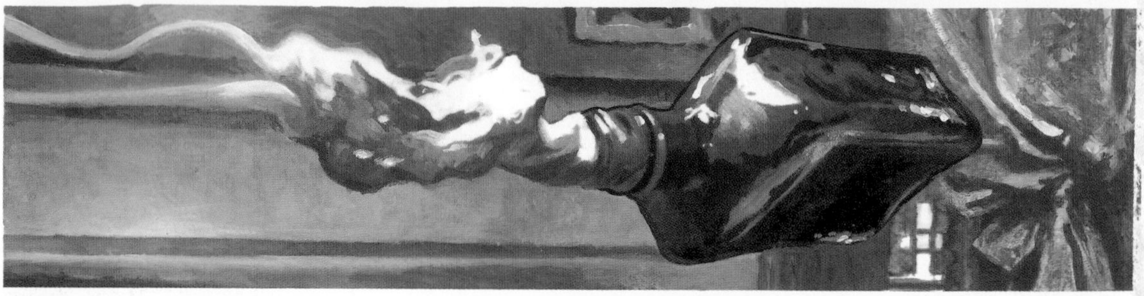

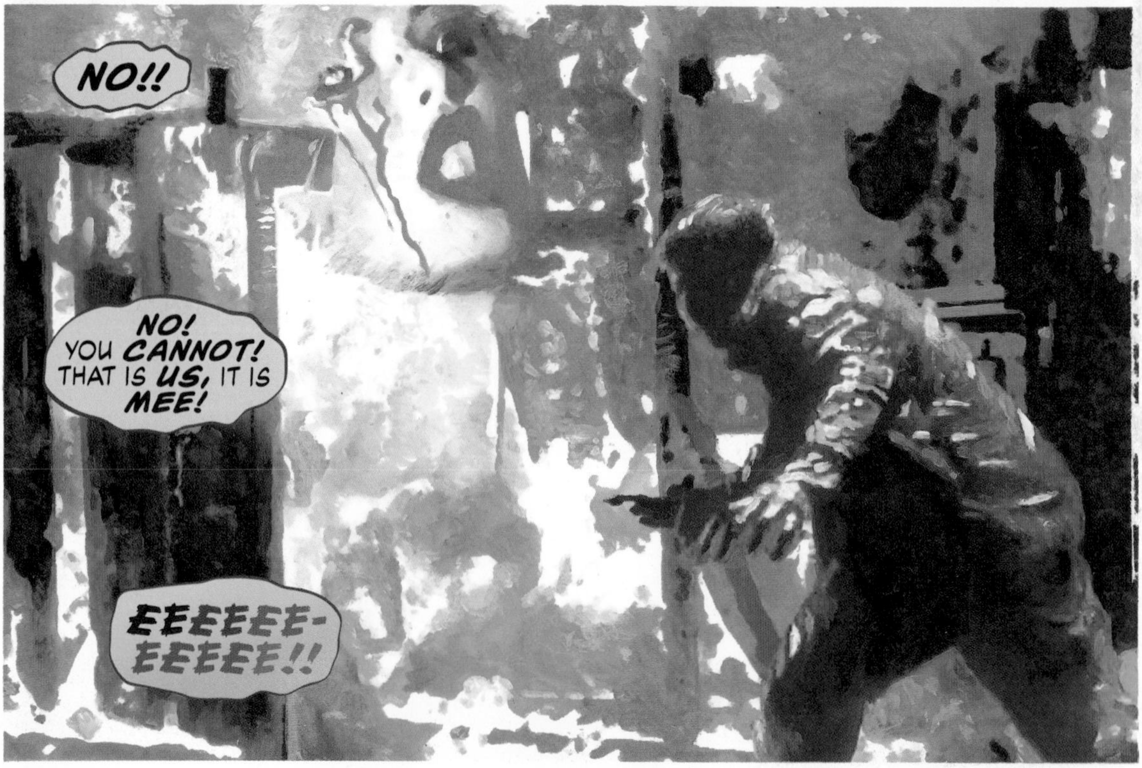
NO!!
NO! YOU CANNOT! THAT IS US, IT IS MEE!
EEEEEE-EEEEEE!!

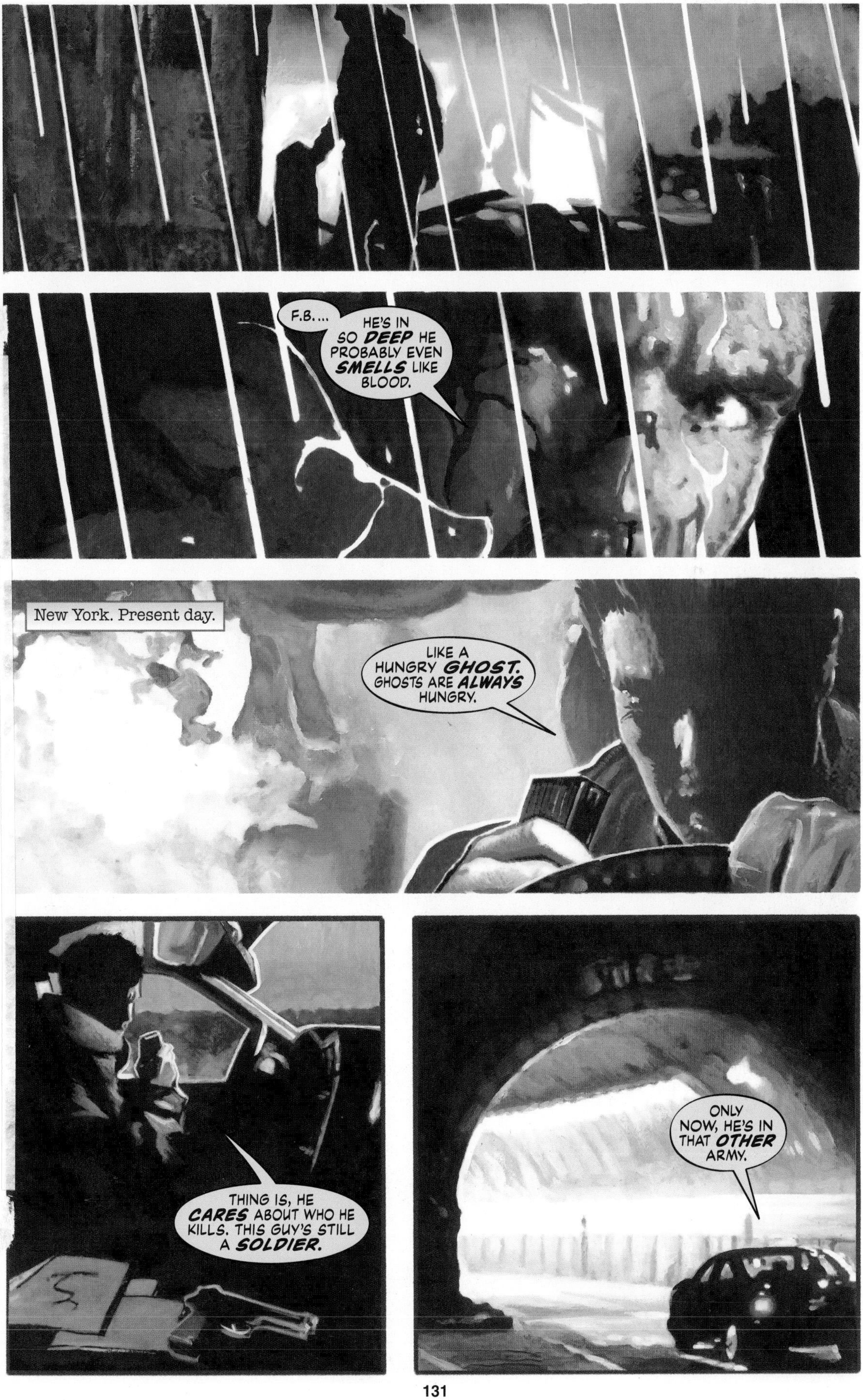
F.B....
HE'S IN SO DEEP HE PROBABLY EVEN SMELLS LIKE BLOOD.
New York. Present day.
LIKE A HUNGRY GHOST. GHOSTS ARE ALWAYS HUNGRY.
THING IS, HE CARES ABOUT WHO HE KILLS. THIS GUY'S STILL A SOLDIER.
ONLY NOW, HE'S IN THAT OTHER ARMY.

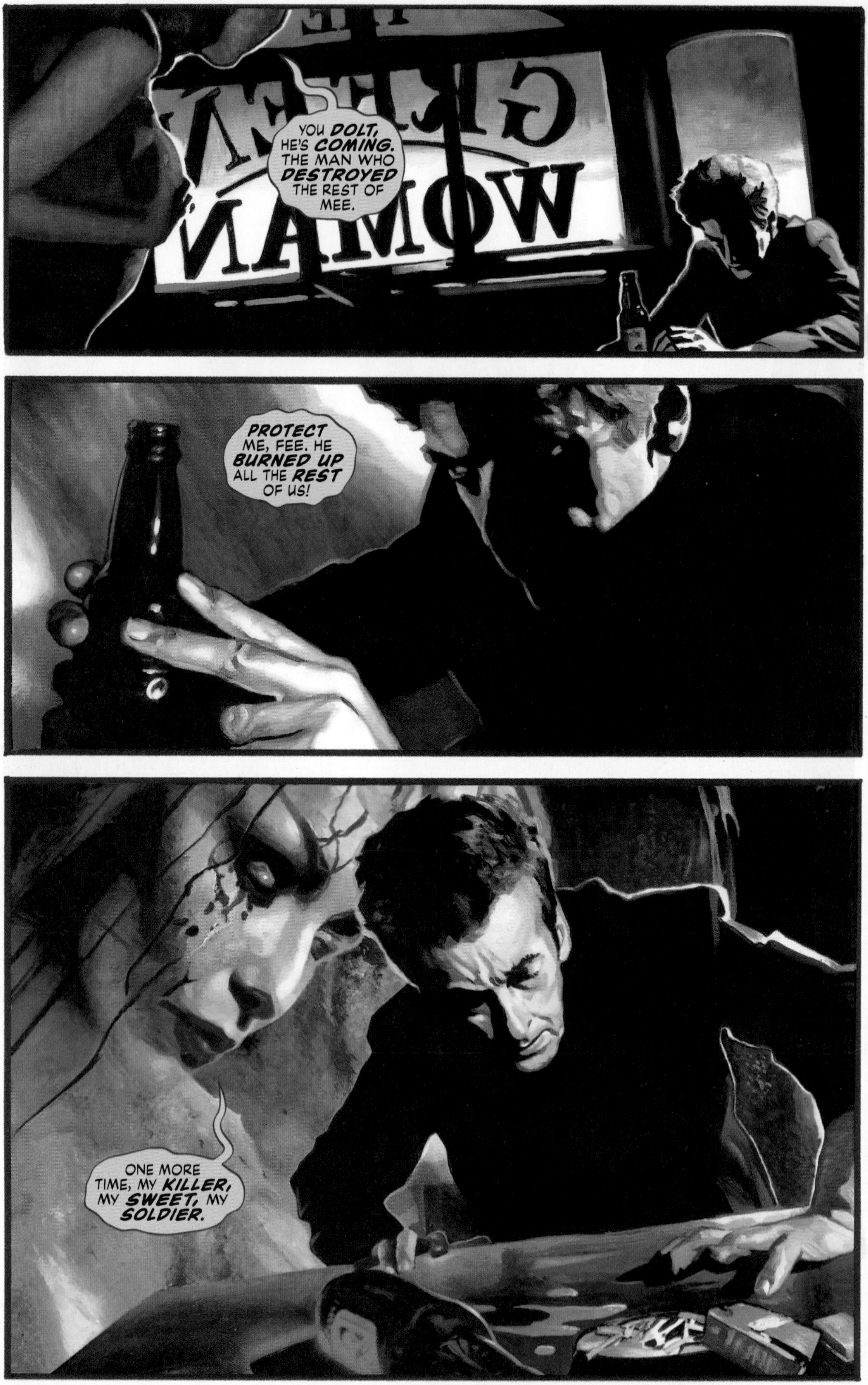
YOU DOLT, HE'S COMING. THE MAN WHO DESTROYED THE REST OF MEE.
PROTECT ME, FEE. HE BURNED UP ALL THE REST OF US!
ONE MORE TIME, MY KILLER, MY SWEET, MY SOLDIER.

FRANK?
FRANK, YOU HAVE TO STOP. IT MUST BE OVER.
BUT DO YOU KNOW WHAT I JUST UNDERSTOOD? THAT I NEVER HAD A CHOICE.

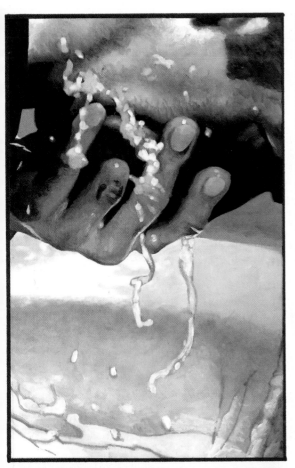

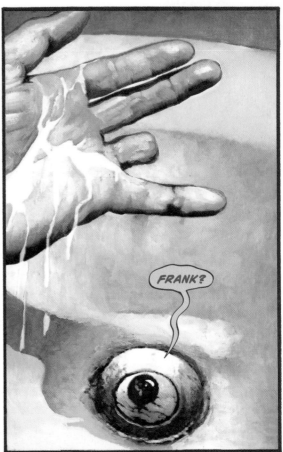

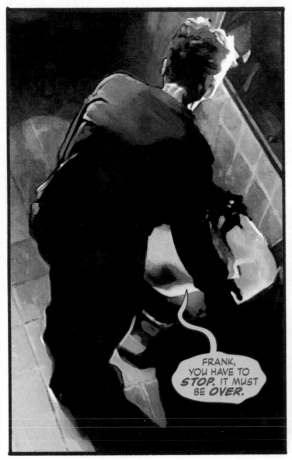

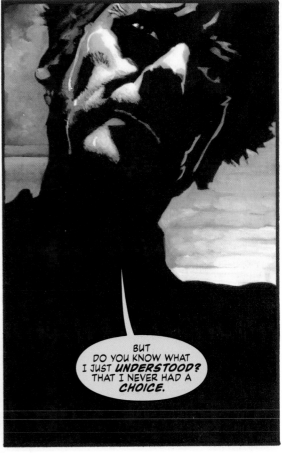

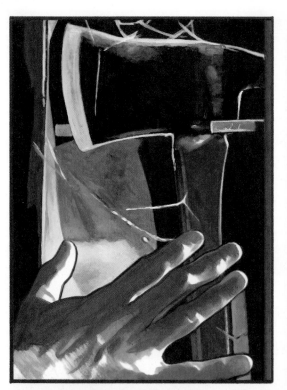

SMASH!

THWACK!!
CHOKK!
I...I CAN'T.

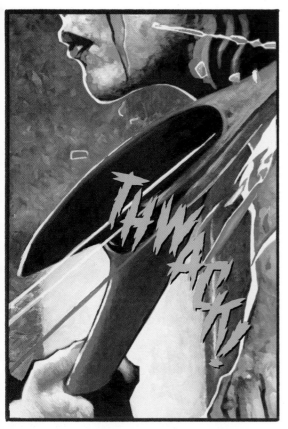

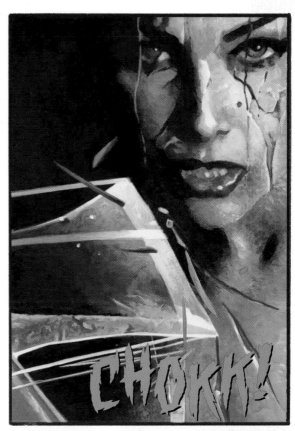

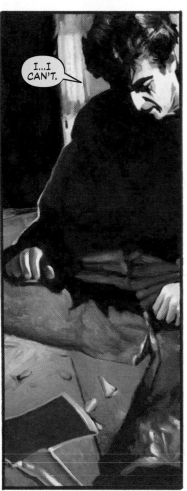

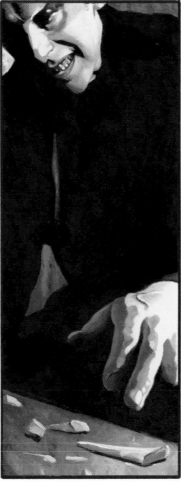

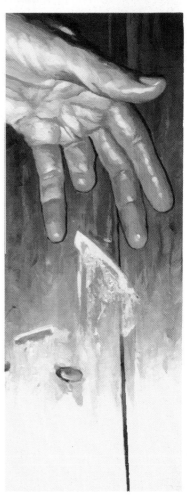

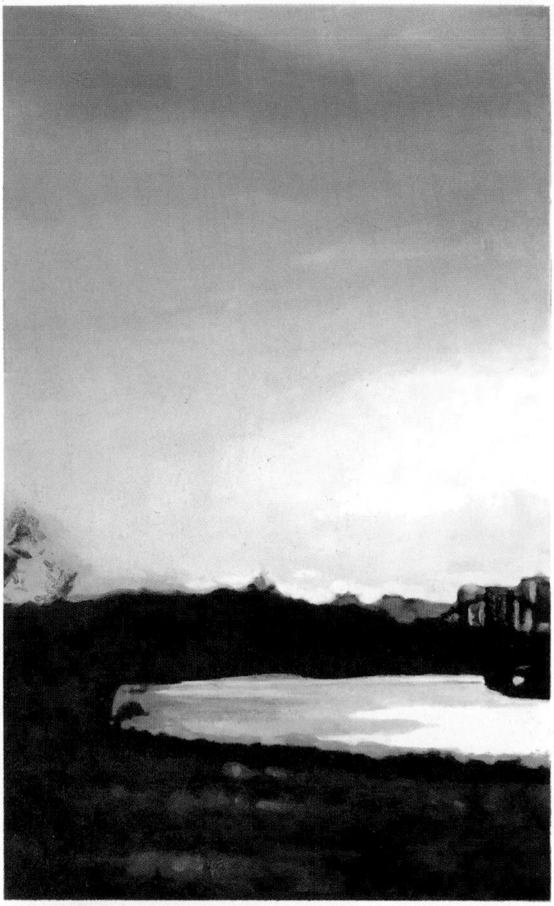

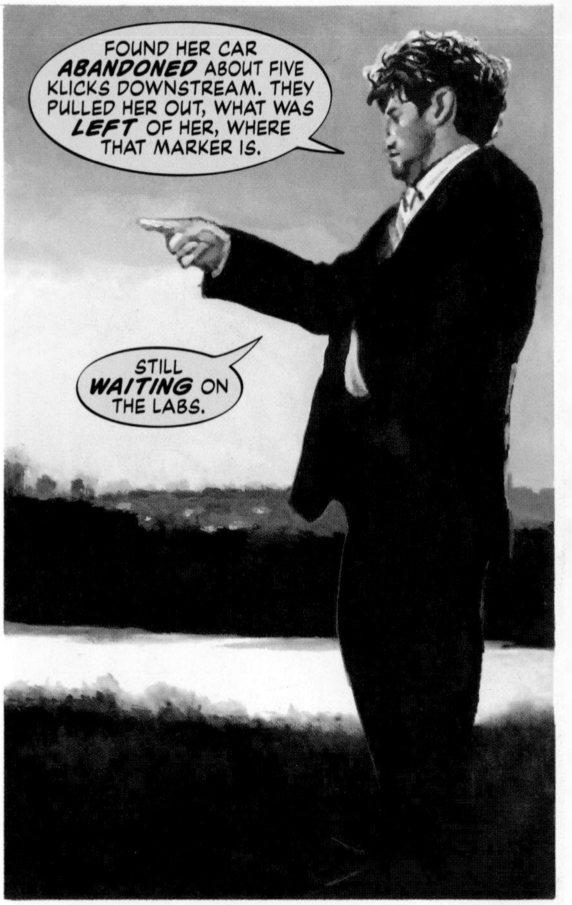
FOUND HER CAR ABANDONED ABOUT FIVE KLICKS DOWNSTREAM. THEY PULLED HER OUT, WHAT WAS LEFT OF HER, WHERE THAT MARKER IS.
STILL WAITING ON THE LABS.

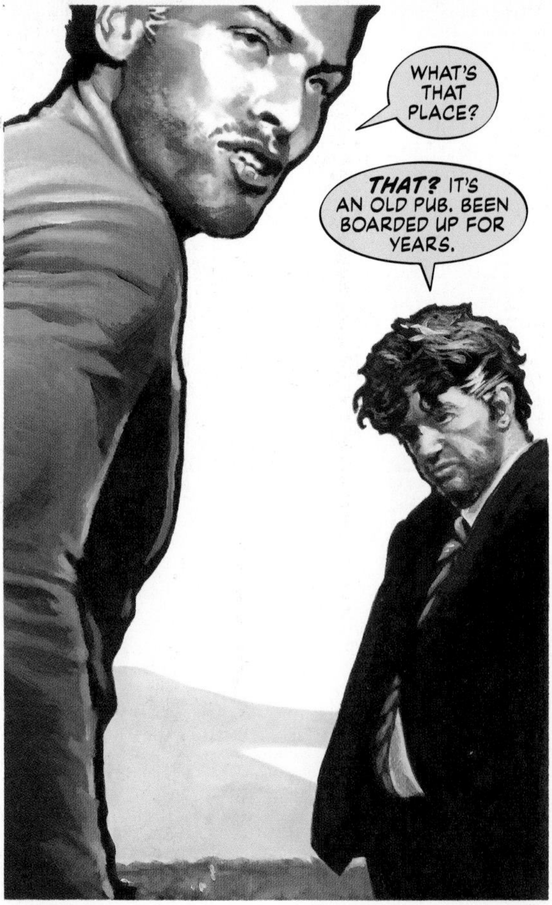
WHAT'S THAT PLACE?
THAT? IT'S AN OLD PUB. BEEN BOARDED UP FOR YEARS.

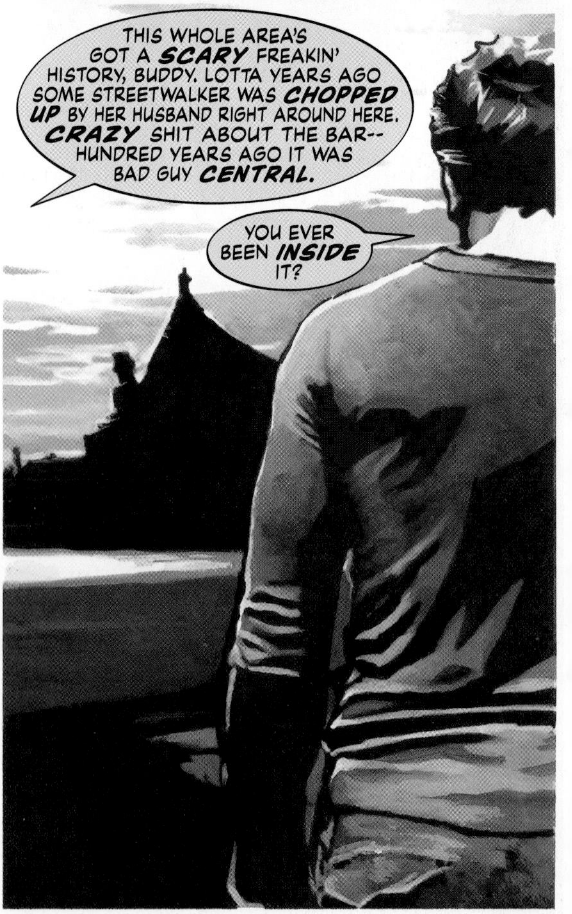
THIS WHOLE AREA'S GOT A SCARY FREAKIN' HISTORY, BUDDY. LOTTA YEARS AGO SOME STREETWALKER WAS CHOPPED UP BY HER HUSBAND RIGHT AROUND HERE. CRAZY SHIT ABOUT THE BAR-- HUNDRED YEARS AGO IT WAS BAD GUY CENTRAL.
YOU EVER BEEN INSIDE IT?

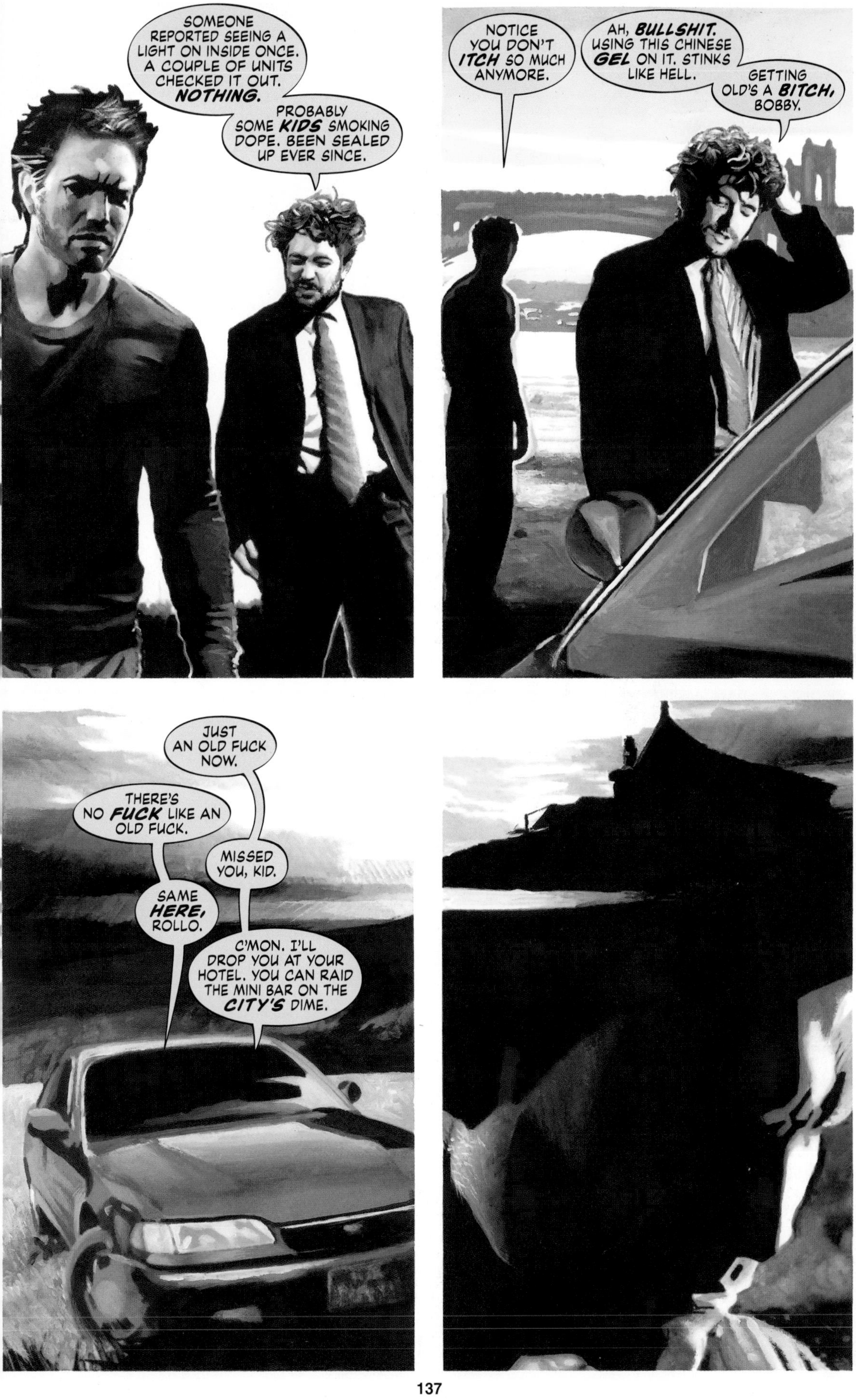
SOMEONE REPORTED SEEING A LIGHT ON INSIDE ONCE. A COUPLE OF UNITS CHECKED IT OUT. NOTHING.
PROBABLY SOME KIDS SMOKING DOPE. BEEN SEALED UP EVER SINCE.
NOTICE YOU DON'T ITCH SO MUCH ANYMORE.
AH, BULLSHIT. USING THIS CHINESE GEL ON IT. STINKS LIKE HELL.
GETTING OLD'S A BITCH, BOBBY.
JUST AN OLD FUCK NOW.
THERE'S NO FUCK LIKE AN OLD FUCK.
MISSED YOU, KID.
SAME HERE, ROLLO.
C'MON. I'LL DROP YOU AT YOUR HOTEL. YOU CAN RAID THE MINI BAR ON THE CITY'S DIME.

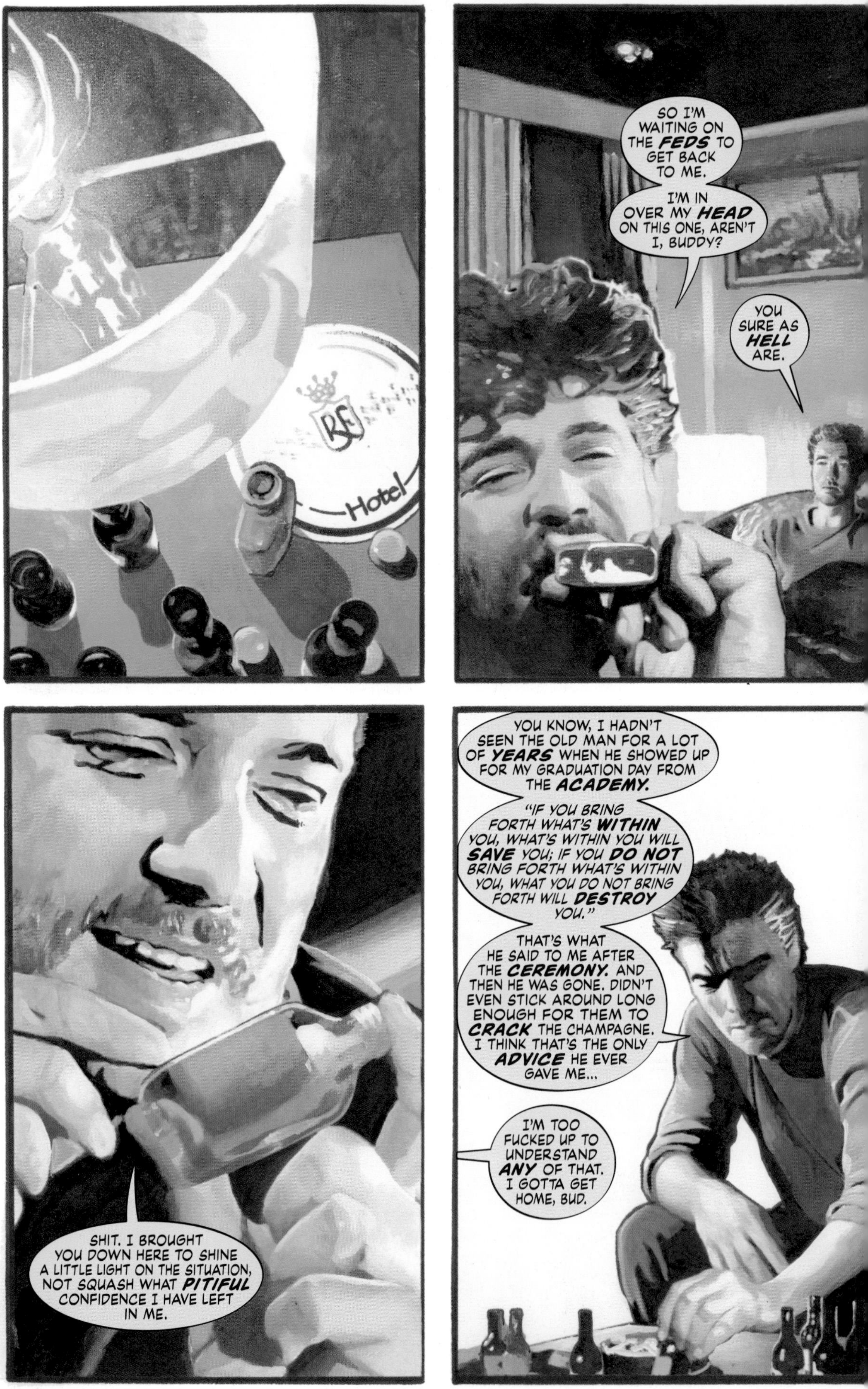
SO I'M WAITING ON THE FEDS TO GET BACK TO ME.
I'M IN OVER MY HEAD ON THIS ONE, AREN'T I, BUDDY?
YOU SURE AS HELL ARE.
SHIT. I BROUGHT YOU DOWN HERE TO SHINE A LITTLE LIGHT ON THE SITUATION, NOT SQUASH WHAT PITIFUL CONFIDENCE I HAVE LEFT IN ME.
YOU KNOW, I HADN'T SEEN THE OLD MAN FOR A LOT OF YEARS WHEN HE SHOWED UP FOR MY GRADUATION DAY FROM THE ACADEMY.
"IF YOU BRING FORTH WHAT'S WITHIN YOU, WHAT'S WITHIN YOU WILL SAVE YOU; IF YOU DO NOT BRING FORTH WHAT'S WITHIN YOU, WHAT YOU DO NOT BRING FORTH WILL DESTROY YOU."
THAT'S WHAT HE SAID TO ME AFTER THE CEREMONY. AND THEN HE WAS GONE. DIDN'T EVEN STICK AROUND LONG ENOUGH FOR THEM TO CRACK THE CHAMPAGNE. I THINK THAT'S THE ONLY ADVICE HE EVER GAVE ME...
I'M TOO FUCKED UP TO UNDERSTAND ANY OF THAT. I GOTTA GET HOME, BUD.

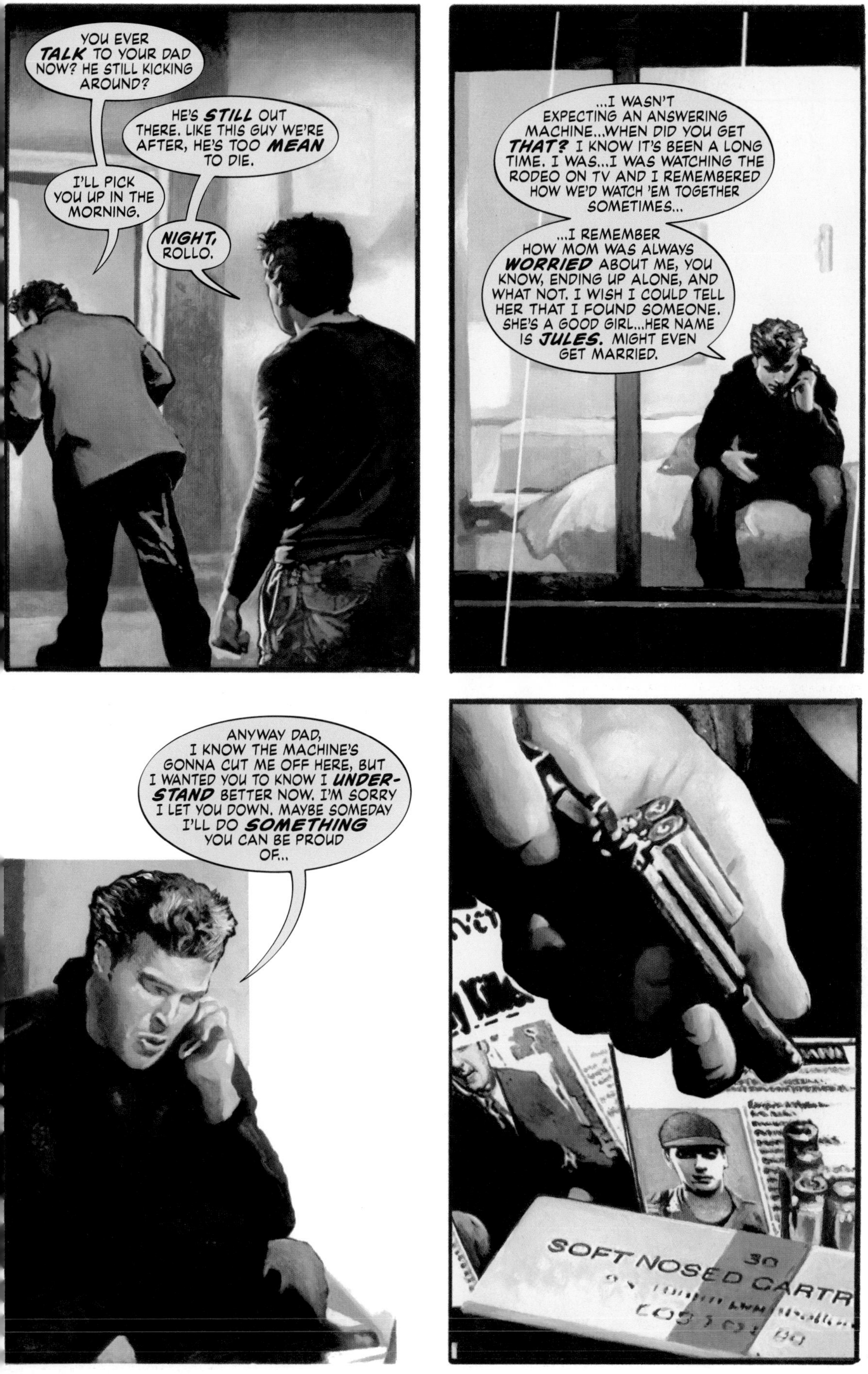
YOU EVER TALK TO YOUR DAD NOW? HE STILL KICKING AROUND?
HE'S STILL OUT THERE. LIKE THIS GUY WE'RE AFTER, HE'S TOO MEAN TO DIE.
I'LL PICK YOU UP IN THE MORNING.
NIGHT, ROLLO.
...I WASN'T EXPECTING AN ANSWERING MACHINE...WHEN DID YOU GET THAT? I KNOW IT'S BEEN A LONG TIME. I WAS...I WAS WATCHING THE RODEO ON TV AND I REMEMBERED HOW WE'D WATCH 'EM TOGETHER SOMETIMES...
...I REMEMBER HOW MOM WAS ALWAYS WORRIED ABOUT ME, YOU KNOW, ENDING UP ALONE, AND WHAT NOT. I WISH I COULD TELL HER THAT I FOUND SOMEONE. SHE'S A GOOD GIRL...HER NAME IS JULES. MIGHT EVEN GET MARRIED.
ANYWAY DAD, I KNOW THE MACHINE'S GONNA CUT ME OFF HERE, BUT I WANTED YOU TO KNOW I UNDERSTAND BETTER NOW. I'M SORRY I LET YOU DOWN. MAYBE SOMEDAY I'LL DO SOMETHING YOU CAN BE PROUD OF...
30
SOFT NOSED CARTR

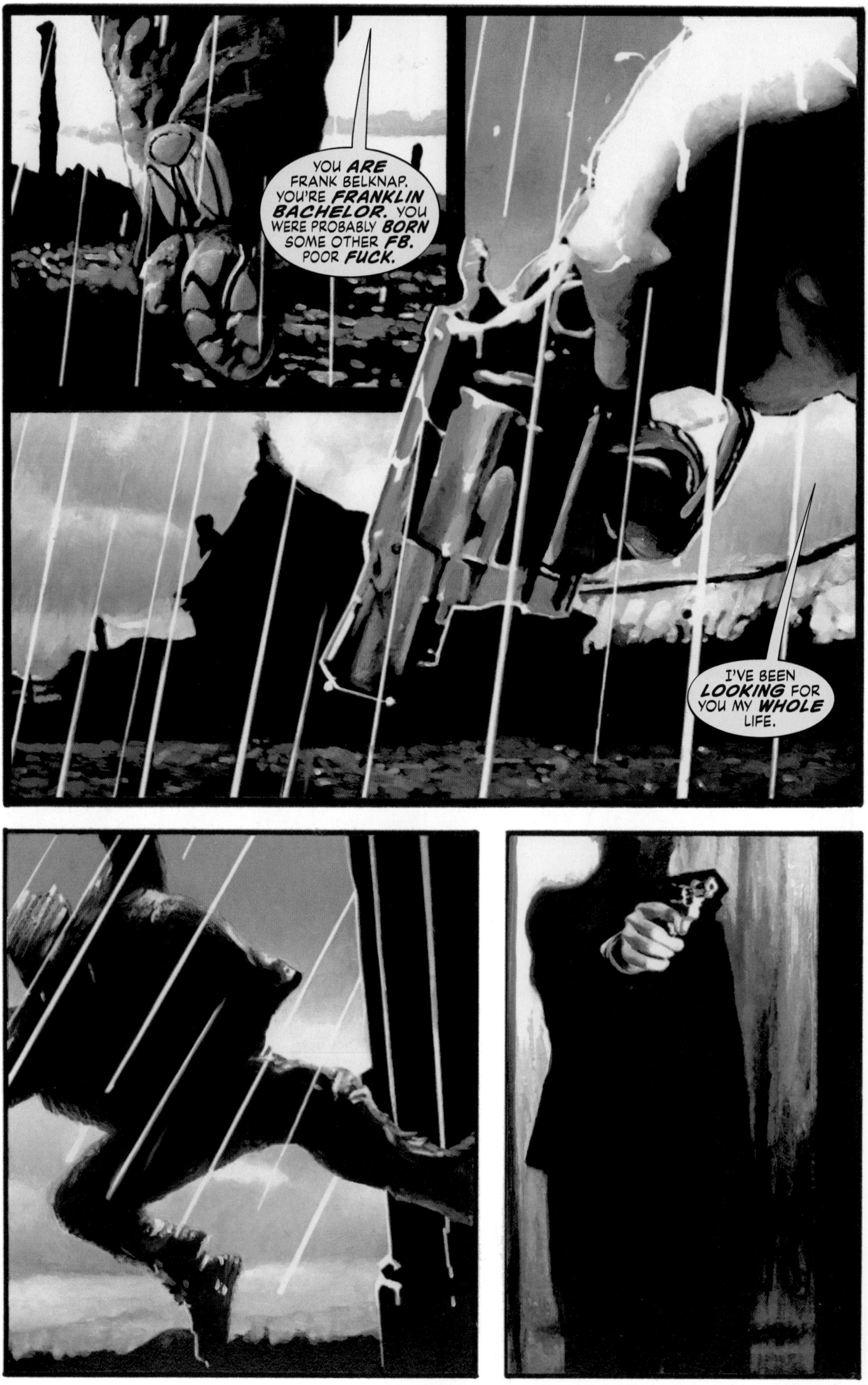

YOU ARE FRANK BELKNAP. YOU'RE FRANKLIN BACHELOR. YOU WERE PROBABLY BORN SOME OTHER FB. POOR FUCK.
I'VE BEEN LOOKING FOR YOU MY WHOLE LIFE.

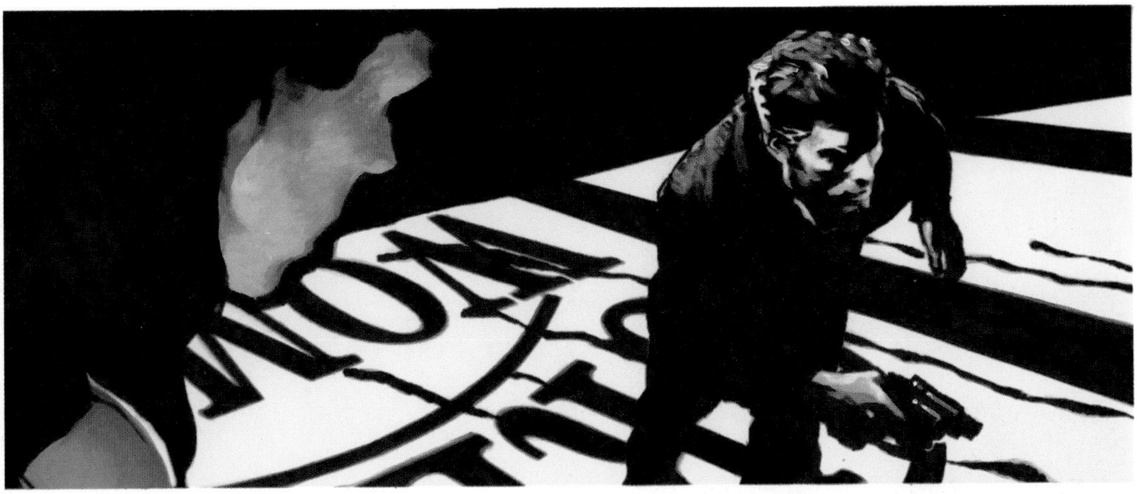

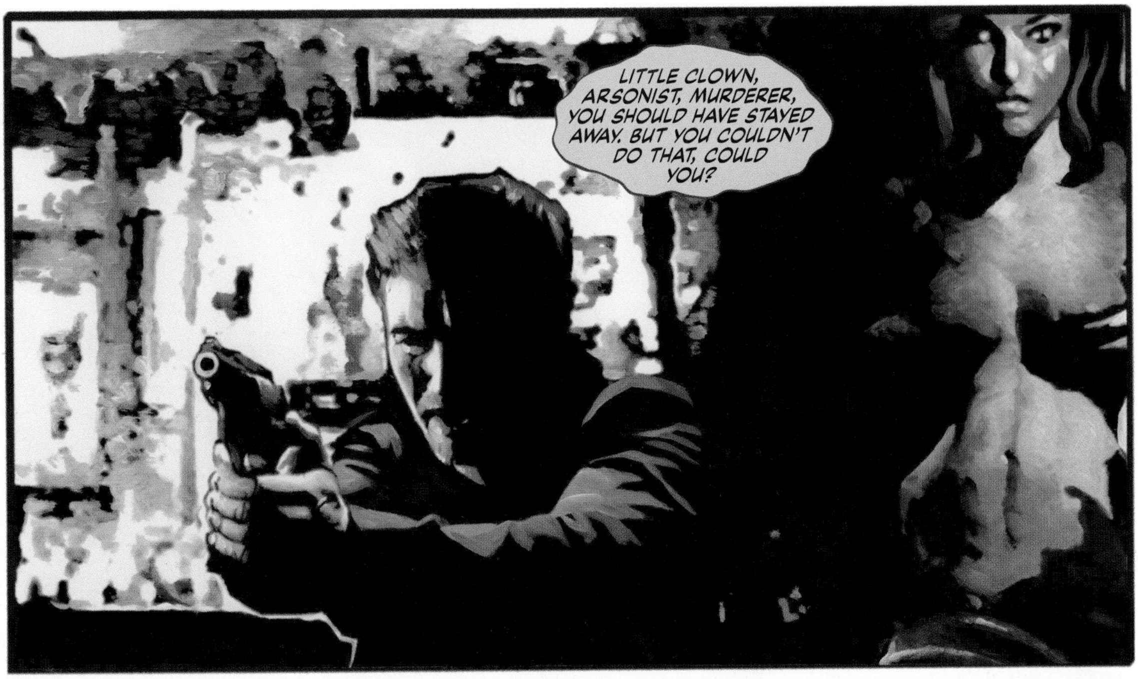

LITTLE CLOWN, ARSONIST, MURDERER, YOU SHOULD HAVE STAYED AWAY. BUT YOU COULDN'T DO THAT, COULD YOU?

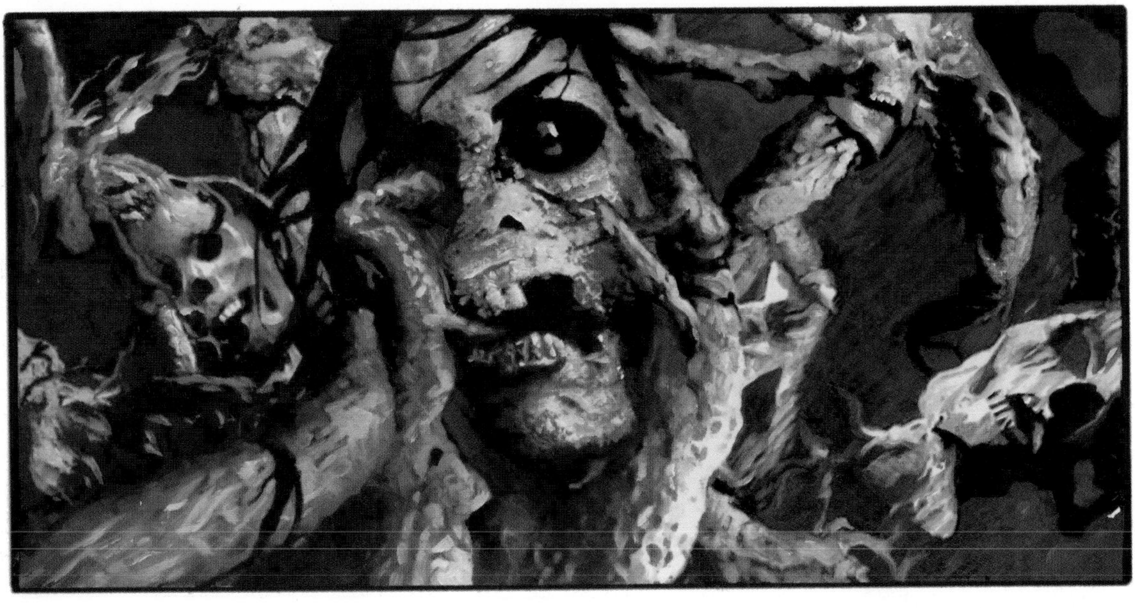

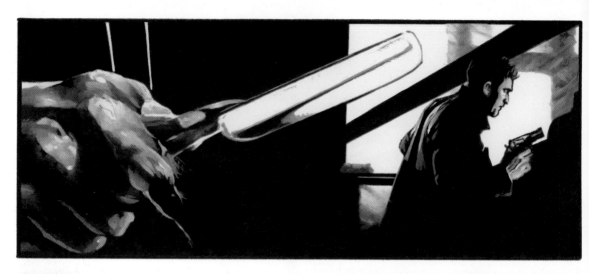

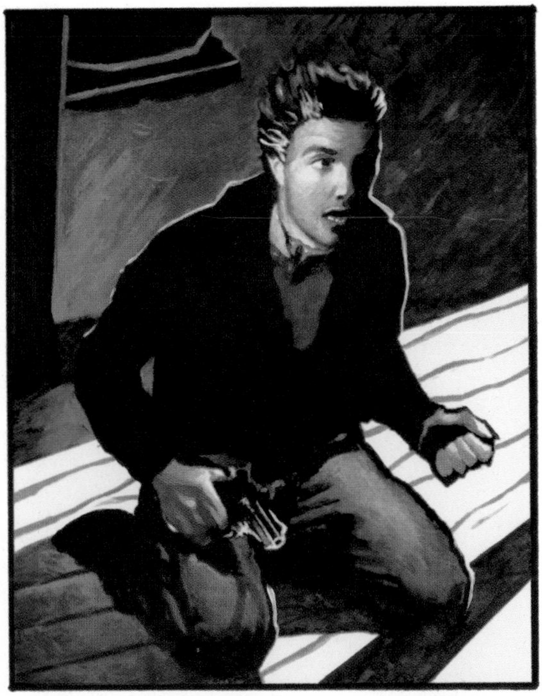

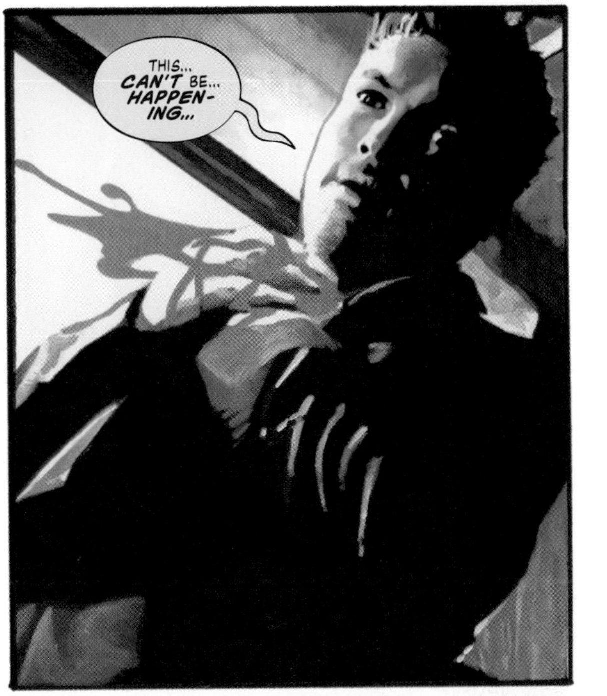
THIS... CAN'T BE... HAPPEN-ING...

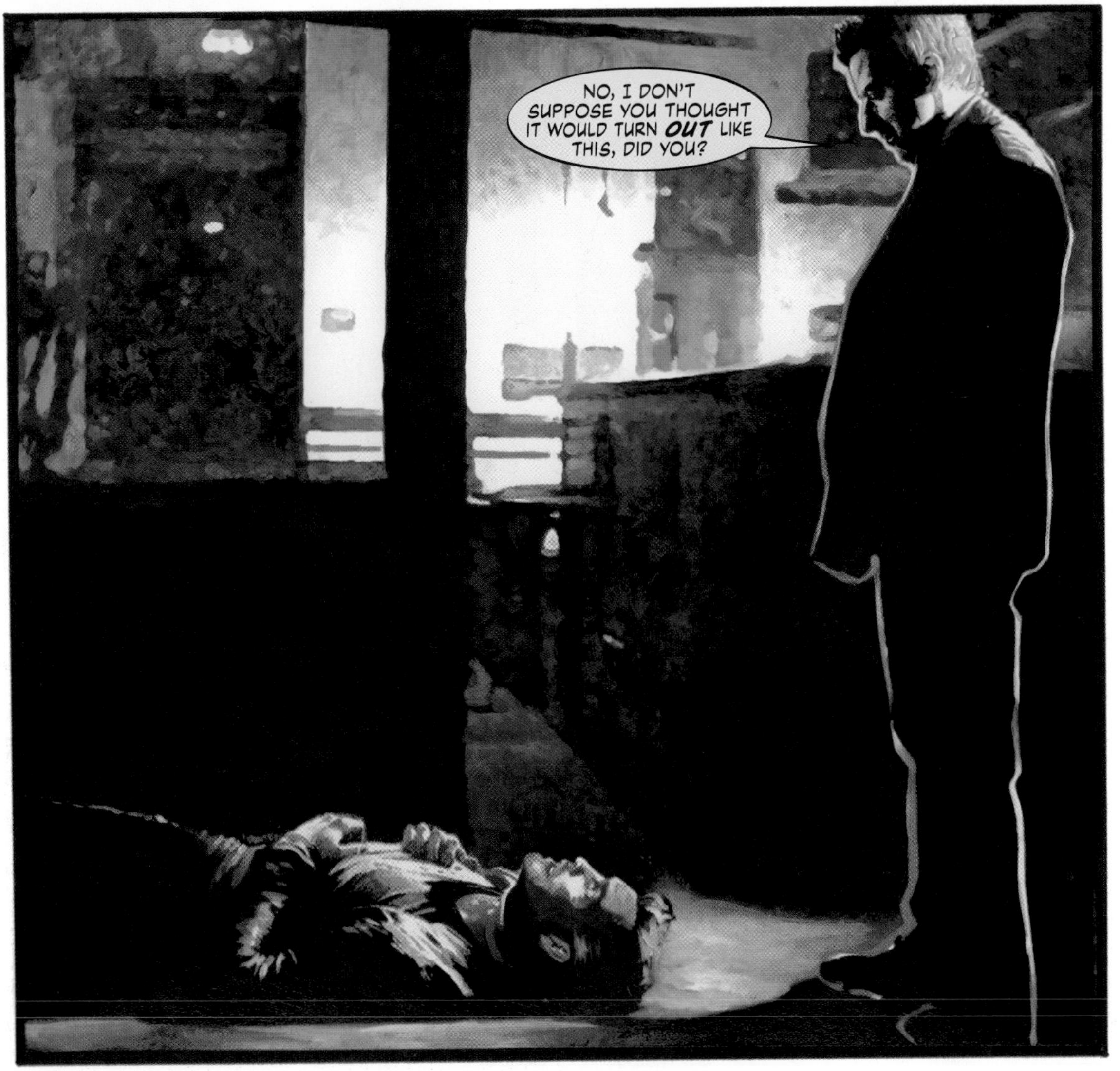
NO, I DON'T SUPPOSE YOU THOUGHT IT WOULD TURN OUT LIKE THIS, DID YOU?

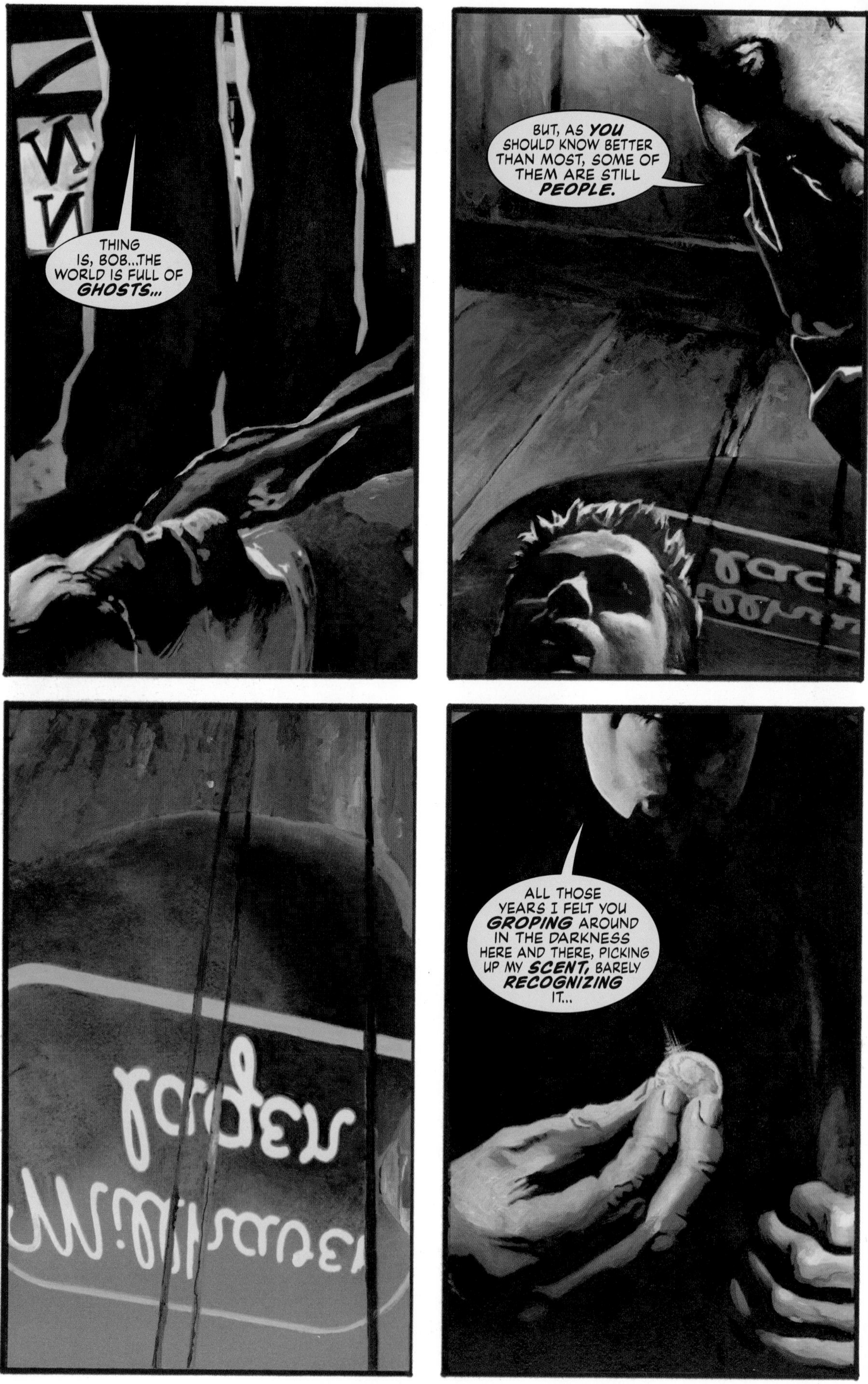
THING IS, BOB...THE WORLD IS FULL OF GHOSTS...
BUT, AS YOU SHOULD KNOW BETTER THAN MOST, SOME OF THEM ARE STILL PEOPLE.
ALL THOSE YEARS I FELT YOU GROPING AROUND IN THE DARKNESS HERE AND THERE, PICKING UP MY SCENT, BARELY RECOGNIZING IT...

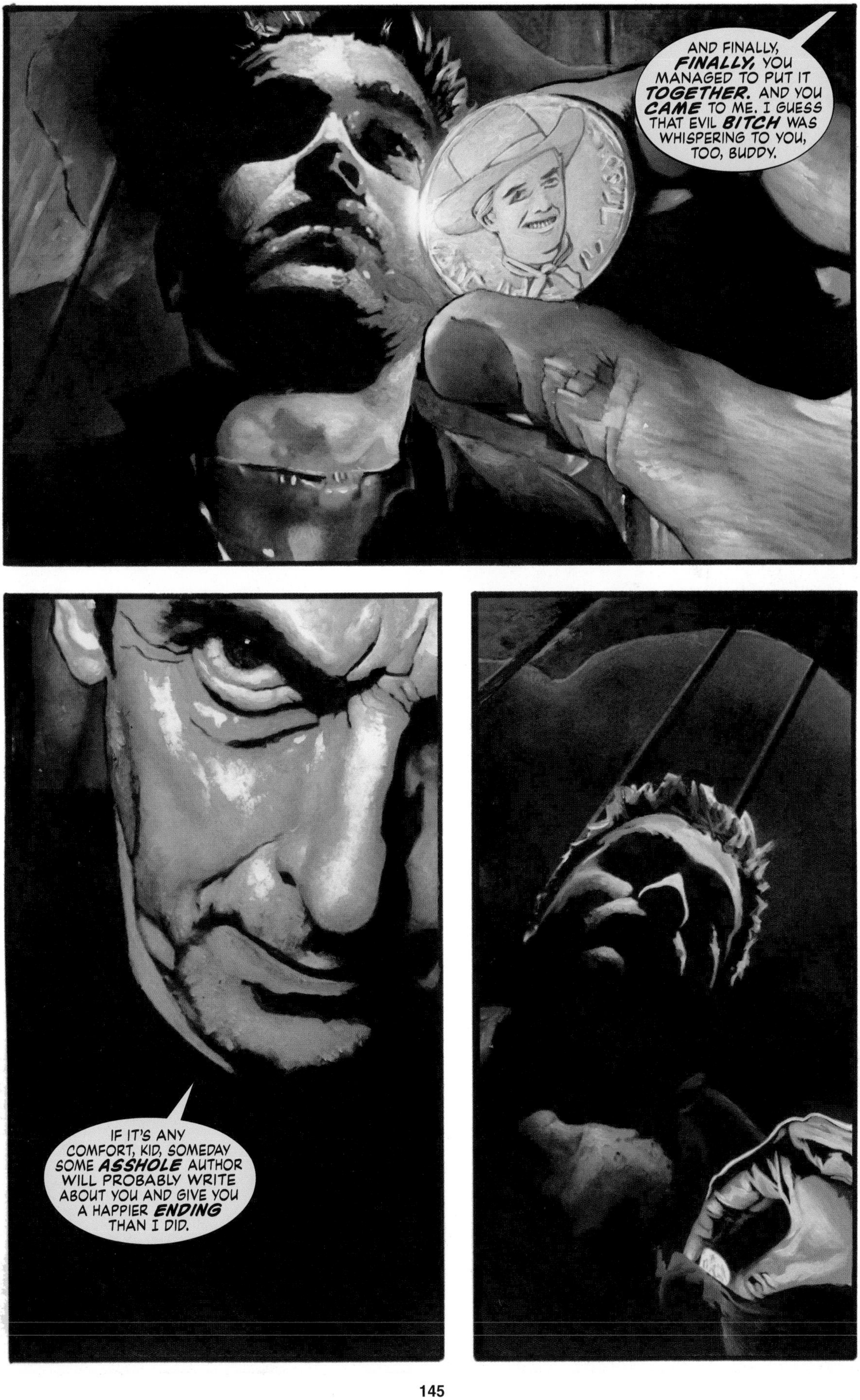
AND FINALLY, FINALLY, YOU MANAGED TO PUT IT TOGETHER. AND YOU CAME TO ME. I GUESS THAT EVIL BITCH WAS WHISPERING TO YOU, TOO, BUDDY.
IF IT'S ANY COMFORT, KID, SOMEDAY SOME ASSHOLE AUTHOR WILL PROBABLY WRITE ABOUT YOU AND GIVE YOU A HAPPIER ENDING THAN I DID.

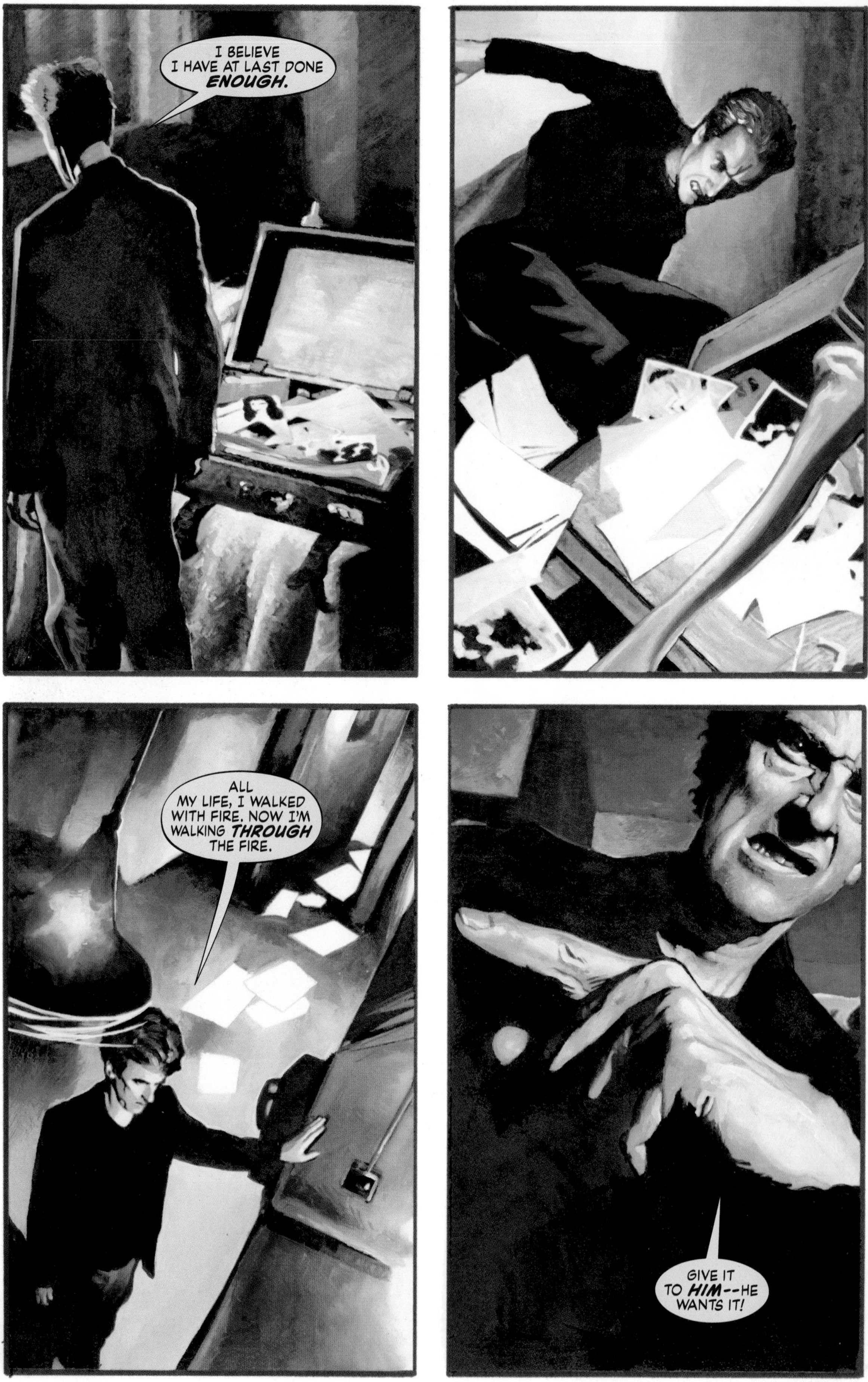
I BELIEVE I HAVE AT LAST DONE ENOUGH.
ALL MY LIFE, I WALKED WITH FIRE. NOW I'M WALKING THROUGH THE FIRE.
GIVE IT TO HIM--HE WANTS IT!

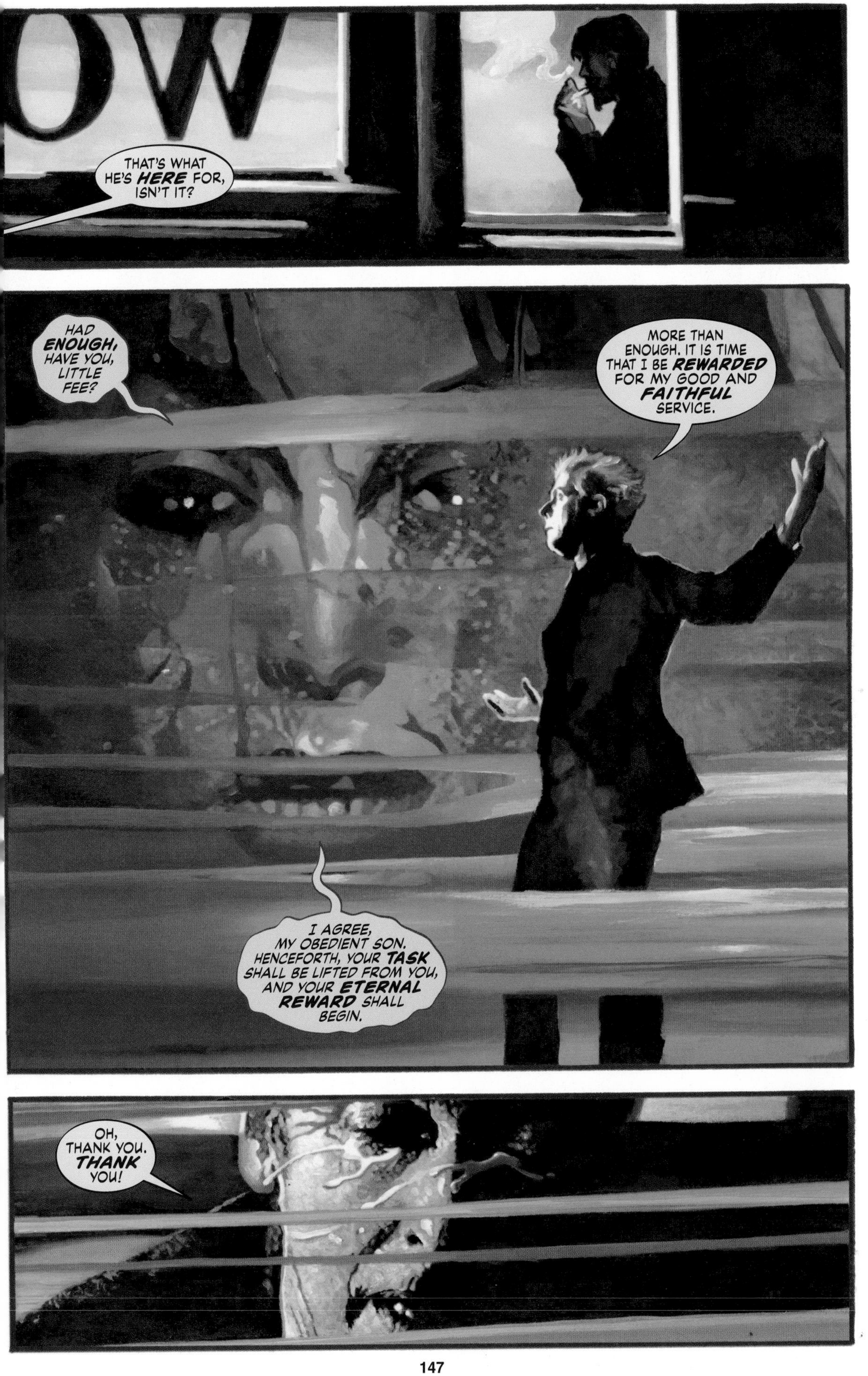
THAT'S WHAT HE'S **HERE** FOR, ISN'T IT?
HAD **ENOUGH,** HAVE YOU, LITTLE FEE?
MORE THAN ENOUGH. IT IS TIME THAT I BE **REWARDED** FOR MY GOOD AND **FAITHFUL** SERVICE.
I AGREE, MY OBEDIENT SON. HENCEFORTH, YOUR **TASK** SHALL BE LIFTED FROM YOU, AND YOUR **ETERNAL REWARD** SHALL BEGIN.
OH, THANK YOU. **THANK** YOU!

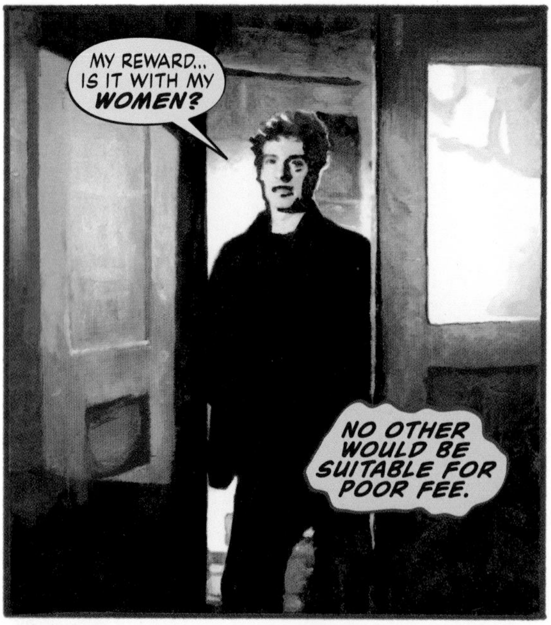
MY REWARD... IS IT WITH MY *WOMEN?*
NO OTHER WOULD BE SUITABLE FOR POOR FEE.

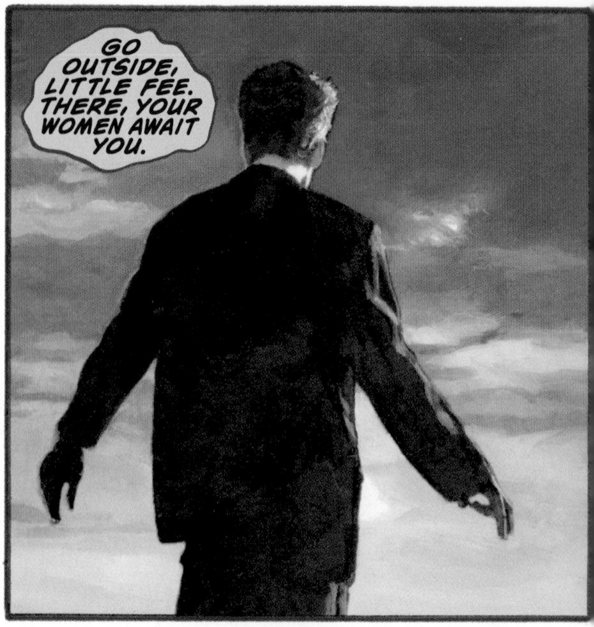
GO OUTSIDE, LITTLE FEE. THERE, YOUR WOMEN AWAIT YOU.

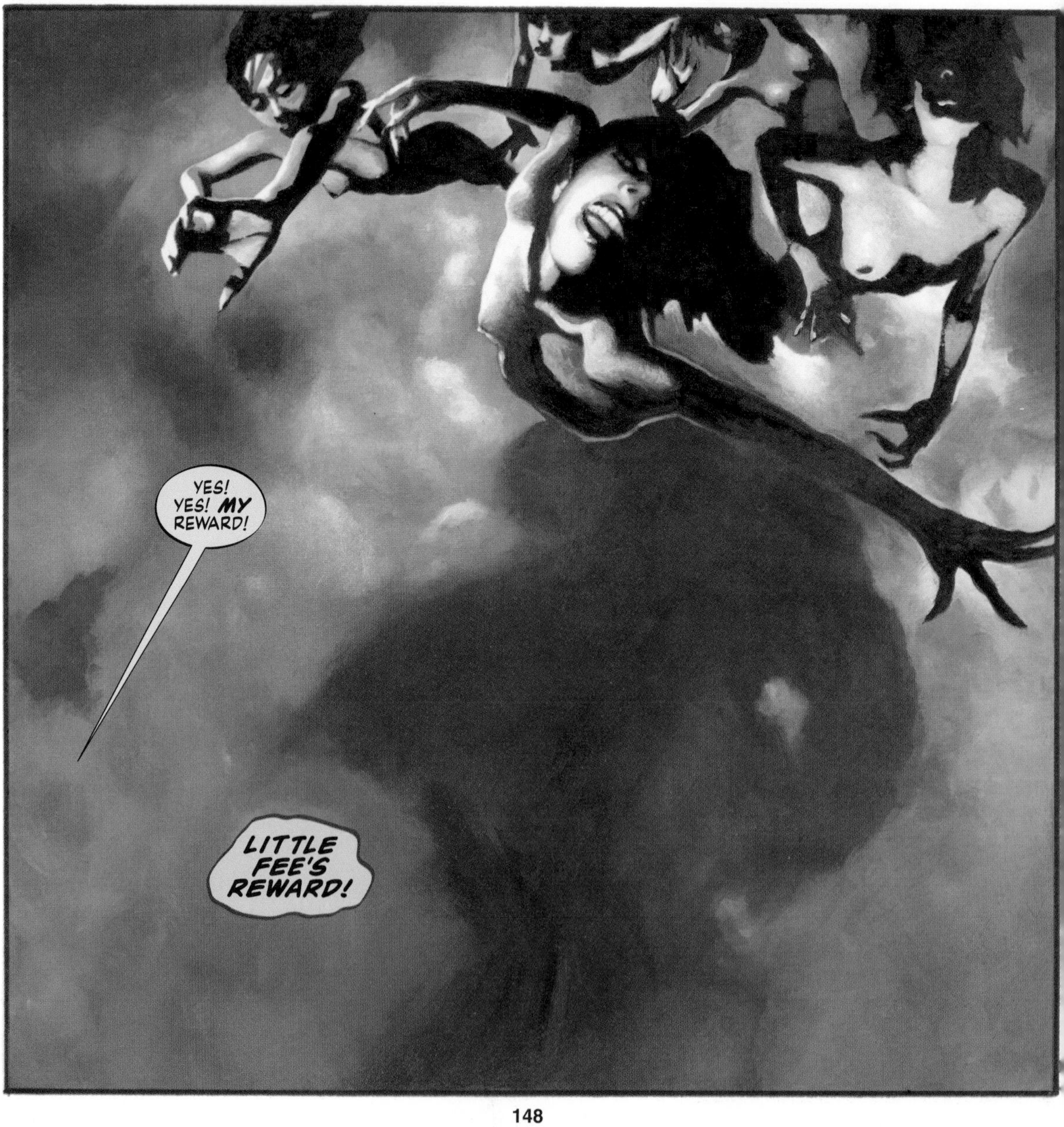
YES! YES! *MY* REWARD!
LITTLE FEE'S REWARD!

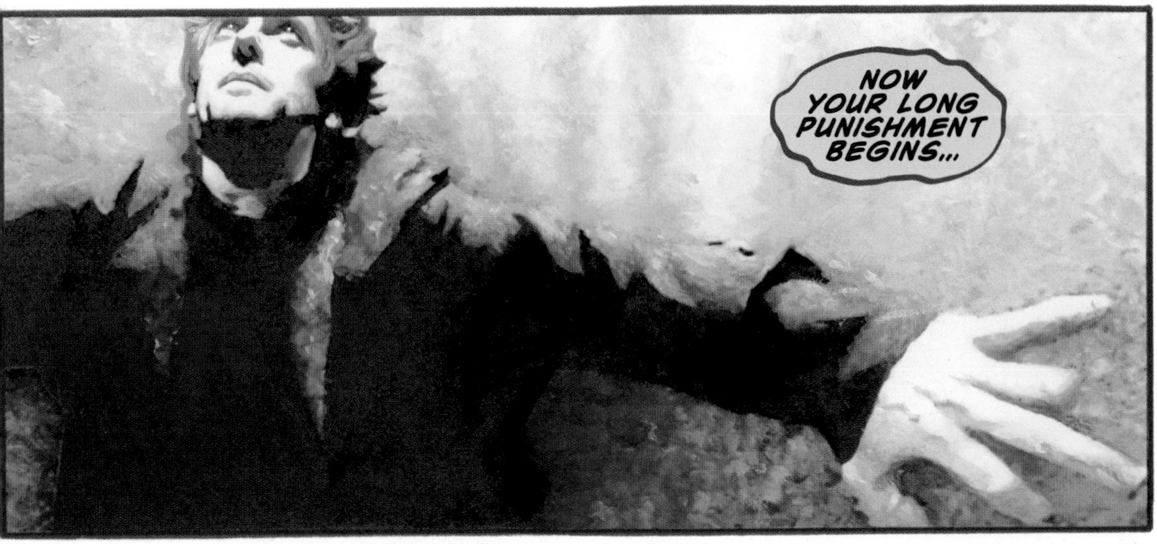
NOW YOUR LONG PUNISHMENT BEGINS...

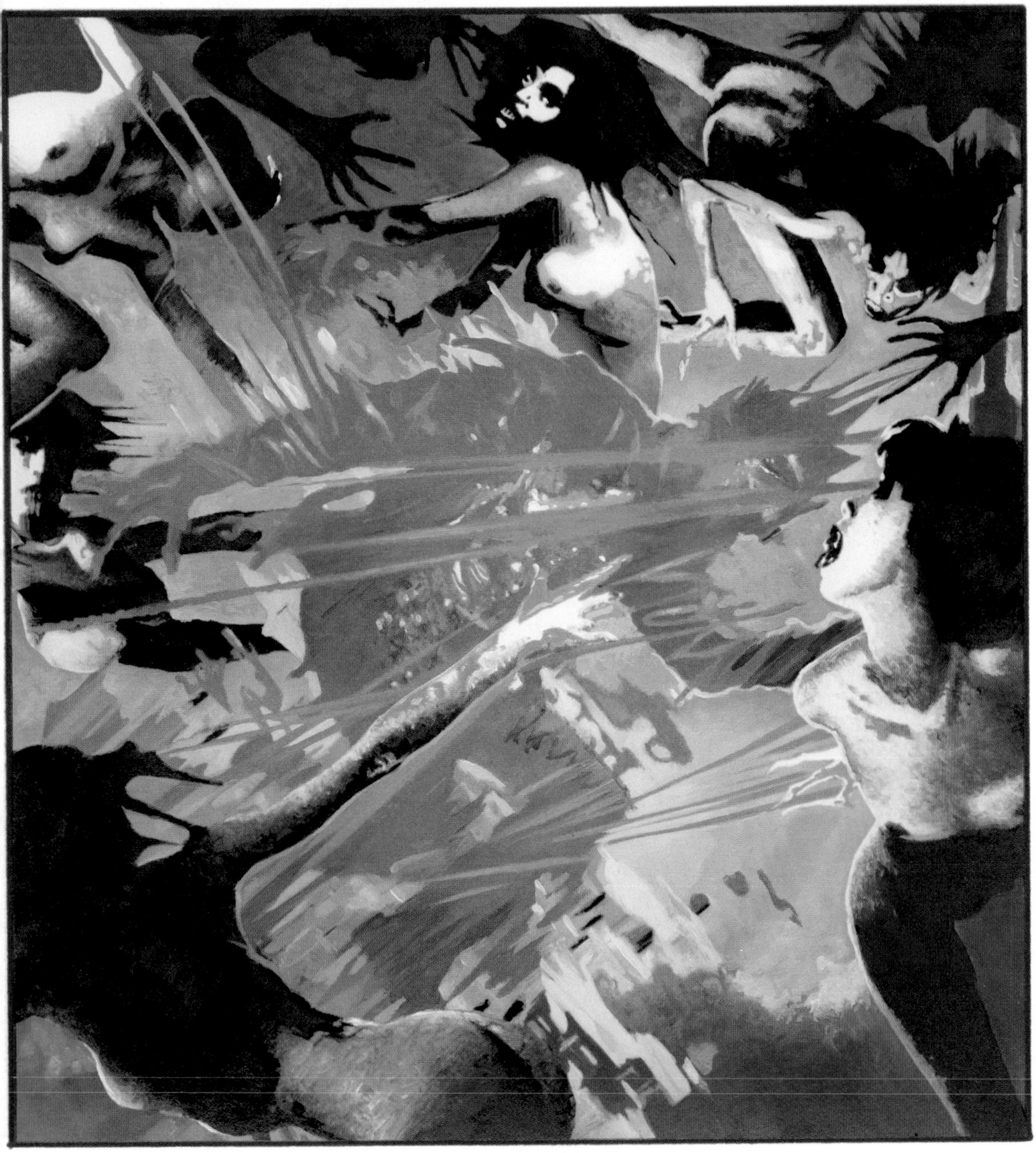

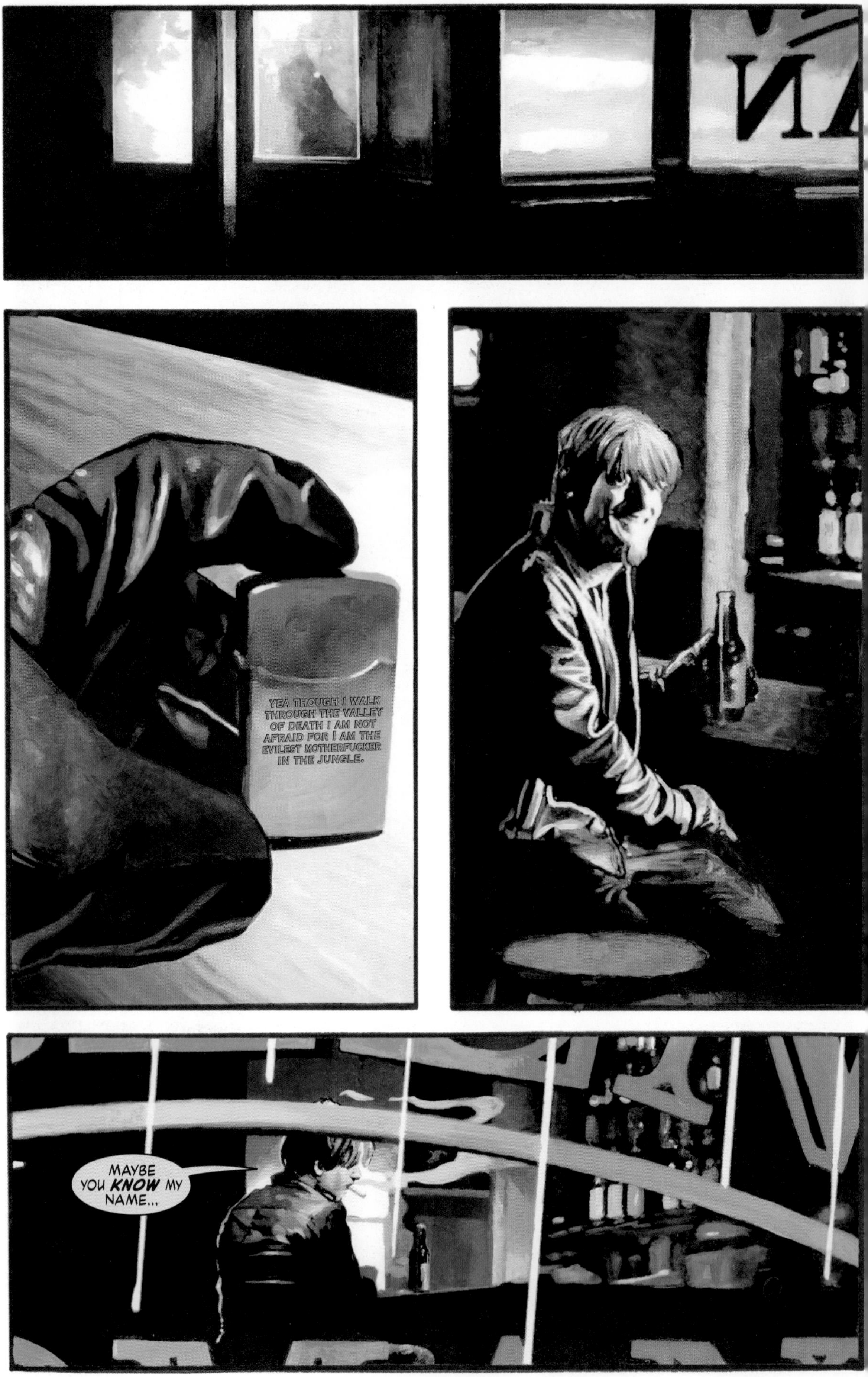
YEA THOUGH I WALK THROUGH THE VALLEY OF DEATH I AM NOT AFRAID FOR I AM THE EVILEST MOTHERFUCKER IN THE JUNGLE.
MAYBE YOU **KNOW** MY NAME...

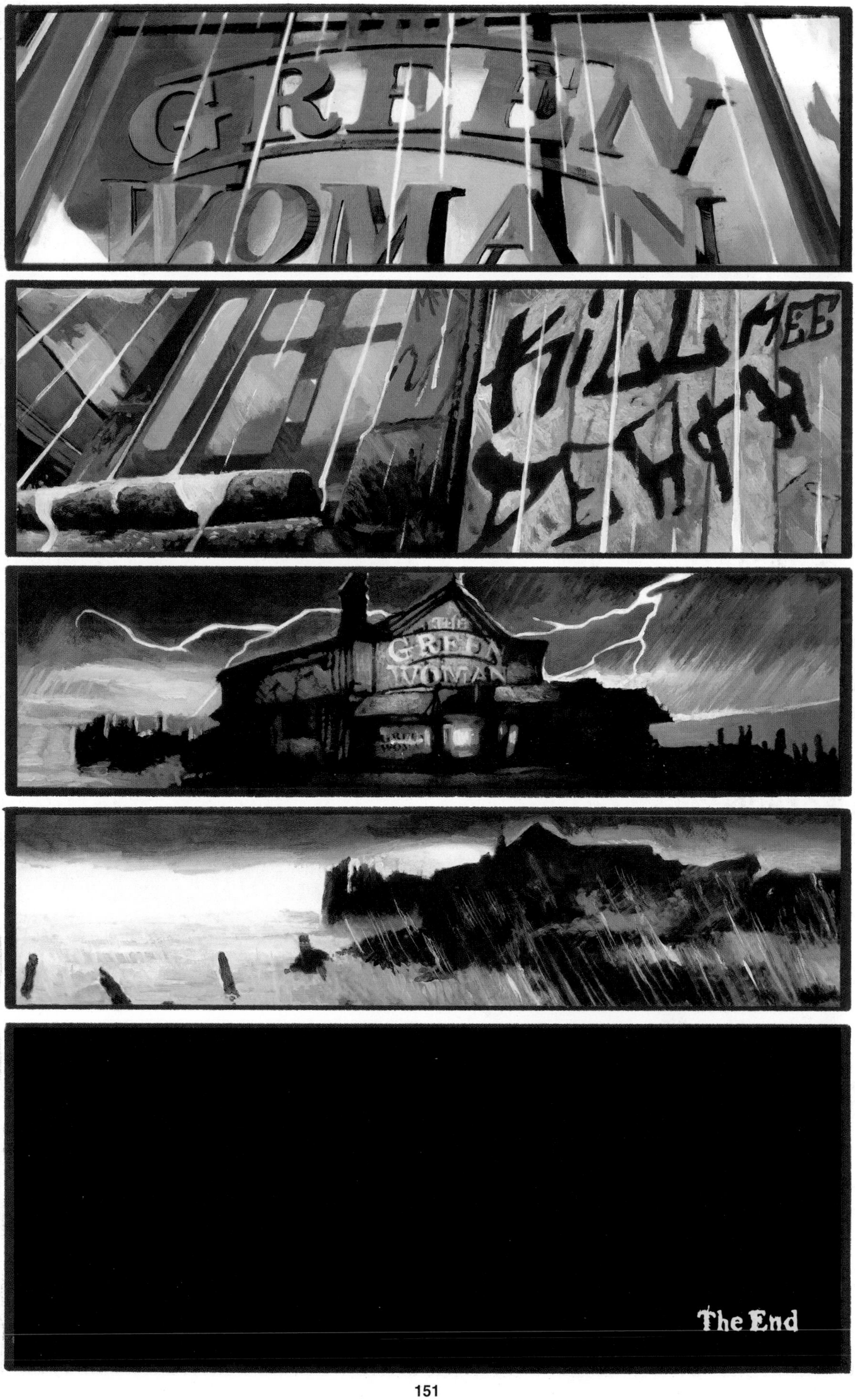
THE GREEN WOMAN
The End

Photo by Kyle Cassidy

Peter Straub is the author of seventeen novels, which have been translated into more than twenty languages. They include *Ghost Story, Koko, Mr. X, In the Night Room*, and two collaborations with Stephen King, *The Talisman* and *Black House*. He has written two volumes of poetry and two collections of short fiction, and he edited the Library of America's edition of H. P. Lovecraft's *Tales* and the forthcoming Library of America's 2-volume anthology *American Fantastic Tales*. He has won the British Fantasy Award, eight Bram Stoker Awards, two International Horror Guild Awards, and two World Fantasy Awards. In 1998, he was named Grand Master at the World Horror Convention. In 2006, he was given the Horror Writers Association's Life Achievement Award. In 2008, he was given the Barnes & Noble Writers for Writers Award by Poets & Writers.

Photo by Lori Dorn

Michael Easton is the author of the critically acclaimed graphic novel trilogy *Soul Stealer* as well as the collection of poetry *Eighteen Straight Whiskeys*. He lives in New York.

Photo by L. Carelli

John Bolton was seven when he first encountered a paint brush and it was love at first sight, offering him an outlet to visualize and create what he saw in his mind and put it to paper. Thus began a lifelong mission of creativity, with influences acquired from a wide variety of sources, but all connected by one underlying theme — the interesting and bizarre.

John has been painting professionally for three decades. His painting displays a thorough understanding of each medium and subject he chooses to tackle, horror being one of his favorites. John has collaborated with some of the industry's most prestigious comic writers, including Neil Gaiman, Mike Carey and Mark Verheiden. In the film world he has worked with Robert Zemeckis, Sam Raimi and Jonathan Glazer. He lives and works in London, England.